GACE History

034
035

Teacher Certification Exam

By: Sharon Wynne, M.S.
Southern Connecticut State University

"And, while there's no reason yet to panic, I think it's only prudent that we make preparations to panic."

XAMonline, INC.
Boston

SOCIAL STUDIES

XAMonline, Inc.
21 Orient Ave.
Melrose, MA 02176
Toll Free 1-800-509-4128
Email: info@xamonline.com
Web www.xamonline.com
Fax: 1-781-662-9268

Library of Congress Cataloging-in-Publication Data

Wynne, Sharon A.
    GACE: History 034, 035   Teacher Certification / Sharon A. Wynne.
    ISBN: 978-1-58197-545-1
    1. GACE: History 034, 035   2. Study Guides.   3. GACE
    4. Teachers' Certification & Licensure.   5. Careers

Disclaimer:
The opinions expressed in this publication are the sole works of XAMonline and were created independently from the National Education Association, Educational Testing Service, or any State Department of Education, National Evaluation Systems or other testing affiliates.

Between the time of publication and printing, state specific standards as well as testing formats and website information may change that is not included in part or in whole within this product. Sample test questions are developed by XAMonline and reflect similar content as on real tests; however, they are not former tests. XAMonline assembles content that aligns with state standards but makes no claims nor guarantees teacher candidates a passing score. Numerical scores are determined by testing companies such as NES or ETS and then are compared with individual state standards. A passing score varies from state to state.

Printed in the United States of America   œ-1

GACE: History 034, 035
ISBN: 978-1-58197-685-4

Table of Contents

COMPETENCY 11.0   UNDERSTAND THE ORIGINS, EVENTS, AND EFFECTS OF THE CIVIL WAR AND RECONSTRUCTION AND THE GROWTH AND DEVELOPMENT OF THE UNITED STATES THROUGH THE BEGINNING OF THE TWENTIETH CENTURY.

SUBAREA V.   US HISTORY 1914 TO THE PRESENT

COMPETENCY 12.0   UNDERSTAND THE ORIGINS, EVENTS, AND
                   EFFECTS OF US INVOLVEMENT IN WORLD WARS I
                   AND II, AND MAJOR POLITICAL, CULTURAL, AND
                   ECONOMIC DEVELOPMENTS IN THE UNITED
                   STATES BETWEEN 1914 AND 1945.

SUBAREA VI.   GEORGIA HISTORY

COMPETENCY 15.0   UNDERSTAND MAJOR DEVELOPMENTS IN GEORGIA'S HISTORY AND GEORGIA'S ROLE IN THE HISTORY OF THE UNITED STATES TO 1877.

Great Study and Testing Tips!

What to study in order to prepare for the subject assessments is the focus of this study guide but equally important is *how* you study.

You can increase your chances of truly mastering the information by taking some simple, but effective steps.

Study Tips:

1. Some foods aid the learning process. Foods such as milk, nuts, seeds, rice, and oats help your study efforts by releasing natural memory enhancers called CCKs (*cholecystokinin*) composed of *tryptophan*, *choline*, and *phenylalanine*. All of these chemicals enhance the neurotransmitters associated with memory. Before studying, try a light, protein-rich meal of eggs, turkey, and fish. All of these foods release the memory enhancing chemicals. The better the connections, the more you comprehend.

Likewise, before you take a test, stick to a light snack of energy boosting and relaxing foods. A glass of milk, a piece of fruit, or some peanuts all release various memory-boosting chemicals and help you to relax and focus on the subject at hand.

2. Learn to take great notes. A by-product of our modern culture is that we have grown accustomed to getting our information in short doses (e.g.,. TV news soundbites or USA Today style newspaper articles.)

Consequently, we've subconsciously trained ourselves to assimilate information better in neat little packages. If your notes are scrawled all over the paper, it fragments the flow of the information. Strive for clarity. Newspapers use a standard format to achieve clarity. Your notes can be much clearer through use of proper formatting. A very effective format is called the *"Cornell Method."*

> Take a sheet of loose-leaf lined notebook paper and draw a line all the way down the paper about 1-2" from the left-hand edge.

> Draw another line across the width of the paper about 1-2" up from the bottom. Repeat this process on the reverse side of the page.

Look at the highly effective result. You have ample room for notes, a left hand margin for special emphasis items or inserting supplementary data from the textbook, a large area at the bottom for a brief summary, and a little rectangular space for just about anything you want.

3. <u>Get the concept then the details</u>. Too often we focus on the details and don't gather an understanding of the concept. However, if you simply memorize only dates, places, or names, you may well miss the whole point of the subject.

A key way to understand things is to put them in your own words. If you are working from a textbook, automatically summarize each paragraph in your mind. If you are outlining text, don't simply copy the author's words.

Rephrase them in your own words. You remember your own thoughts and words much better than someone else's, and subconsciously tend to associate the important details to the core concepts.

4. <u>Ask Why?</u> Pull apart written material paragraph by paragraph and don't forget the captions under the illustrations.

Example: If the heading is "Stream Erosion", flip it around to read "Why do streams erode?" Then answer the questions.

If you train your mind to think in a series of questions and answers, not only will you learn more, but it also helps to lessen the test anxiety because you are used to answering questions.

5. <u>Read for reinforcement and future needs</u>. Even if you only have 10 minutes, put your notes or a book in your hand. Your mind is similar to a computer; you have to input data in order to have it processed. *By reading, you are creating the neural connections for future retrieval.* The more times you read something, the more you reinforce the learning of ideas.

Even if you don't fully understand something on the first pass, *your mind stores much of the material for later recall.*

6. <u>Relax to learn, so go into exile</u>. Our bodies respond to an inner clock called biorhythms. Burning the midnight oil works well for some people, but not everyone.

If possible, set aside a particular place to study that is free of distractions. Shut off the television, cell phone, and pager and exile your friends and family during your study period.

If you really are bothered by silence, try background music. Light classical music at a low volume has been shown to aid in concentration over other types. Music that evokes pleasant emotions without lyrics are highly suggested. Try just about anything by Mozart. It relaxes you.

7. <u>**Use arrows not highlighters**</u>. At best, it's difficult to read a page full of yellow, pink, blue, and green streaks.

Try staring at a neon sign for a while and you'll soon see that the horde of colors obscures the message.

A quick note, a brief dash of color, an underline, and an arrow pointing to a particular passage is much clearer than a horde of highlighted words.

8. <u>**Budget your study time**</u>. Although you shouldn't ignore any of the material, *allocate your available study time in the same ratio that topics may appear on the test.*

Testing Tips:

1. <u>Get smart, play dumb</u>. Don't read anything into the question. Don't assume that the test writer is looking for something other than what is asked. Stick to the question as written and don't read extra things into it.

2. <u>Read the question and all the choices *twice* before answering the question</u>. You may miss something by not carefully reading, and then re-reading both the question and the answers.

If you really don't have a clue as to the right answer, leave it blank on the first time through. Go on to the other questions, as they may provide a clue as to how to answer the skipped questions.

If, later on, you still can't answer the skipped questions . . . **Guess.**

The only penalty for guessing is that you *might* get it wrong. Only one thing is certain; if you don't put anything down, you will get it wrong!

3. <u>Turn the question into a statement</u>. Look at the way the questions are worded. The syntax of the question usually provides a clue. Does it seem more familiar as a statement rather than as a question? Does it sound strange?

By turning a question into a statement, you may be able to spot if an answer sounds right, and it may also trigger memories of material you have read.

4. <u>Look for hidden clues</u>. It's actually very difficult to compose multiple-foil (choice) questions without giving away part of the answer in the options presented.

In most multiple-choice questions you can often readily eliminate one or two of the potential answers. This leaves you with only two real possibilities and automatically your odds go to Fifty-Fifty for very little work.

5. <u>Trust your instincts</u>. For every fact you have read, you subconsciously retain something of that knowledge. On questions you aren't really certain about, go with your basic instincts. **Your first impression on how to answer a question is usually correct.**

6. <u>Mark your answers directly on the test booklet</u>. Don't bother trying to fill in the optical scan sheet on the first pass through the test.

Be careful not to miss-mark your answers when you transcribe them to the scan sheet.

7. <u>Watch the clock</u>! You have a set amount of time to answer the questions. Don't get bogged down trying to answer a single question at the expense of 10 questions you can more readily answer.

THIS PAGE BLANK

SUBAREA I.   **HISTORICAL CONCEPTS AND SKILLS**

COMPETENCY 1.0   **UNDERSTAND IMPORTANT HISTORICAL TERMS, CONCEPTS, AND PERSPECTIVES**

Skill 1.1   **Demonstrate knowledge of basic historical terms and concepts.**

History is the study of the past, especially the aspects of the human past, political and economic events as well as cultural and social conditions. Students study history through textbooks, research, field trips to museums and historical sites, and other methods. Most nations set the requirements in history to study the country's heritage, usually to develop an awareness and feeling of loyalty and patriotism. History is generally divided into the three main divisions: (a) time periods, (b) nations, and (c) specialized topics. Study is accomplished through research, reading, and writing.

History is without doubt an integral part of every other discipline in the social sciences. Knowing historical background on anything and anyone anywhere goes a long way towards explaining that what happened in the past leads up to and explains the present.

Causality: The reason something happens, its cause, is a basic category of human thinking. We want to know the causes of some major event in our lives. Within the study of history, causality is the analysis of the reasons for change. The question we are asking is why and how a particular society or event developed in the particular way it did given the context in which it occurred.

Conflict: Conflict within history is opposition of ideas, principles, values or claims. Conflict may take the form of internal clashes of principles or ideas or claims within a society or group or it may take the form of opposition between groups or societies.

Bias: A prejudice or a predisposition either toward or against something. In the study of history, bias can refer to the persons or groups studied, in terms of a society's bias toward a particular political system, or it can refer to the historian's predisposition to evaluate events in a particular way.

Interdependence: A condition in which two things or groups rely upon one another; as opposed to independence, in which each thing or group relies only upon itself.

Identity: The state or perception of being a particular thing or person. Identity can also refer to the understanding or self-understanding of groups, nations, etc.

Nation-state: A particular type of political entity that provides a sovereign territory for a specific nation in which other factors also unite the citizens (e.g., language, race, ancestry, etc.).

Culture: The civilization, achievements, and customs of the people of a particular time and place.

Middle Age

The system of **feudalism** became a dominant feature of the economic and social system in Europe. It was a system of loyalty and protection. The strong protected the weak who returned the service with farm labor, military service, and loyalty. Life was lived out on a vast estate, owned by a nobleman and his family, called a "manor." It was a complete village supporting a few hundred people, mostly peasants. Improved tools and farming methods made life more bearable although during a peasant's lifetime, very few left the manor or traveled outside of their village.

Feudalism was the organization of people based on the ownership of land by a *Lord* or other *Noble* who allowed individuals known as *peasants* or *serfs* to farm the land, giving the majority of the farmed goods to the manor and kept a smaller portion for themselves. The Lord or Noble, in return for the serfs' loyalty, offered them his protection. In practical effect, the serf was considered owned by his lord with little or no rights at all. The lord's sole obligation to the serfs was to protect them so they could continue to work for him (most, though not all lords were men). This system would last for many centuries. In Russia it would last until the 1860s.

Skill 1.2   Place historical events in chronological order and recognize major historical developments that took place at the same time in different parts of the world

Chronology is the ordering of events through time. Chronologies are often listed along a timeline or in a list by date. Chronologies allow for easy visualization of a wide expanse of history in one place. This allows a student to quickly get an overview of the major events and changes over time. By including important related events, the cause and effect of major developments can be emphasized. By placing chronologies for different societies parallel to one another, comparisons in relative development can be quickly interpreted, providing material for further historical exploration.

Pre-Historic Period

Fully modern humans evolved in Africa between 200,000 and 100,000 years ago. Early humans were primarily hunger-gatherers, able to communicate, organize in groups, and had rudimentary tool-making skills. The end of the Ice Age brought climate change. Population increased due to warmer temperatures, increased rainfall, more abundant and diverse food supplies. Hunters began to form communities, while rituals and symbols of group identity began to emerge.

<u>The Americas</u>: humans crossed the Bering land bridge from Siberia to the Americas 25,000 BCE; hunter-gatherers developed large stone hunting points (Clovis points) capable of piercing Mammoth hides; 15,000 BCE – Meadowcroft Rock shelter in Pennsylvania; 13,000 BCE – settlement at Bluefish Cave, Yukon; 12,000 BCE – humans reached southern South America; 11,000 BCE – evidence of a village at Monte Verde, Chile; 10,000 BCE – evidence of pottery; 9000 BCE – herds of mammoths were near extinction.

<u>Africa</u>: 42,000 BCE – mining of red ocher from Lion Cave in Southern Africa (body ornamentation); 35,000 BCD – tropical rain forests of Africa colonized by early humans; 30,000 BCE – new tool technology; 24,000 BCE – rock art produced at Apollo 11 Cave in southern Africa; 20,000 BCE – terra-cotta figurines from Algeria and engraved objects from South Africa; 10,000 BCE – more settled lifestyles developing in Nile and Niger valleys.

<u>Europe</u>: 1 million years ago – first hominids traveled to Europe from Africa through the Strait of Gibraltar; 120,000 BCE – Neanderthals present; 35,000 BCE – settled by modern humans; new tool technology; 25,000 BCE – sculptures and engravings on bone and antlers; 10,000 BCE – large animals (woolly rhinoceros, giant deer and mammoth) became extinct; retreat of glaciers provides marine and land resources.

<u>West Asia</u>: 100,000 BCE – earliest known burial in Israel – evidence of complex social organization; 45,000 BCE – flint tools developed in Israel and spread across Southern Europe; 40,000 BCE – Neanderthals still present in Southwest Asia; 17,000 BCE – wild cereal gathering in Israel; 13,000 BCE – people in Israel intensively harvesting, grinding and storing wild grains; 12,000 BCE – first use of grindstones; 11,000 BCE – domestication of dogs in the Middle East.

<u>South and East Asia</u>: seafood becomes important in the diet and settlements develop in coastal areas; 1.7 million years ago – first hominid civilization; 90,000 BCE – first evidence of humans; 60,000 BCE – modern humans throughout the region; 40,000 BCE – first stone tools; 11,000 BCE – earliest portable art in the region; 10,000 BCE – Jomon people of Honshu island, Japan make first known pottery; rock shelter paintings in Central India that include buffalo.

<u>Australasia</u>: 60,000 BCE – first humans arrived in boats from southeast Asia, settling along the coasts and rivers; 45,000 BCE – worlds first known rock art; 25,000 BCE – first evidence of human cremation; 20,000 BCE – settlement reaches south coast of Tasmania; 16,000 BCE – extinction of giant marsupials.

Emergence of Human Civilization 10,000 – 5,000 BCE

By 7000 BCE farming was the primary means of subsistence in Western Asia, while hunter-gathering predominated elsewhere. Over the next 5000 years farming became established independently in other areas. This agricultural revolution had monumental impact on the lives of humans: (1) farming could support much larger populations; (2) sizes of settlements became increasingly larger; (3) larger communities generated needs and opportunities that gave rise to new activities; (4) trade in raw materials and finished goods developed between communities; and (5) cooperation became normalized through communal efforts. Some people were able to develop craft skills, to engage in long-distance trade, and to experiment with technology, such as pottery kilns, metallurgy and irrigation. Communities established permanent villages with material goods and equipment, which led to the beginnings of social differentiation. Various regions developed a dependence on different staple crops. Animals were domesticated and selective breeding began to enhance useful traits. Permanent dwellings were produced. Communities created identifying symbols and rituals, including burial. Communal living, however, also exposed people to disease and epidemics.

Between 7000 and 5000 BCE communities in west Asia and southeastern Europe discovered independently that metals can be extracted from rock by heating. The first metals used were copper, gold and lead. But tools made of these soft metals could not compete with flint and stone for tools. Copper became used for decorative items.

Americas: experiments with cultivation of potatoes, squash and beans began to supplement hunting and gathering; 8500 – evidence in the Andes of harvesting grains and vegetables; 8000 – evidence of use of grindstones; 7500 – earliest known cemetery in North America; 5500 – squash avocados and chili's were stapes in the Central American diet.

Europe: 7000 – farming reached southeast Europe, spreading west along the Mediterranean and north into central and northwest Europe; new strains of cereals were developed in northern Europe; cattle and pigs replaced goats as the main domestic animals; 5000 – cereal farming villages arose in western Europe; 5400 – farming spreads to central Europe; fishing supplemented hunting-gathering in northern Europe; farming villages in southern Anatolia traded flint, obsidian, timber, shells and copper.

West Asia: earliest farmers settled in a fertile arc of land from the Persian Gulf to the eastern Mediterranean; 9000 – wheat harvested in Mesopotamia; 8000 – large-seeded grains cultivated at Jericho; 7000 – villages of mud-brick houses in Anatolia and central Mesopotamia; goats are main domesticated animal; 6000 – craftsmen smelt copper and lead; painted pottery in northern Mesopotamia; 5500 – farmers of southern Mesopotamia using irrigation.

East Asia: 7000 – agriculture in northern China; grain kept in storage pits, pigs and dogs domesticated; 6000 – rice cultivated in lowlands of Yangtze delta; 5000 – jade imported into northern Manchuria from Central Asia or Siberia.

South and Southeast Asia: 7000 – drainage and cultivation practiced in New Guinea; 6000 – pottery in grave goods indicates trade with central Asia; first pottery production in southeast Asia; 5000 – cultivation of wheat and barley in northern India; cultivation of rice south of Ganges Valley; 2000 – farming established in the region.

Africa: 9000 – hunter-gatherers moved into the Sahara as ice age ended; 8000 – Saharan rock art; 7000 – wavy-line pottery produced; 6500 – cattle domesticated in northern Africa; 6000 – Sahara becomes arid again and people move out; wheat and barley cultivation spreads to the Nile valley from the Middle East.

Development of cultures and cities 5000 – 500 BCE

The first great urban civilization developed in the fertile river valleys of the Nile, Tigris, Euphrates, Indus and Yellow Rivers. Despite the fact that they developed independently, they shared several characteristics:
- Hierarchical societies
- Complex division of labor
- Administered by an elite class
- Divine monarchy emerged in some
- Monuments began to symbolize the powers of the ruling elite
- Farming communities came together to create ritual centers and burial sites
- High degree of social organization

By 2500 cities were established in 2 major centers: Nile Valley, Mesopotamia, and the Indus Valley, with a scattering of other cities. In each case, lack of important natural resources, such as timber, metal and stone, forced these civilizations to establish trade networks. Where trade contacts led, cultural exchange followed. Cities soon developed in Anatolia and the Iranian Plateau. By 3500 BCE wheeled vehicles were in use in southwest Asia and by 3000 BCE their use had spread to Europe and India. The primary mode of transportation for trade was by ship, but wheeled carts pulled by recently-domesticated beasts of burden were also used for overland trade. Mesopotamia first used sails in 4500 BCE, and began to use the plow in 4000 BCE.

Writing evolved primarily to record trade transactions, but its use quickly spread to other functions. First written texts found in Mesopotamia are receipts dating to about 4000 BCE. There is also evidence of writing in the royal tombs at Abydos in Upper Egypt at about the same time. By 3100 Mesopotamia had developed a cuneiform script.

South America: 4750 – first agriculture in the Americas was corn grown in Central America's Tehuacan valley; 4000 – first pottery in the Amazon basin; 3500 – cotton cultivated in Central America for fishing nets and textiles; 2600 – regional ritual centers appear; 2500 – agriculture is supporting larger communities, permanent settlements appear, and there is evidence of long-distance trade along the Andean coast.

Africa: 3400 – first walled towns appear; 3100 – King Narmer unifies Pharaonic Egypt into a state; belief in life after death is documented and elaborate well-appointed tombs are built for the afterlife; 3000 – first evidence of hieroglyphic writing; 2650 – pyramids (royal tombs) built near capital city of Memphis (this investment of labor and resources demonstrates the ruler's control over the people); 2530 – construction of the Great Pyramid at Giza.

Europe: increasing social organization is demonstrated by elaborate burials; 4500 – large cemeteries along the cost of the Black Sea contain gold jewelry; 3800 – ditched enclosures around settlements in central Europe; 3500 – metallurgy practiced in eastern Europe; 3000 – small farming communities gather to build defensive enclosures and to create regional centers for social, economic and ritual life; 2900 – burials with corded-ware pottery; 2500 – Stonehenge built.

East Asia: 4000 – planned villages in China with distinct residential, labor and burial areas; 3000 – potters wheel invented; distinction appears in burial of rich and poor; walled settlements; evidence of farming in Korea; 2750 – Chinese bronze artifacts; 2700 – cultivation of silkworms and weaving silk; 2500 – Banshan culture produces boldly painted burial urns.

South Asia: 5000 – use of pottery in Indus Valley; 4000 – irrigation practiced in Indus Valley; 3500 – walled towns appear in Indus Valley; 2500 – true cities emerge and reach their height with a population of 40,000, a network of residential streets, houses built of standardized bricks, a sophisticated drainage and sewer system, and merchandise traded as far as Mesopotamia.

West Asia: 3500 – Uruk, first city-state of Mesopotamia; cities built around raised mud-brick temple complex and administered by priestly elite; 3250 – pictographic writing; 3100 – City of Byblos on Levantine coast; 2500 – City of Ur in southern Mesopotamia; Ebla in western Mesopotamia trades with Mediterranean peoples; city-states arise throughout Mesopotamia and the Levant with extensive trade links.

As cities expanded and others arose, states developed, populations grew, and economic pressures intensified. Rivalry for territory and power emerged. States became militaristic which made warfare, weapons development and diplomacy critical. Early societies become increasingly stratified and distinct classes emerged. Scattered agricultural communities in Europe were becoming more sophisticated, developing metallurgy and trade and beginning to compete for land and resources. At this time symbolic representations of the sun were found in almost all cultures.

The Americas: precursors of urban civilizations began to emerge in Central and South America; 2000 BCE – ceramics and large-scale cultivation of corn in Peru; 1800 – construction of La Florida ceremonial center in Peru; Olmec center of San Lorenzo developing on the Gulf Coast of Central America; in eastern North America agriculture was being practiced; 1500 – small settled communities in river valleys of Mississippi system; metalworking in Peru.

Africa: Egyptian civilization reached its height during the New Kingdom, 1560 – 1085 BCE. In 1633 much of Egypt was ruled by an Adriatic people, the Hyksos; 1417 – the New Kingdom reached the high point of power, wealth and prestige under Amenophis III; 1350, Pharaoh Akhenaton introduced sun worship in Egypt; Egypt's wealth was based on gold in Nubia and its domination of Palestine and southern Syria; the New Kingdom fell as a result of corruption and decline of royal power, unrest in Palestine and foreign attacks, particularly by the Hittites.

Europe: new types of bronze weapons indicated the emergence of a warrior elite as increased need for land created conflict between cities. 2250 – Minoan civilization built the palace of Knoxxos on Crete, the first Mediterranean state; several small cities of Mycenean Greece grew wealthy on trade, but all were destroyed or abandoned by the 12th Century BCE. 2000 – fortified settlements in Central and Eastern Europe; 1650 – Linear A script appears on Crete; 1550 – Myceneans became the dominant power of the Greek mainland.

West Asia: northern Mesopotamia was dominated by several city-states – Ashur and Mari – centered on palaces and religious complexes. In central Anatolia, Hittites ruled a powerful kingdom and their efforts to control trading cities of the Levant caused conflict with Egypt. 2300 – city states of southern Mesopotamia were temporarily united against Sargon of Agade; 1760 – Babylon gains temporary control of the region; 1650 – emergence of the Hittite kingdom; 1600 – Phoenicians start to use Canaanite script (first alphabetic script); 1250 – battle of Kadesh between Egypt and the Hittites.

East Asia: 1900 BCE – first Chinese city at Erlitou on the Yellow River; 1800 – urban civilization of Shang in China in which the Shang dynasty exercised absolute power based on labor of farmers; elsewhere the transition to agriculture was slow. However agricultural villages in Thailand produced bronze objects with techniques similar to those used in China; 1400 – first written inscriptions.

Oceania: 2500 – dingo introduced to Australia from Southeast Asia; 1500 – one of the great population movements of history, when the Lapita people, originally settlers from the East Indies began to explore and colonize the Pacific islands. They spread culture quickly, reaching Tonga and Samoa by 1000 BCE.

Cities evolved in several ways, depending upon the culture from which they emerged, the nature of outside pressures, and the interests of the rulers. This was a period of increasing social stratification throughout the world, and all cities were structured in ways that reflected the gulf between ruler and ruled, sacred and secular. A quest for new territory and greater wealth also began to emerge.

The Assyrians formed the world's first large empire. It was ruled with great efficiency. The Assyrians used cavalry and iron technology to make more powerful weapons and armor. Iron revolutionized tools and weapons in Europe and Asia. More efficient farming produced higher crop yields and supported larger populations. Long-distance trade networks disseminated political and cultural influences.

By 750 civilizations covered a belt from the Mediterranean to China. Trade and cultural exchange were well established across this belt of cities, and iron working spread from the Middle East to China. By the 6th Century BCE, Chinese silk began to appear in Europe. But tribes of nomads were spreading across Central Asia, eastern Europe and Siberia, attacking the cities. By 500, the Classical Age was beginning in Greece – a high point in the history of western civilization.

The Americas: Between 750 and 500 BCE the Olmec civilization flourished in Mexico, and other cultures emerged in Central America. The Zapotec civilization produced hieroglyphics and calendar calculations that reflect the earliest known writing in the Americas. The Adena burials in the eastern woodlands of North America were furnished with grave goods. These people produced gigantic earthworks – such as the Great Serpent Mound – which indicate a stratified and politically organized society. Permanent villages of people practicing horticulture arose in southeastern and southwestern North America. By 600 BCE jade artifacts were being traded in Central America, and by 500 the Paracas culture was emerging in South America.

Africa: 1168 BCE – death of Rameses III; 1085 marks the end of the 20th Dynasty in Egypt and the end of stable rule. Rival kings rule from different cities with brief periods of stability amid long civil wars; 900 – foundation of the Nubian kingdom of Cush; 814 – Carthage founded by Phoenicians (Semitic people from the east Mediterranean) along with other trading centers along the north African coast; knowledge of iron working carried along the trans-Siberian trade routes to agricultural communities to the south; mid 8th century – Nubian Cushites control all of Egypt and extend power north by 750; 671 – Assyrians attack Egypt, sack Memphis and Thebes; Cushites retreat and build new capital at Meroe, burying kings in pyramid-shaped tombs and worshipping Egyptian gods; 663 – Egypt regains independence under Saite dynasty until conquered by the Persians in 525; by 500 – iron working technology takes hold in sub-Saharan region; Darius I of Persia completes construction of a canal linking the Nile and the Red Sea.

Europe: Independent city-states arose throughout Greece and western Asia Minor. Trade with Italy and the Levant brings wealth and population. Colonists build trading cities along the Mediterranean. In Italy, the Etruscans build fortified hilltop cities and establish extensive trade with Africa and Europe. 1200 BCE – New Urnfield culture in Danube area; 1150 – Collapse of Mycenean Greece; 1000 – colonists from mainland Greece settle coastal areas of Asia Minor and the islands of the Aegean; 900 – end of the dark ages in Greece; 850 – earliest village on Rome's Palatine Hill; 800 – Rise of Etruscan city-states in central Italy; first phase of Celtic Iron Age; 776 – first Pan-Hellenic athletic games at Olympia's sanctuary of Zeus. As city-states of Greece became more wealthy, civic pride was demonstrated through construction of magnificent buildings. Greek colonies reached from the Black Sea to the Iberian Peninsula. The expanding population of Europe moved into more marginal areas, using iron tools. Northern Europe was occupied by Celtic and Germanic peoples. 750 – first evidence of use of the Greek alphabet; 700 – Scythians from Central Asia begin to settle in eastern Europe and the Black Sea region; 600 – trade between the Greeks and the Celts; defensive hilltop fortresses are built throughout southern Germany and eastern France; 510 – Romans expel Etruscan overlords and establish a Republic; 505 – democracy established in Athens.

<u>West Asia:</u> The Babylonians systematically studied the skies and developed the ability to plot the path of the sun and planets and to predict lunar eclipses by 1000 BCE. Power struggles between established states of west Asia allowed barbarian tribes to enter the region (Medes, Chaldeans, Philistines, Hebrews, and Phrygians). Hebrews briefly created a kingdom, but it collapsed by 926. From the 9th century the dominant power in east Asia is Assyria. By the 8th century, the Assyrian empire reached from the Levant to the Persian Gulf. Subject peoples were ruled by provincial governors, who ruthlessly suppressed resistance. The only kingdom in the region that was outside Assyrian control was the Armenian kingdom of Urartu. Assyria's enemies united to overthrow the empire in 612. Babylon briefly dominated Mesopotamia until the arrival of the Medes and Persians. In 550 Cyrus, a Persian king, defeated the Medes and established the Achaemenid Empire, which became the largest state the world had seen, reaching from the Nile to the Indus. Darius I, a later Persian ruler consolidated imperial rule, dividing subject peoples into provinces, levying taxes, and building the Royal Road from Sardis to Susa for communication. 1200 BCE – Collapse of Hittite empire; Jewish exodus from Egypt and settlement in Palestine; 1100 – Syria and Palestine settled by nomadic tribes; 1000 – Phoenicians dominated trade of Levant and developed an alphabetic script; King David unites Israel and Judea, with a capital at Jerusalem; 950 – foundation of the Assyrian Empire; 900 – Urartu resists Assyrian aggression; 700 – Scythians establish settlements; 663 – Assyrian Empire reaches its greatest extent with the sack of Thebes in Egypt; 612 – Babylonians and Medes sack Nineveh and Nimrud, ending the Assyrian empire; 604 – Nebuchadnezzar II rebuilds Babylon and captures Jerusalem; 550 – Cyrus the Great of Persia defeats the Medes and forms the Achaemenid Empire; 539 – Cyrus takes Babylon and its empire without bloodshed; 521 – Persian Empire reaches its greatest extent under Darius I.

The Age of Empires 500 BCE – 1000 CE

The years between 500 BCE and 500 CE witnessed the rise of several great empires. Periods of creativity and accomplishment alternated with periods of intense conflict between rival empires. This was the period Classical Greece flourished. It was a climactic period for the Persian Empire. The amazing empire of Alexander the Great not only became the largest empire yet created, but accomplished in its wake the fertile cultural cross-pollination that changed the world. Rome transitioned from Republic to Empire, while the first Chinese empire was born. In Africa and the Americas, other political structures united people previously isolated from one another. The Byzantine Empire arose, as did Charlemagne's Carolingian Empire. India and Africa were deeply impacted by the rise and growth of the Islamic Empire. China's internal struggles came to an end with the rise of the Tang and Song dynasties, and in the Americas the Mayan Culture entered its classical period.

This period was also typified by active trade across constantly increasing spans of distance and culture. Religions blossomed throughout the world, becoming, in many cases, truly global in their influence. Religion and politics began to influence one another in new ways, and these great world religions came into conflict with each other. The period was rich in the development and rapid advance of various technologies, fields of learning, and the arts.

Africa: 500-250 BCE, the Phoenician city of Carthage controlled the trans-Saharan trade with West Africa; ironworking was well established; The Nok of the Niger Delta was the most famous culture of the period; Egypt had become a Persian satrapy that was conquered by Alexander the Great in 332 BCE; after Alexander's death, Egypt fell to Ptolemy, who founded the Ptolemaic dynasty; about 500, Bantus began to spread from Niger to the East African lakes region and down the west coast of Africa; 146, Rome defeated Carthage and brought North Africa into the empire; 100, Romans introduce Camel into the Sahara; 31, Octavian's defeat of Antony and Cleopatra at the battle of Actium made Egypt a Roman province; Cleopatra's death marked the end of the Ptolemaic dynasty in Egypt; Kingdom of Meroe in South Africa prospered, exporting frankincense to Rome; by 1 BCE the Bantu had reached southern Africa, introducing agriculture and ironworking; 1-250 CE – Egypt underwent remarkable economic recovery under Roman rule; as ancient Egyptian cults and traditions declined, Christianity found many converts in Egypt; the Romans extended their control to the Berber kingdoms of Numidia and Mauretania; by 100 Axum had become a major power based on control of the incense trade; 44, Mesopotamia annexed by Rome; 69, Romans defeat the Saharan kingdom of Garamantes, but do not absorb it into the empire; 100, Alexandria emerged as a center of Christian scholarship and becomes the seat of one of the first Christian bishops; 150, Christianity began to spread westward to Roman provinces; 250-500, Christian Egypt linked the Mediterranean world with the various kingdoms of the Upper Nile; camels revolutionized trans-Saharan trade in West Africa; Berber nomads dominated the trade, bringing West African gold, ivory and ostrich feathers to the Mediterranean coast; 311-400 the Christian Donatist controversy led African bishops to rebel against the Christian church; 397, Berbers rebel against Roman rule; 429, Nomadic Vandals invade North Africa from Spain resulting in the fall of Carthage in 439 and the establishment of a North African kingdom; 969, Fatimid rulers of North Africa declared Egypt independent of Baghdad and made Cairo the capital; kingdoms of west Africa become prosperous on caravans crossing the Sahara to provide gold to Arabs; Arab trading settlements reached Zanzibar and Madagascar.

<u>Americas</u>: 500-250 BCE – Influence of Chavin culture waned and distinct local cultures emerged in South America; 400, Early Zapotec culture flourishing; 350, beginning of the Nazca culture in southern Peru; 250 BCE – 1 CE – Nazca and Moche cultures become increasingly sophisticated in Peru; Teotihuacan in Mexico became one of the most populous cities in the world, with a population of 40,000 by 50 CE; 200, Nazca Lines carved into the surface of the southern Peruvian desert; 100, Adena culture in North America reaches its height; 1-250 CE, Moche civilization thrives and expands through military conquest, building structures of adobe brick; Teotihuacan controlled production and distribution of obsidian through a city of 200,000; construction of the Pyramid of the Sun; 250-500, the great civilizations of Central America, Teotihuacan, the Maya and the Zapotecs were flourishing; 300-900, flourishing of the Maya civilization, the only fully literate culture in pre-Columbian America; cities of stone were built in the rain forests; between 500 and 750 CE two civilizations emerged in South America: the city of Tiahuanaco near Lake Titicaca and Huari, which was well fortified; in Central America, Teotihuacan collapsed, though it remained a pilgrimage center until the Spanish conquest in the 16th century; 700, beginning of Puebloan culture; 750-1000 CE – Mayan civilization begins to decline; Toltecs developing a state in Mexico, migrating into central Mexico; in North America, the Mogollon, Anasazi and Hohokam cultures emerged, building pueblos in the desert canyons; 750, first towns appear in the Mississippi valley; 900, advanced culture among Inuit of Alaska.

Europe: 500-250 BCE -- Greece reaches the pinnacle of the classical period in the 5th century; the Peloponnesian Wars between Athens and Sparta significantly weakened both of the major city-states, enabling Philip of Macedon to conquer them in 338; Philip's son, Alexander the Great, conquered the Persian Empire, creating the most important empire to date in history. Alexander's Hellenizing policies made Greek culture the predominant force in the empire. By 264 Rome was poised to become a major power; 250 BCE – 1 CE – after the fall of Carthage, Rome began a period of constant expansion, eventually controlling all of the Greek territories and reaching to Gaul to the north; a period of brief civil wars in which various military leaders attempted to control Rome occurred in the 1st century BCE; 27 CE, Octavian became emperor and reunited the Roman empire, creating a period of peace and prosperity that lasted for two centuries; 1-250 CE – during the second century, uprisings and internal strife weakened the structure of the Roman empire; Pompeii was destroyed by a volcanic eruption, famine and disease began to spread, and weak emperors began to lose control of the vast empire; 250-500 CE – various migrations and attacks by nomadic peoples, including the Huns and the Goths eventually destroyed the great empires; 284, Diocletian divided the Roman empire into Eastern and Western sections; the influence of Christianity and the founding of Constantinople moved power to the eastern part of the Empire; Germanic and Slavic peoples infiltrated and conquered much of the Roman empire; the Western Empire collapsed in 476; 500-1000 CE – The Franks became the most powerful of the Germanic tribes; Constantinople became the Christian capital of the Byzantine Empire; the emperor Justinian re-conquered North Africa and most of Italy, although most of this territory was lost to the Islamic empire or to Slavic peoples over the following 200 years; Charlemagne brought most of Western Europe into a single kingdom of the Franks; after his death the empire was divided into three parts, becoming the Saxon kingdom, the Holy Roman Empire, and the Carolingian Empire.

<u>West Asia</u>: 490-390 BCE, Persian empire weakened by strife and rebellion; Darius I of Persia attached Athens and other Greek cities, but was defeated at Marathon; 331, Alexander the Great defeated Darius III and ended the Persian empire; 323, Alexander's empire divided among his 3 successors, most of West Asia becoming part of the Seleucid empire; 247, founding of the Parthian dynasty; 171, Mithridates I founded the Parthian empire, which lasted about 500 years; 141 Parthians control Mesopotamia; 53, Parthians had heavily armored cavalry and were able to hold off Rome at the battle of Carrhae; Parthia controls the Silk Road linking China and Rome; 40, Rome recognized Herod the Great as ruler of Judaea; in the first century CE, the Parthian empire was torn by internal dissent; 114-198, Romans tried to invade Parthia three times; 224, Ardashir Popakan defeated the Parthians and founded the Sassanian dynasty, creating a centralized administration; his son Shapur repelled the Romans and made Sassanian Persia the most stable power of late antiquity; by the end of the 4th century, Sassanian Persia reached from the Euphrates to the Indus; social stability in their empire was fostered by a strong bureaucracy, a healthy agricultural economy and the state religion Zoroastrianism; Sassanian Persia posed a threat to Rome's interest in Asia, and the two were in conflict for 200 years, especially over Armenia; In the 5th century Persia was attacked by the "White Huns" but the empire survived; by the end of the 7th century all of western Asia had been overrun by Arabian armies, spreading the Islamic empire; 570, birth of Muhammed; 622, Start of the Islamic era; 656 Arabians overrun Persia; 661 beginning of the Umayyad Dynasty with Damascus as the center of the Islamic empire; 698 Arabs capture Carthage; 711, Arabs conquer Spain; 750, Abbasid dynasty came to power in the Islamic empire, but its legitimacy and authority were not universally accepted; Persian administrators were ruling much of the Islamic empire; by 969 the Byzantine empire peaked under a new dynasty of Macedonian rulers who came into conflict with the Arabs and regained control of Anatolia and Antioch.

East and South Asia: until 250 BCE the Russian steppe was occupied by nomads who hunted, herded animals and practiced agriculture, with their chieftains possibly acting as middlemen in the trade between Europe and China; 403-221, China was absorbed by internal conflict; in the 5th century the states of the Ganges plain were absorbed into the kingdom of Magadha; 327, Alexander's invasion of Northwest India; shortly after, Chandragupta Maurya claimed the throne and began to expand the empire; 272, Ashoka claimed the throne; by 232, the Mauryans ruled most of the subcontinent and Buddhism became a major force in India; 260, Ashoka converted to Buddhism; 232, death of Ashoka and end of the empire; 221, the Qin unified China and the ruler took the title of "First Emperor;" 210, widespread revolts after his death; 206, Han dynasty achieved power and became prosperous through a state monopoly on iron and salt, combined with opening the Silk Road to Central Asia; 221, the Great Wall was built as a defense against nomadic infiltration and attack; 185, Shunga dynasty begins;136, Confucianism became the state religion of China; 136, opening of the Silk Road; 108, China took military control of Korea; the Greek colony of Bactria became independent and the Bactrians established kingdoms in the Indus Valley where Greek and Indian cultures blended; much of Southeast Asia fell under Indian cultural influence as Hinduism and Buddhism spread east; 90, Bactrian kingdom of Gandhara falls to the Scythians; 30, Shakas take over the Indo-Greek villages of the Indus Valley; by 220 CE, the Chinese empire collapsed and regional warlords created 3 kingdoms; China remained divided for more than 300 years; Korea came to be controlled by small local states; 1st century CE, Yuezhi were pushed from the borders of China; the Kushan tribe united the other tribes, moved into Bactria, and then expanded into northern India; the Kingdom of Kushana crumbled at the end of the second century when native peoples of the region were beginning to assert power; 150, Kushans become Persian vassals; 280, after the period of fragmentation, China is reunited under the Jin, retaining control over southern China; northern China was invaded several times by nomads; during the political uncertainty, Buddhism flourished and many were drawn to the monastic life; Japan's Yamato state emerged in the 4th century, gradually gaining control of the southern part of the country; 386, Toba Wei reunified northern China; 420, Southern Dynasties begin in China with Song rule; the Gupta dynasty grew throughout the 4th century and controlled northern India in an age of religious tolerance; in the mid fifth century the "White Huns" entered India's golden age; in Ceylon, Buddhism became the dominant religion; 350-500 was a period of vast migration and invasion across Europe, Asia and Northern Africa.

The migrations occurred for a number of reasons, including famine, population density, and the search for a better life; major migrating groups included the Huns, Goths, Ostragoths, Visigoths, Alans, Vandals, Burgundians, Franks, Jutes, Angles, Saxons, Irish and Picts; by 526 the map had been completely redrawn by migrations; after centuries of conflict, China was united by the Sui dynasty, 581-617, which was succeeded by the Tang dynasty in 618; Chinese territory was expanded into Central Asia, and the Chinese gained control of most of the Silk Road; Buddhism reached Japan from China in 538; under Chinese influence, Japan underwent a series of reforms, abolishing slavery, adopting a modified form of written Chinese and creating a civil service; during the eighth century, internal rebellion weakened the Tang dynasty, which eventually collapsed in the ninth century; 960-79, China is divided into 10 separate states until reunified by the Song dynasty; both Korea and Japan were governed by strong Buddhist dynasties by 1000 CE.

Oceania: the island of Fiji was first settled around 1500 BCE and was the home of Polynesian culture; descendants of these settlers eventually colonized the entire Pacific region; by 400 Easter Island and the Hawaiian Islands had been settled, but they did not reach New Zealand until about 700.

1000-1500 CE – The Era of Trade, Conflict and Exploration

During the first millennium, navigation of the seas became possible. Three civilizations explored the seas and used the seas to reach and claim new territories: the Vikings used the rivers of Russia to reach the Black Sea and crossed the Atlantic to Iceland and North America; the Arabs discovered a sea route to China in the 8th century and began a new age of trade; they also reached the East Indies and East Africa; and the Polynesians expanded from island to island throughout the Pacific, colonizing every island by 1000 CE.

Religious conflict and territorial wars were intense in many parts of the world. As marginal land was cleared for agriculture, populations expanded and demanded new territory. Trade routes developed across Europe and Asia, and a mercantile economy developed. The growth of Christianity in Europe caused conflict with the Islamic empire and produced the Crusades (1050-1350), which were military efforts to regain control over the Holy Land. For the most part, the Crusades were not successful, but progress was made in Spain and Portugal. Northern India fell into Muslim control and Buddhism was driven from the Indian subcontinent. Nomadic invasions from the north of China shrunk the Song Empire.

In the 13th century, Mongol horsemen, led by Genghis Khan and others, emerged from Central Asia and began to conquer large regions of eastern Europe and Asia. By 1300 they divided their empire into 4 large empires reaching from China to eastern Europe. Their attacks were particularly destructive in China and the Islamic states of southwest Asia. Once the Mongols controlled these regions, however, trade and travel was restored. The Muslim Abbasid Caliphate was ended, but Islam continued to spread as it was adopted by the Mongols. New Muslim states arose in Egypt and India. Europe continued to try to defend itself against Muslim and Mongol incursion, but Venice and Genoa flourished because of trade connections with the East.

Epidemics of bubonic plague moved from China and Korea to the West Coast of Europe. Massive deaths led to economic and social devastation that weakened states throughout Europe, Asia and North Africa. The "Little Ice Age" (which lasted until the nineteenth century) brought bad weather to these plague-devastated areas, causing poor harvests. Mongol empires began to decline and crumble in many areas. The Khanate of the Golden Horde, however, continued in southern Russia until the 15th century. In China and Persia, the Mongols were assimilated into the local populations. In China, the Ming dynasty introduced a Han Chinese aristocratic regime. Imperial expansion, mass migration, cross-cultural trade and long-distance travel enabled the spread of agricultural crops, domesticated animals, and diseases. Chinese rulers extended their authority south of the Yangtze River; Muslim armies penetrated India, Persia and North Africa; Bantu-speaking peoples migrated throughout sub-Saharan Africa. The exchange of culture and biology dramatically changed societies throughout the eastern hemisphere.

By 1500 most of the eastern hemisphere had recovered from the population losses caused by the plague. In southwest Asia, two Turkish groups established strong empires – the Ottomans in Anatolia, and the Safavids in Persia. European states were beginning to build central governments with standing armies and gunpowder weapons. During the 15th century, Portuguese mariners settled the Atlantic islands, explored the West Coast of Africa, and made a sea voyage to India. Columbus crossed from Spain to the Americas, where the Aztec and Inca empires ruled over complex agricultural societies. A new era of exploration had begun, paving the way for further expansion. Each of the major cultural regions had their own unique world views. Ideas, religions, and technologies were spread by trade, migration or cultural and political expansion. Buddhism, Christianity and Islam each had wide areas of influence. Mapping was practiced in one form or another by almost every culture.

<u>Africa</u>: 1050, Berber Muslim Almoravids controlled northwest Africa and part of Muslim Spain, invading Ghana in 1076, until 1147, when another Berber religious sect, the Almohads took control and unified the Maghreb; 1150, emergence of the Zagwe dynasty in Ethiopia revivesdsea trade; 1174, Saladin became ruler of Egypt, ending Fatimid dynasty and founded the Ayyubid dynasty; 1250s, Mali Empire conquered the Kingdom of Ghana and took control of west African trade in gold and slaves with huge camel caravans crossing the Sahara to North Africa; Swahili city-states on the east African Coast exported goods through Indian Ocean trade routes; rulers of Mali and Swahili city-states adopted Islam and built mosques and religious schools; Islam did not reach central or southern Africa, but trade led to the development of several wealthy states like the Kingdom of Great Zimbabwe; 1250, Mamluk military caste takes over Egypt; 1270, expansion of the Christian Kingdom of Ethiopia; 14th century, Mali Empire dominates West Africa, based on trade of gold and slaves for salt, textiles, horses and manufactured goods from the North; 1324 Mansa Musa (Mali ruler) makes pilgrimage to Mecca and word spreads of his wealth; Swahili cities in East Africa escaped the plague, but suffered economically due to trade slow-down; 1344, Ethiopia at its height; 1390, formation of the Kingdom of Kongo; 1460s-90s, Songhay ruler Sunni Ali conquered Mali and took over the Saharan caravan trade; Portuguese explores the west coast, where African rulers laid the foundations for the Akan and Benin states; sailors from the Swahili city-states in East Africa helped Vasco da Gama understand local monsoon winds and finish his voyage to India.

<u>The Americas</u>: the Chimu rose to prominence with their capital at Chan Chan and ruled by semi-divine kings; the empire expanded by military conquest, exerting firm economic control of conquered territories and linking them with a system of roads; in Central America Chichimec tribes sacked the Toltec city of Tula and established several small city-states that were constantly at war with one another; North America's first true towns were established in the Mississippi valley and cliff dwellings were built in the desert southwest; 1000, Leif Ericson (son of Eric the Red) sailed from Greenland to North America; 1100, Anasazi people of the southwest built cliff dwellings at Mesa Verde and Chaco Canyon; 1200, Incas settle in the Andean valley; 1200s, many small city-states competed for power in central Mexico; migrating Mexican people entered Mexico, laying the foundation for what would become the Aztec Empire; in the Andes, local rulers organized independent states; woodland peoples east of the Mississippi built increasingly elaborate ceremonial centers; 1438, Incas began territorial expansion until, 30 years later, the kingdom covered 2500 miles along the Andes and the west coast, linked by systems of roads; the Aztec empire reached its height in the later 1400s; through trade, its influence extended across most of Central America to the pueblo farmers north of the Rio Grande; 1492, Columbus lands on Cuba and Hispaniola; both Aztecs and Incas were consolidating their empires when the first European contact occurred.

<u>Europe</u>: in the 11th century the consolidation of Poland, Hungary and the Scandinavian regions into the world of western Christianity resulted in a new peak of power and influence; Western Europeans began to take control of the Mediterranean from the Arabs and Byzantines; a new era of prosperity based on trade began; 1016, Canute unites England, Denmark and Norway; 1054, final split between the Roman and Orthodox churches; 1066, Norman conquest of England in the Battle of Hastings; 1091, Norman conquest of Sicily; 1119, Bologna University founded; 1154, construction of Chartres Cathedral; in the thirteenth century, feudal monarchies of England and France consolidated large regional states. This did not occur in Italy and Germany due to conflicts between Church and State; 1236, Christians took Cordoba and Seville in Spain, leaving only Moorish Granada in Islamic control; 1237, beginning of the Mongol conquest of Russia; 1261, Byzantine Empire regains Constantinople; 1271, Marco Polo leaves for China; the 14th century was a time of plague and recovery; scarce labor led peasants and workers to demand higher wages and better working conditions, but their efforts were unsuccessful; France suffered from the Hundred Years War; Religious divisions brought conflict; rival popes in Rome and Avignon split the church; the Lollards in England challenged the doctrine and the authority of the Church; 1337, beginning of the Hundred Years' War; 1347, Bubonic plague reached Italy; 1381, Peasants Revolt in England; 1397, Union of Kalmar places Norway, Denmark and Sweden under a single ruler; the 15th century marked the beginning of the Renaissance in Europe; city-states of Italy were the cultural leaders of Europe; political power was shifting to the "New Monarchs" who ruled strong centralized kingdoms in England, France and Spain; Poland dominated eastern Europe; power quickly shifted to Muscovy when Ivan III claimed the title "tsar" in 1472, and began Russian expansion; 1415, English defeat French at Agincourt; 1417, schism in the church ends; 1429, English siege of Orleans ended by Joan of Arc; 1453, end of the Hundred Years War; 1469, marriage of Ferdinand of Aragon and Isabella of Castile; 1492, Muslim Grenada falls to Spain; 1494, Charles VIII of France invades Italy; by the end of the 15th century, Europe was on the cusp of rapid territorial expansion. Europeans had become technologically advanced, resourceful, and had amassed an amazing knowledge of much of the world through travel and trade.

West Asia: in the 11th century the Byzantine Empire lost much of its Asian territory to the Seljuk Turks; 1055, Islamic Turks become established in Baghdad and form a partnership with Persians and Arabs; 1099, the first Crusade retakes Jerusalem and establishes small crusader states; 1187, Muslims led by Saladin and others reclaim Jerusalem; 1258, Mongols sacked Baghdad and overthrew the Abbasid Caliphate, establishing themselves as Il-Khans, subordinate to the Great Khan in China; by 1300, most of them had accepted Islam; 1299, Osman founds the Ottoman state; in the late 14th century, the Turkish warrior Timur claimed a large empire in Central Asia, invaded India, and planned to attack China when he died in 1406; the Ottoman empire expanded during the 14th century; by 1400, the Byzantine empire was reduced to Constantinople and a few coastal areas in Greece and western Anatolia; 1347, the plague reached Baghdad and Constantinople; 1405, Timur's sons divided his empire; a new power was rising in Persia, the Shi'ite Safavids; 1453, Ottomans took Constantinople and ended the Byzantine Empire.

North and East Asia: by 1110, Song China was the most advanced, wealthy, and populous state in the world; in Japan, the emperors lost power to the Fujiwara family in the mid 12th century, triggering a period of internal warfare that ended with the victory of the Minamoto clan as Shoguns; 1045, moveable type printing was invented in China; 1191, beginning of Zen Buddhism in Japan; 1211, Genghis Khan invaded northern China, but the southern Song empire did not fall until 1279; 1264, Kublai Khan became emperor and founded the Yuan dynasty in 1270; 1292, Marco Polo left China; 1294, Kublai Khan's death; 14th century, plague, floods and famine raised Chinese resentment of Mongol rule; 1356, a rebellion in southeast China put the Ming dynasty in Power; Mongols were eventually driven out of China; 1333, Japan's Kamakura shogunate collapsed; 1351, massive floods of the Yellow River; 1392, Yi dynasty begins in Korea.

South and Southeast Asia: during the 11th and 12th centuries the Khmer Empire was at its height; during the 11th century, Northern India was repeatedly invaded by Ghazni Muslims of Afghanistan; 1186, last Ghanzi ruler was deposed by Turkish leader Muhammad al Ghur; southeast India was controlled by the Chola dynasty, who also controlled the sea route between west Asia and China; the Khmer Empire and the Kingdom of Pagan experienced a golden age; 1044, first Burmese state established at Pagan; 1152, Temple of Angkor Wat finished; 1206, Qutb al-din and his Islamic raiders, after terrorizing northern India for 30 years, established a new sultanate with its capital at Delhi; during the 14th century the sultanate of Delhi reached its greatest extent, but lost control of most of the peninsula by century's end; 14th century, new Thai kingdom of Siam is founded; 1398, Delhi sacked by Timur; 14th century, southeast Asia was increasingly controlled by the Majapahit empire in Java; 15th century, Ming dynasty consolidated its power in China; 1400, Malacca founded; by 1500, Malacca's populations was 50,000 and was a major center of world trade.

1500 – 1815 European Expansion

1500-1600, Spain seized a huge land empire that included much of South and Central America, the Philippine Islands, and the West Indies; Portugal built a sailing empire that reached from Brazil to Malacca and Macao; Magellan proved that the oceans were linked; sea lanes were established through the Indian, Atlantic and Pacific oceans, marking the beginning of global trade; Portugal traded with China and Japan, but cultural contact between Europe and East Asia was minimal; European contact barely reached beyond the cost in Africa; missionaries took the Catholic faith to many parts of the Spanish and Portuguese empires; the Church faced the threat of the Protestant Reformation in Europe; Catholic kingdoms struggled to halt the expansion of the Ottoman empire in the Mediterranean and into Central Europe; the Dutch and English began to build their overseas empires.

Africa: The Songhai are defeated by the Ottomans, who also gained control of the trans-Saharan caravan trade; 1505, first Portuguese trading posts in East Africa; 1517, Ottomans conquer Egypt; 1546, Songhai destroys Mali Empire; 1570, Portugal establishes a colony in Angola; 1591, Songhai empire falls to Morocco.

The Americas: Spanish arrive, with horses, iron weapons and guns; they also introduce devastating diseases to the native populations; by 1511, the Spanish had control of all of the major Caribbean Islands; 1519-22, Cortes conquered the Aztecs; 1531-32, Pizarro defeats the Incas; 1530's, Portugal began to gradually colonize the coast of Brazil.

Europe: the Protestant Reformation was the primary concern, with Scandinavia, England, Scotland and many German States abandoning Catholicism, taking over church lands and monasteries, and governing state religions; Russia's territory expanded to the Caspian and to western Siberia.
West Asia: the Ottoman navy ruled the Mediterranean until 1571; Muslims dominated commercial shipping.

South and Southeast Asia: 1523, Chagatai Turks invaded northern India, creating the Mughal dynasty of Muslim rulers; Portugal gained control of the Spice Islands; Burma remained the leading power in Southeast Asia, conquering Siam and Laos.

1501, first black slaves brought to the Americas by Spanish; 1520, Suleiman the Magnificent rules Ottoman Empire; 1527, end of the Italian Renaissance; Medici family expelled from Florence; 1543, Copernicus publishes theory that earth revolves around the sun; 1547, Ivan IV (the Terrible) crowned in Russia; 1580, Drake circumnavigates the globe; 1588, England defeats the Spanish Armada; 1598, Edict of Nantes ends three decades of religious fighting in France; 1600, English East India company founded.

<u>1600-1700</u>: Dutch, French and British explorers create settlements and trade networks; British and French seamen searched for a northwest and northeast passage from Europe to Asia.

<u>Africa</u>: slave trade affected African politics and society; populations grew because of the introduction of food crops from the Americas; 2 million slaves exported; 1620, African slaves taken to the English colony at Jamestown; 1652, Dutch colony established at the Cape of Good Hope.

<u>The Americas</u>: in this period of rapid colonization, Spain controls much of Central America and the Andes, Portugal builds a plantation society along the coast of northeastern South America; English colonies are planted along the east coast of North America and sugar plantations on Jamaica and other Caribbean Islands, and French and Dutch colonists build forts and trading posts in North America with sugar plantations in the Caribbean and Guiana; French hunters and traders explore the Great Lakes regions and the upper Mississippi valley; indigenous peoples remain independent; 1604, French colony of Arcadia founded; 1630, English Massachusetts Bay colony founded; 1654, England seizes Jamaica from Spain; 1664, England gains control of New Amsterdam from the Dutch; 1695, God discovered in Brazil.

<u>Europe</u>: 1618-48, Thirty years war in Germany; Treaty of Westphalia established a system of states based on a balance of power, which maintained relative stability until the French Revolution; the Russian Empire expanded to the Pacific Ocean by mid-century; 1643; Louis XIV becomes king of France; 1682, Peter the Great becomes tsar of Russia; 1683, siege of Vienna ends the Ottoman empire.

<u>East Asia</u>: 1644, a Manchu army defeated the Ming dynasty and established the Qing dynasty, which endured until 1911; in Japan, the Tokugawa dynasty introduced a centralized government; foreign trade was carefully controlled by China and Japan; 1603, Tokugawa dynasty established;
<u>South and Southeast Asia</u>: English and Dutch trading companies consolidated their holdings in the Indian Ocean; 1619, Dutch founded Batavia as trading center in Southeast Asia; 1663, Dutch expel the Portuguese from Ceylon; 1642-48, English Civil War' 1665, Great Plague in London kills 75,000.

<u>1700-1815</u>: new ideas began to emerge in science, philosophy and politics; the enlightenment fomented rebellion in many places; improvements in agriculture increased food production, which fueled population growth; technological innovations led to the Industrial Revolution and urban growth; European expansion continued, and Britain established its power in India and Australia; rapid population growth, the emergence of industrial societies, and the developing of the American colonies combined with new ideas about government and individual freedom to create uprisings and demands for political change in the late eighteenth century; the success of the American Revolution and the rejection of royal authority in favor of representative government during the French revolution, laid the groundwork for significant change in Europe and throughout the world; the aftermath of the French and American revolutions and the Napoleonic Wars gave rise to a new nationalism and new demands for democracy and freedom. The colonial regimes of South America were overthrown and in Europe Belgium and Greece achieved independence.

<u>Africa</u>: Islamic influence spread in North Africa; the Asante and Yoruba dominated West Africa; the slave trade flourished, with over 13.5 million people transported from Africa; Xhosa resistance in the south limited British and Dutch expansion; 1779-80, war between Boers and Bantu in southern Africa; 1795, British take over the Cape of Good Hope; 1798, Napoleon occupies Egypt.

<u>The Americas</u>: rivalries between French, Spanish, English and Dutch for territory in North America; 1775, the American Revolution begins; 1783, division between the US and Canada; Portuguese and Spanish territorial rivalry in South America; Spain and Portugal both trying to control gold mines in Brazil; struggles between settlers and native peoples; 1728, Bering explores Alaska.

<u>Europe</u>: throughout Europe governments became stronger, particularly Peter the Great in Russia and Frederick the Great in Prussia; the Bourbon monarchy reached its peak in France; 1789, French Revolution begins; 1799, a coup brings Napoleon to power in France; 1701, War of Spanish Succession begins; 1707, the United Kingdom of Great Britain formed (England, Wales, and Scotland); 1756, beginning of the Seven Years War and the French and Indian Wars in America; in India, more than 100 British prisoners die in the "Black Hole of Calcutta;" 1757, beginning of the British Empire in India; 1765, invention of the Steam engine; 1769, production of the spinning machine marks an early step in the Industrial Revolution; 1778, Cook discovers Hawaii; 1793, Louis XVI and Marie Antoinette executed; reign of Terror begins in France; 1803, the Louisiana Purchase; 1804, Haiti declares independence from France; France creates a law code; 1819, Simon Bolivar liberates New Granada;

Skill 1.3   Recognize the multiple sources of major historical events and analyze cause-and-effect relationships among important events from an era.

Chronology is the ordering of events through time. Chronologies are often listed along a timeline or in a list by date.

Chronologies allow for easy visualization of a wide expanse of history in one place. This allows a student to quickly get an overview of the major events and changes over time. By including important related events, the causes and effects of major developments can be emphasized. By placing chronologies for different societies parallel to one another, comparisons in relative development can be quickly interpreted, providing material for further historical exploration.

Historic causation is the concept that events in history are linked to one another by and endless chain of cause and effect. The root causes of major historical events cannot always be seen immediately, and are only apparent when looking back from many years later.

When Columbus landed in the New World in 1492, the full effect his discovery could not have been measured at that time. By opening the Western Hemisphere to economic and political development by Europeans, Columbus changed the face of the world. The native populations that had existed before Columbus arrived were quickly decimated by disease and warfare. Over the following century, the Spanish conquered most of South and Central America, and English and French settlers arrived in North America, eventually displacing the native people. This gradual displacement occurred over many years and could not have been foreseen by those early explorers. Nevertheless, looking back, it can be said that Columbus caused a series of events that had a great impact on world history.

In some cases, individual events had an immediate, clear effect. In 1941, Europe was embroiled in war. On the Pacific Rim, Japan was engaged in military occupation of Korea and other Asian countries. The United States took a position of isolation, choosing not to become directly involved with the conflicts. This position changed rapidly, however, on the morning of December 7, 1941, when Japanese forces launched a surprise attack on a US naval base at Pearl Harbor in Hawaii. The United States immediately declared war on Japan, and became involved in Europe shortly afterwards. The entry of the United States into the Second World War undoubtedly contributed to the eventual victory of the Allied forces in Europe, and the defeat of Japan after two atomic bombs were dropped there by the US. The surprise attack on Pearl Harbor affected the outcome of the war and the shape of the modern world.

Interaction between cultures, either by exploration, migration or war, often contribute directly to major historical events, but other forces can influence the course of history, as well. Religious movements such as the rise of Catholicism in the middle ages created social changes throughout Europe and culminated in the Crusades and the expulsion of Muslims from Spain. Technological developments can lead to major historical events, as in the case of the Industrial Revolution, which was driven by the replacement of water power with steam power.

Social movements can also cause major historical shifts. Between the Civil War and the early 1960s in the United States, racial segregation was practiced legally in many parts of the country through "Jim Crow" laws. Demonstrations and activism opposing segregation began to escalate during the late 1950s and early 1960s, eventually leading to the passage in the US Congress of the Civil Rights Act of 1964, which ended legal segregation in the United States.

Skill 1.4   Recognize specialized fields of historical study and demonstrate knowledge of ways in which historians use concepts and theories from other disciplines

Specialized fields of historical study include the following:

- Social history – the approach to the study of history that views a period of time through the eyes of everyday people and is focused on emerging trends.
- Archaeology: study of prehistoric and historic human cultures through the recovery, documentation and analysis of material remains and environmental data.
- Art History: the study of changes in the social context of art.
- Big History: study of history on a large scale across long time frames (since the Big Bang and up to the future) through a multi-disciplinary approach.
- Chronology: science of localizing historical events in time.
- Cultural history: the study of culture in the past.
- Diplomatic history: the study of international relations in the past.
- Economic History: the study of economies in the past.
- Military History: the study of warfare and wars in history and what is sometimes considered to be a sub-branch of military history, Naval History.
- Paleography: study of ancient texts.
- Political history: the study of politics in the past.
- Psychohistory: study of the psychological motivations of historical events.
- Historiography of science: study of the structure and development of science.
- Social History: the study of societies in the past.
- World History: the study of history from a global perspective.

Skill 1.5   Analyze historical events from a variety of conceptual perspectives

The practice of dividing time into a number of discrete periods or blocks of time is called "periodization." Because history is continuous, all systems of periodization are arbitrary to a greater or lesser extent. However, dividing time into segments facilitates understanding of changes that occur over time and identifying similarities of events, knowledge, and experience within the defined period. Further, some divisions of time into these periods apply only under specific circumstances.

Divisions of time may be determined by date, by cultural advances or changes, by historical events, by the influence of particular individuals or groups, or by geography. Speaking of the World War II era defines a particular period of time in which key historical, political, social and economic events occurred. Speaking of the Jacksonian Era, however, has meaning only in terms of American history. Defining the "Romantic period" makes sense only in England, Europe and countries under their direct influence.

Many of the divisions of time that are commonly used are open to some controversy and discussion. The use of BC and AD dating, for example, has clear reference only in societies that account time according to the Christian calendar. Similarly, speaking of "the year of the pig" has greatest meaning in China.

An example of the kind of questions that can be raised about designations of time periods can be seen in the use of "Victorian." Is it possible to speak of a Victorian era beyond England? Is literature that is written in the style of the English poets and writers "Victorian" if it is written beyond the borders of England?

Some designations also carry both positive and negative connotations. "Victorian" is an example of potential negative connotations, as well. The term is often used to refer to class conflict, sexual repression, and heavy industry. These might be negative connotations. The term "Renaissance" is generally read with positive connotations.

Sometimes several designations can be applied to the same period. The period known as the "Elizabethan Period" in English history is also called "the English Renaissance." In some cases the differences in designation refer primarily to the specific aspect of history that is being considered. For example, one designation may be applied to a specific period of time when one is analyzing cultural history, while a different designation is applied to the same period of time when considering military history.

COMPETENCY 2.0   UNDERSTAND SOCIAL SCIENCE SKILLS TO LOCATE, ANALYZE, AND SYNTHESIZE INFORMATION RELATED TO HISTORICAL TOPICS.

Skill 2.1   Recognize the characteristics and uses of various social science reference resources and types of historical evidence.

Reference sources can be of great value and by teaching students how to access these first, they will later have skills that will help them access more in—depth databases and sources of information.

Encyclopedias are reference materials that appear in book or electronic form. Encyclopedias can be considered general or specific. General encyclopedias peripherally cover most fields of knowledge; specific encyclopedias cover a smaller amount of material in greater depth. Encyclopedias are good first sources of information for students. While their scope is limited, they can provide a quick introduction to topics so that students can get familiar with the topics before exploring the topics in greater depth.

Almanacs provide statistical information on various topics. Typically, these references are rather specific. They often cover a specific period of time. One famous example is the *Farmer's Almanac.* This annual publication summarizes, among many other things, weather conditions for the previous year.

An **atlas** is a collection of maps usually bound into a book and contain geographic features, political boundaries, and perhaps social, religious and economic statistics. Atlases can be found at most libraries but they are widely available on the Internet. The United States Library of Congress holds more than 53,000 atlases, most likely the largest and most comprehensive collection in the world.

Bibliographies contain references for further research. Bibliographies are usually organized topically. They point people to the in-depth resources they will need for a complete review of a topic.

Databases, typically electronic, are collections of material on specific topics. For example, teachers can go online and find many databases of science articles for students in a variety of topics.

The Internet and other research resources provide a wealth of information on thousands of interesting topics for students preparing presentations or projects. Using search engines like Google, Microsoft and Infotrac, students can search multiple Internet resources or databases at one time. Students should have an outline of the purpose of a project or research presentation that includes:

- Purpose - identity the reason for the research information
- Objective - having a clear thesis for a project will allow the students opportunities to be specific on Internet searches
- Preparation - when using resources or collecting data, students should create folders for sorting through the information. Providing labels for the folders will create a system of organization that will make construction of the final project or presentation easier and less time consuming
- Procedure - organized folders and a procedural list of what the project or presentation needs to include will create A+ work for students and A+ grading for teachers
- Visuals or artifacts - choose data or visuals that are specific to the subject content or presentation. Make sure that poster boards or Power Point presentations can be visually seen from all areas of the classroom. Teachers can provide laptop computers for Power Point presentations.

Finally, periodical guides categorize articles and special editions of journals and magazines to help archive and organize the vast amount of material that is put in periodicals each year.

Statistical **surveys** are used in social sciences to collect information on a sample of the population. With any kind of information, care must be taken to accurately record information so the results are not skewed or distorted.

Opinion Polls are used to represent the opinions of a population by asking a number of people a series of questions about a product, place, person, event or perhaps the president and then using the results to apply the answers to a larger group or population. Polls, like surveys are subject to errors in the process. Errors can occur based on who is asked the question, where they are asked, the time of day or the biases one may hold in relevance to the poll being taken.

Refer to Skill 2.2 for further discussion.

Skill 2.2 **Distinguish between primary and secondary sources and demonstrate knowledge of the advantages and limitations of each**

Primary sources include the following kinds of materials:

Documents that reflect the immediate, everyday concerns of people: memoranda, bills, deeds, charters, newspaper reports, pamphlets, graffiti, popular writings, journals or diaries, records of decision-making bodies, letters, receipts, snapshots, etc.

Theoretical writings which reflect care and consideration in composition and an attempt to convince or persuade. The topic will generally be deeper and have more pervasive values than is the case with "immediate" documents. These may include newspaper or magazine editorials, sermons, political speeches, philosophical writings, etc.

Narrative accounts of events, ideas, trends, etc. written with intention by someone contemporary with the events described.

Statistical data, although statistics may be misleading.

Literature and nonverbal materials, novels, stories, poetry and essays from the period, as well as coins, archaeological artifacts, and art produced during the period. Guidelines for the use of primary resources:

1. Be certain that you understand how language was used at the time of writing and that you understand the context in which it was produced.
2. Do not read history blindly; but be certain that you understand both explicit and implicit referenced in the material.
3. Read the entire text you are reviewing; do not simply extract a few sentences to read.
4. Although anthologies of materials may help you identify primary source materials, the full original text should be consulted.

Secondary sources include the following kinds of materials:
- Books written on the basis of primary materials about the period of time
- Books written on the basis of primary materials about persons who played a major role in the events under consideration
- Books and articles written on the basis of primary materials about the culture, the social norms, the language, and the values of the period
- Quotations from primary sources
- Statistical data on the period
- The conclusions and inferences of other historians
- Multiple interpretations of the ethos of the time

Guidelines for the use of secondary sources:
- Do not rely upon only a single secondary source.
- Check facts and interpretations against primary sources whenever possible.
- Do not accept the conclusions of other historians uncritically.
- Place greatest reliance on secondary sources created by the best and most respected scholars.
- Do not use the inferences of other scholars as if they were facts.
- Ensure that you recognize any bias the writer brings to his/her interpretation of history.
- Understand the primary point of the book as a basis for evaluating the value of the material presented in it to your questions.

Skill 2.3 **Demonstrate knowledge of research skills and procedures used in the social sciences.**

There are many different ways to find ideas for **research problems**. One of the most common ways is through experiencing and assessing relevant problems in a specific field. Researchers are often involved in the fields in which they choose to study, and thus encounter practical problems related to their areas of expertise on a daily basis. The can use their knowledge, expertise and research ability to examine their selected research problem. For students, all that this entails is being curious about the world around them. Research ideas can come from one's background, culture, education, experiences etc. Another way to get research ideas is by exploring literature in a specific field and coming up with a question that extends or refines previous research.

Once a **topic** is decided, a research question must be formulated. A research question is a relevant, researchable, feasible statement that identifies the information to be studied. Once this initial question is formulated, it is a good idea to think of specific issues related to the topic. This will help to create a hypothesis. A research **hypothesis** is a statement of the researcher's expectations for the outcome of the research problem. It is a summary statement of the problem to be addressed in any research document. A good hypothesis states, clearly and concisely, the researchers expected relationship between the variables that they are investigating. Once a hypothesis is decided, the rest of the research paper should focus on analyzing a set of information or arguing a specific point. Thus, there are two types of research papers: analytical and argumentative.

Analytical papers focus on examining and understanding the various parts of a research topic and reformulating them in a new way to support your initial statement. In this type of research paper, the research question is used as both a basis for investigation as well as a topic for the paper. Once a variety of information is collected on the given topic, it is coalesced into a clear discussion.

Argumentative papers focus on supporting the question or claim with evidence or reasoning. Instead of presenting research to provide information, an argumentative paper presents research in order to prove a debatable statement and interpretation.

The **scientific method** is the process by which researchers over time endeavor to construct an accurate (that is, reliable, consistent and non-arbitrary) representation of the world. Recognizing that personal and cultural beliefs influence both our perceptions and our interpretations of natural phenomena, standard procedures and criteria minimize those influences when developing a theory.

The scientific method has four steps:

1. Observation and description of a phenomenon or group of phenomena.
2. Formulation of a hypothesis to explain the phenomena.
3. Use of the hypothesis to predict the existence of other phenomena or to predict quantitatively the results of new observations.
4. Performance of experimental tests of the predictions by several independent experimenters and properly performed experiments.

While the researcher may bring certain biases to the study, it's important that bias not be permitted to enter into the interpretation. It's also important that data that doesn't fit the hypothesis not be ruled out. This is unlikely to happen if the researcher is open to the possibility that the hypothesis might turn out to be null. Another important caution is to be certain that the methods for analyzing and interpreting are flawless. Abiding by these mandates is important if the discovery is to make a contribution to human understanding.

Skill 2.4   Evaluate historical information.

Primary sources are works, records, etc. that were created during the period being studied or immediately after it. Secondary sources are works written significantly after the period being studied and based upon primary sources.

Suppose you are preparing for a presentation on the Civil War and you intend to focus on causes, an issue that has often been debated. If you are examining the matter of slavery as a cause, a graph of the increase in the number of slaves by area of the country for the previous 100 years would be very useful in the discussion. If you are focusing on the economic conditions that were driving the politics of the age, graphs of GDP, distribution of wealth geographically and individually, and relationship of wealth to ownership of slaves would be useful.

If you are discussing the war in Iraq, detailed maps with geopolitical elements would help clarify not only the day-to-day happenings but also the historical features that led up to it. A map showing the number of oil fields and where they are situated with regard to the various political factions and charts showing output of those fields historically would be useful. If you are teaching the history of space travel, photos of the most famous astronauts will add interest to the discussion.

Graphs showing the growth of the industry and charts showing discoveries and their relationship to the lives of everyday Americans would be helpful.

Making a decision based on a set of given information requires a careful interpretation of the information to decide the strength of the evidence supplied and what it means.

A chart showing that the number of people of foreign birth living in the US has increased annually over the last ten years might allow one to make conclusions about population growth and changes in the relative sizes of ethnic groups in the US The chart would not give information about the reason the number of foreign-born citizens increased, or address matters of immigration status. Conclusions in these areas would be invalid based on this information.

Social studies provide an opportunity for students to broaden their general academic skills in many areas. By encouraging students to ask and investigate questions, they gain skill in making meaningful inquiries into social issues. Providing them with a range of sources requires students to make judgments about the best sources for investigating a line of inquiry and develops the ability to determine authenticity among those sources. Collaboration develops the ability to work as part of a team and to respect the viewpoints of others.

Historic events and social issues cannot be considered only in isolation. People and their actions are connected in many ways, and events are linked through cause and effect over time. Identifying and analyzing these social and historic links is a primary goal of the social sciences. The methods used to analyze social phenomena borrow from several of the social sciences. Interviews, statistical evaluation, observation and experimentation are just some of the ways that people's opinions and motivations can be measured. From these opinions, larger social beliefs and movements can be interpreted, and events, issues and social problems can be placed in context to provide a fuller view of their importance.

Also Refer to Skill 2.3 for additional information.

Skill 2.5   Interpret graphic presentations of historical information.

We use **illustrations** of various sorts because it is often easier to demonstrate a given idea visually instead of orally. Sometimes it is even easier to do so with an illustration than a description. This is especially true in the areas of education and research because humans are visually stimulated. It is a fact that any idea presented visually in some manner is always easier to understand and to comprehend than simply getting an idea across verbally, by hearing it or reading it. Among the more common illustrations used are various types of **maps, graphs and charts**.

Photographs and globes are useful as well, but as they are limited in what kind of information that they can show, so they are rarely used. Unless, as in the case of a photograph, it is of a particular political figure or a time that one wishes to visualize.

Although maps have advantages over globes and photographs, they do have one major disadvantage. The major problem of all maps comes about because most maps are flat and the Earth is a sphere. It is impossible to reproduce exactly on a flat surface an object shaped like a sphere. In order to put the earth's features onto a map they must be stretched in some way. This stretching is called **distortion.**

Distortion does not mean that maps are wrong it simply means that they are not perfect representations of the Earth or its parts. **Cartographers,** or mapmakers, understand the problems of distortion. They try to design them so that there is as little distortion as possible in the maps.

Information can be gained looking at a map that might take hundreds of words to explain otherwise. Maps reflect the great variety of knowledge covered by social sciences. To show such a variety of information, maps are made in many different ways. Because of this variety, maps must be understood in order to make the best sense of them. Once they are understood, maps provide a solid foundation for social science studies.

To apply information obtained from **graphs** one must understand the two major reasons why graphs are used:

1. To present a <u>model or theory</u> visually in order to show how two or more variables interrelate.
2. To present <u>real world</u> data visually in order to show how two or more variables interrelate.

Most often used are those known as **bar graphs** and **line graphs**. (Charts are often used for similar reasons and are explained in the next section).

Graphs themselves are most useful when one wishes to demonstrate the sequential increase, or decrease of a variable or to show specific correlations between two or more variables in a given circumstance.

Most common is the **bar graph**, because it is easy to see and an understandable way of visually showing the difference in a given set of variables. However it is limited in that it can not really show the actual proportional increase, or decrease, of each given variable to each other. (In order to show a decrease, a bar graph must show the "bar" under the starting line, thus removing the ability to really show how the various different variables would relate to each other).

Thus, in order to accomplish this, one must use a **line graph**. Line graphs can be of two types: a **linear** or **non-linear** graph. A linear line graph uses a series of straight lines; a non-linear line graph uses a curved line. Though the lines can be either straight or curved, all of the lines are called **curves**.

To use **charts** correctly, one should remember the reasons one uses graphs. The general ideas are similar. It is usually a question as to which, a graph or chart, is more capable of adequately portraying the information one wants to illustrate. One can see the difference between them and realize that in many ways graphs and charts are interrelated. One of the most common types, because it is easiest to read and understand, even for the lay person, is the **pie-chart**.

You can see pie-charts used often, especially when one is trying to illustrate the differences in percentages among various items, or when one is demonstrating the divisions of a whole.

Posters. The power of the political poster in the 21st century seems trivial considering the barrage of electronic campaigning, mudslinging, and reporting that seems to have taken over the video and audio media in election season. Even so, the political poster has been a powerful propaganda tool, and it has been around for a long time. For example, in the 1st century AD, a poster that calls for the election of a Satrius as quinquennial has survived to this day. Nowhere have political posters been used more powerfully or effectively than in Russia in the 1920s in the campaign to promote communism. Many of the greatest Russian writers of that era were the poster writers. Those posters would not be understood at all except in the light of what was going on in the country at the time.

However, today we see them primarily at rallies and protests where they are usually hand-lettered and hand-drawn. The message is rarely subtle. Understanding the messages of posters requires little thought as a rule. However, they are usually meaningless unless the context is clearly understood. For example, a poster reading "Camp Democracy" can only be understood in the context of the protests of the Iraq War near President George W. Bush's home near Crawford, Texas. "Impeach" posters are understood in 2006 to be directed at President Bush, not a local mayor or representative.

Cartoons. The political cartoon (aka editorial) presents a message or point of view concerning people, events, or situations using caricature and symbolism to convey the cartoonist's ideas, sometimes subtly, sometimes brashly, but always quickly. A good political cartoon will have wit and humor, which is usually obtained by exaggeration that is slick and not used merely for comic effect. It will also have a foundation in truth; that is, the characters must be recognizable to the viewer and the point of the drawing must have some basis in fact even if it has a philosophical bias. The third requirement is a moral purpose.

Using political cartoons as a teaching tool enlivens lectures, prompts classroom discussion, promotes critical thinking, develops multiple talents and learning styles, and helps prepare students for standardized tests. It also provides humor. However, it may be the most difficult form of literature to teach. Many teachers who choose to include them in their social studies curricula caution that, while students may enjoy them, it's doubtful whether they are actually getting the cartoonists' messages.

The best strategy for teaching such a unit is through a sub-skills approach that leads students step-by-step to higher orders of critical thinking. For example, the teacher can introduce caricature and use cartoons to illustrate the principles. Students are able to identify and interpret symbols if they are given the principles for doing so and get plenty of practice, and cartoons are excellent for this. It can cut down the time it takes for students to develop these skills, and many of the students who might lose the struggle to learn to identify symbols may overcome the roadblocks through the analysis of political cartoons. Many political cartoons exist for the teacher to use in the classroom and they are more readily available than ever before.

A popular example of an editorial cartoon that provides a way to analyze current events in politics is the popular comic strip "Doonesbury" by Gary Trudeau. For example, in the time period prior to the 2004 presidential election, Alex, the media savvy teenager does her best for political participation. In January she rallies her middle school classmates to the phones for a Deanathon and by August she is luring Ralph Nader supporters into discussions on Internet chat rooms. Knowledgeable about government, active in the political process, and willing to enlist others, Alex has many traits sought by the proponents of civics education.

Skill 2.6   Evaluate the appropriateness of alternative graphic formats for conveying historical information.

In other words, how do you choose when to use words, when to use charts, when to use graphs or when to use maps and/or illustrations (photos, etc.)? This is sometimes a difficult choice to make. To a large extent, it depends on the audience. A picture is worth a thousand words to most audiences; however, for children they are vital, as they are sometimes for older people. Also, if some members of the audience are speakers of English as a second language, graphics are extremely useful in increasing understanding of principles and events.

Another important factor in such a choice is how complicated the information is. Charts can go a long way in simplifying even complex ideas. Maps can defog a discussion of a geographical area that is not familiar to the audience. Photographs of people, places, or happenings can bring ideas to life.

Another factor is retention. If an idea is reinforced by a visual, it will be remembered longer because the listener has had access to it through more than one sense.

Suppose you are preparing for a presentation on the Civil War and you intend to focus on causes, an issue that has often been debated. If you are examining the matter of slavery as a cause, a graph of the increase in the number of slaves by area of the country for the previous 100 years would be very useful in the discussion. If you are focusing on the economic conditions that were driving the politics of the age, graphs of GDP, distribution of wealth geographically and individually, and relationship of wealth to ownership of slaves would be useful.

If you are discussing the war in Iraq, detailed maps with geopolitical elements would help clarify not only the day-to-day happenings but also the historical features that led up to it. A map showing the number of oil fields and where they are situated with regard to the various political factions and charts showing output of those fields historically would be useful.

If you are teaching the history of space travel, photos of the most famous astronauts will add interest to the discussion. Graphs showing the growth of the industry and charts showing discoveries and their relationship to the lives of everyday Americans would be helpful.

Geography and history classes are notoriously labeled by students as dull. With all the visual resources available nowadays, those classes have the potential for being the most exciting courses in the curriculum.

SUBAREA II.   **WORLD HISTORY TO 1600**

COMPETENCY 3.0   **UNDERSTAND THE ORIGINS, STRUCTURES, DEVELOPMENT, AND INTERACTIONS OF ANCIENT SOCIETIES.**

Skill 3.1   **Demonstrate knowledge of the religious, cultural, economic, and political development of Mesopotamian societies**

The earliest known civilizations developed in the Tigris-Euphrates valley of Mesopotamia (modern Iraq) and the Nile valley of Egypt between 4000 BCE and 3000 BCE. Because these civilizations arose in river valleys, they are known as **fluvial civilizations.** Geography and the physical environment played a critical role in the rise and the survival of both of these civilizations. The Fertile Crescent was bounded on the West by the Mediterranean, on the South by the Arabian Desert, on the north by the Taurus Mountains, and on the east by the Zagros Mountains.

First, the rivers provided a source of water that would sustain life, including animal life. The hunters of the society had ample access to a variety of animals, initially for hunting to provide food, as well as hides, bones, antlers, etc. from which clothing, tools and art could be made. Second, the proximity to water provided a natural attraction to animals which could be herded and husbanded to provide a stable supply of food and animal products. Third, the rivers of these regions overflowed their banks each year, leaving behind a deposit of very rich soil. As these early people began to experiment with growing crops rather than gathering food, the soil was fertile and water was readily available to produce sizeable harvests. In time, the people developed systems of irrigation that channeled water to the crops without significant human effort on a continuing basis.

The designation **Fertile Crescent** was applied by the famous historian and Egyptologist James Breasted to the part of the Near East that extended from the Persian Gulf to the Sinai Peninsula. It included Mesopotamia, Syria and Palestine. This region was marked by almost constant invasions and migrations. These invaders and migrants seemed to have destroyed the culture and civilization that existed.

The first empire in history was probably in **Mesopotamia**, and it was probably the Akkadians, led by Sargon, conqueror of Sumeria. However, Sargon didn't last long as an emperor. He was succeeded as the master of Mesopotamia by a host of famous names, including the Amorite leader Hammurabi, he of the famous Code. Another of the famous leaders of the Middle Eastern peoples was Nebuchadnezzar, leader of the Chaldeans. We know this name better for two famous episodes in world history: the building of the Hanging Gardens of Babylon and the Babylonian Captivity, the capture of and transport of the ancient Israelites.

The culture of **Mesopotamia** was definitely autocratic in nature. The various civilizations that criss-crossed the Fertile Crescent were very much top-heavy, with a single ruler at the head of the government and, in many cases, also the head of the religion. The people followed his strict instructions or faced the consequences, which were usually dire and often life-threatening.

The civilizations of the Sumerians, Amorites, Hittites, Assyrians, Chaldeans, and Persians controlled various areas of the land we call Mesopotamia. With few exceptions, tyrants and military leaders controlled the vast majority of aspects of society, including trade, religions, and the laws. Each Sumerian city-state (and there were a few) had its own god, with the city-state's leader doubling as the high priest of worship of that local god. Subsequent cultures had a handful of gods as well, although they had more of a national worship structure, with high priests centered in the capital city as advisers to the tyrant.

Trade was vastly important to these civilizations, since they had access to some but not all of the things that they needed to survive. Some trading agreements led to occupation, as was the case with the Sumerians, who didn't bother to build walls to protect their wealth of knowledge. Egypt and the Phoenician cities were powerful and regular trading partners of the various Mesopotamian cultures.

Legacies handed down to us from these people include:

The first use of writing, the wheel, and banking (Sumeria);
The first written set of laws (Code of Hammurabi);
The first epic story (*Gilgamesh*);
The first library dedicated to preserving knowledge (instituted by the Assyrian leader Ashurbanipal);
The Hanging Gardens of Babylon (built by the Chaldean Nebuchadnezzar)

The ancient civilization of the **Sumerians** invented the wheel; developed irrigation through use of canals, dikes, and devices for raising water; devised the system of cuneiform writing; learned to divide time; and built large boats for trade. The Babylonians devised the famous **Code of Hammurabi**, a code of laws. Other rulers of the Fertile Crescent include the warrior-tribes the Hittites and the Assyrians, both powerful and successful in their day. But the Middle East empire-building phase didn't really build until Darius the Great came onto the scene.

Darius was the man who built a collection of cities and satraps into the Persian Empire, one of the largest the world had ever seen. It stretched from Egypt, which it conquered eventually, to the boundaries of India. Millions of people owed their lives and their allegiances to Darius and to his successors. The head of the Persian Empire was the most powerful man in the world. He was also the head of the various religions that dotted his large empire, with various locations believing in local gods and spirits representing aspects of Nature.

As big as the Persian Empire was, the Persians always wanted more. They grew covetous of the growing Greek civilization, which was looking to expand in all directions, especially to the east, to areas already claimed by the Persians. A series of disagreements escalated into a series of battles and then a full-blown war, which the Greeks refer to as the Persian Wars. Some of the most famous battles in the world occurred during this war, including Marathon (in which the Greeks won despite being vastly outnumbered), Thermopylae (in which a valiant group of Spartans held off thousands of Persian warriors for several days), Salamis (a naval battle that the Greeks won despite being outgunned and outnumbered), and Plataea (in which the Greeks sealed the deal by finally outnumbering the Persians). These victories convinced the Persians not to attempt another invasion of Greece, but it didn't mean the end of the Empire.

Skill 3.2   Recognize the relationship between religion and political authority in ancient Egypt and the development of a long-enduring, monumental state system.

Egypt made numerous significant contributions, including construction of the great pyramids; development of hieroglyphic writing; preservation of bodies after death; making paper from papyrus; contributing to developments in arithmetic and geometry; the invention of the method of counting in groups of 1-10 (the decimal system); completion of a solar calendar; and laying the foundation for science and astronomy.

The earliest historical record of **Kush** is in Egyptian sources. They describe a region upstream from the first cataract of the Nile as "wretched." This civilization was characterized by a settled way of life in fortified mud-brick villages. They subsisted on hunting and fishing, herding cattle, and gathering grain. Skeletal remains suggest that the people were a blend of Negroid and Mediterranean ancestry. This civilization appears to be the second-oldest in Africa (after Egypt).

In government, the king ruled through a law of custom that was interpreted by priests. The king was elected from the royal family. Descent was determined through the mother's line (as in Egypt). But in *an unparalleled innovation,* the Kushites were ruled by a series of female monarchs. The Kushite religion was polytheistic, including all of the primary Egyptian gods. There were, however, regional gods which were the principal gods in their regions. Derived from other African cultures, there was also a lion warrior god. This civilization was vital through the last half of the first millennium BC, but it suffered about 300 years of gradual decline until it was eventually conquered by the Nuba people.

The ancient **Assyrians** were warlike and aggressive due to a highly organized military and used horse drawn chariots.

Skill 3.3   Identify early trading networks and writing systems among eastern Mediterranean societies and explain the development and importance of writing.

Refer to Skill 3.1 and Skill 4.4.

Skill 3.4   Demonstrate knowledge of the development of Indian civilization, explaining the effects of Buddhism and Hinduism on India, and examine the subsequent diffusion of Buddhism

Hinduism began by people called Aryans around 1500 BC and spread into India. The Aryans blended their culture with the culture of the Dravidians, natives they conquered. Today it has many sects, promotes worship of hundreds of gods and goddesses and belief in reincarnation. Though forbidden today by law, a prominent feature of Hinduism in the past was a rigid adherence to and practice of the infamous caste system.

Buddhism developed in India from the teachings of Prince Gautama and spread to most of Asia. Its beliefs opposed the worship of numerous deities, the Hindu caste system and the supernatural. Worshippers must be free of attachment to all things worldly and devote themselves to finding release from life's suffering.

Skill 3.5   Demonstrate knowledge of the development of Chinese civilization under the Zhou and Qin dynasties, analyze the contributions of Confucianism to Chinese culture, and examine its diffusion to Southeast Asia, Japan, and Korea

Two of the world's most important religions originated in China: Taoism and Confucianism. Confucius, especially, is one of the most famous figures in world history; his ethic teachings continue to form the basis of thought for many Chinese people. In literature, the poetry of the period is generally considered the best in the entire history of Chinese literature. The rebirth of Confucianism led to the publication of many commentaries on the classical writings. Encyclopedias on several subjects were produced, as well as histories and philosophical works.

Confucianism is a Chinese religion based on the teachings of the Chinese philosopher Confucius. There is no clergy, no organization, and no belief in a deity or in life after death. It emphasizes political and moral ideas with respect for authority and ancestors. Rulers were expected to govern according to high moral standards.

Shinto the native religion of Japan developed from native folk beliefs worshipping spirits and demons in animals, trees, and mountains. According to its mythology, deities created Japan and its people, which resulted in worshipping the emperor as a god. Shinto was strongly influenced by Buddhism and Confucianism but never had strong doctrines on salvation or life after death.

The Han Dynasty in China lasted from 206 BCE to 220 CE. The Dynasty was founded by the family known as the Liu clan. Within China, the period of the Han Dynasty (some 400 years) is generally considered one of the greatest periods in Chinese history. During this period China officially became a Confucian state. The empire was prosperous and commerce flourished. The empire also extended its influence, both culturally and politically, over Mongolia, Korea, Vietnam and Central Asia.

Major accomplishments of the Han Dynasty include:

- Development of a strong military,
- Westward expansion,
- Enabling of secure caravan traffic across Central Asia,
- Development of a "tributary system" with non-Chinese local powers that allowed these non-Chinese states autonomy in exchange for symbolic recognition of Han overlordship,
- Creation of the Silk Road,
- Conversion to a Confucian state,
- The invention of paper,
- Intellectual, literary and artistic revival,
- Introduction of a policy of the government buying surplus commodities and selling them in periods of want to prevent hunger and speculation,
- Restricting the coining of metal to the government,
- Ssu-ma Chien's narrative of the history of China up to his own time,
- Production of one of the world's first dictionaries,
- The scientists of the period came close to working out the true length of the solar year,
- First observation of sunspots,
- The assertion that eclipses were not the warnings of Providence, but natural phenomena,
- Artistic carving in stone depicted realistic action,
- Making of mirrors, glass and lacquered objects, and
- The introduction of Buddhism into China.

Skill 3.6   Analyze and compare the origins and structure of the Greek polis, the Roman Republic, and the Roman Empire and analyze factors that led to the collapse of the Western Roman Empire.

The classical civilization of **Greece** reached the highest levels in man's achievements based on the foundations already laid by ancient groups such as the Egyptians, Phoenicians, Minoans, and Mycenaeans. Among the more important contributions from Greece were: the Greek alphabet derived from the Phoenician letters, which formed the basis for the Roman and our present-day alphabets; extensive trading and colonization resulting in the spread of the Greek civilization; the love of sports with emphasis on a sound body, leading to the tradition of the Olympic games; the rise of independent, strong city-states; the complete contrast between independent, freedom-loving Athens with its practice of pure democracy (direct, personal, active participation in government by qualified citizens) and rigid, totalitarian, militaristic Sparta; important accomplishments in drama, epic and lyric poetry, fables, myths centered around the many gods and goddesses, science, astronomy, medicine, mathematics, philosophy, art, architecture, writing about and recording historical events; the conquests of Alexander the Great spreading Greek ideas to the areas he conquered and bringing to the Greek world many ideas from Asia; and above all, the value of ideas, wisdom, curiosity, and the desire to learn as much about the world as was possible.

Ancient Greece is often called the **Cradle of Western Civilization** because of the enormous influence it had not only on the time in which it flourished, but on western culture ever since.

Early Greek institutions have survived for thousands of years and have influenced the entire world. The **Athenian** form of democracy, with each citizen having an equal vote in his own government, is a philosophy upon which all modern democracies are based. In the United States, the Greek tradition of democracy was honored in the choice of Greek architectural styles for the nation's government buildings. The modern Olympic Games are a revival of an ancient Greek tradition, and many of the events are recreations of original contests.

The works of the Greek epic poet **Homer** are considered the earliest in western literature, and are still read and taught today. The tradition of the theater was born in Greece, with the plays of Aristophanes and others. In philosophy, Aristotle developed an approach to learning that emphasized observation and thought, and Socrates and Plato contemplated the nature of being and the origins and ideals of government and political relations. Greek mythology has been the source of inspiration for literature into the present day.

In the field of mathematics, Pythagoras and Euclid laid the foundation of geometry and Archimedes calculated the value of pi. Herodotus and Thucydides were the first to apply research and interpretation to written history.

In the arts, Greek sensibilities were held as perfect forms to which others might strive. In sculpture, the Greeks achieved an idealistic aesthetic that had not been perfected before that time. The Greek civilization served as an inspiration to the Roman Republic, which followed in its tradition of democracy, and was directly influenced by its achievements in art and science. Later, during the Renaissance, European scholars and artists would rediscover ancient Greece's love for dedicated inquiry and artistic expression, leading to a surge in scientific discoveries and advancements in the arts.

Rome was the next and most successful of the ancient empires, building itself from one town that borrowed from its Etruscan neighbors into a worldwide empire stretching from the wilds of Scotland to the shores of the Middle East. Building on the principles of Hellenization, Rome imported and exported goods and customs galore, melding the production capabilities and the belief systems of all it conquered into a heterogeneous yet distinctly Roman civilization. Like no other empire before it, Rome conquered and absorbed what it got. Trade, religion, science, political structure—all these things were incorporated into the Roman Empire, with all of the benefits that assimilation brought being passed on to the Empire's citizens.

The ancient civilization of Rome lasted approximately 1,000 years including the periods of republic and empire, although its lasting influence on Europe and its history extended for a much longer period. There was a very sharp contrast between the curious, imaginative, inquisitive Greeks and the practical, simple, down-to-earth, no-nonsense Romans, who spread and preserved the ideas of ancient Greece and other culture groups. The contributions and accomplishments of the Romans are numerous but their greatest included language, engineering, building, law, government, roads, trade, and the **Pax Romana**. Pax Romana was the long period of peace enabling free travel and trade, spreading people, cultures, goods, and ideas over a vast area of the known world. In the end, though, Rome grew too big to manage and its enemies too numerous to turn back. The sprawling nature of the Empire made it too big in the end to protect and the heterogeneity dissolved into chaos and violence.

The official end of the **Roman Empire** came when Germanic tribes took over and controlled most of Europe. The five major tribes were the Visigoths, Ostrogoths, Vandals, Saxons, and the Franks. In later years, the Franks successfully stopped the invasion of southern Europe by Muslims by defeating them under the leadership of Charles Martel at the Battle of Tours in 732 AD. Thirty-six years later in 768 AD, the grandson of Charles Martel became King of the Franks and is known throughout history as Charlemagne. Charlemagne was a man of war but was unique in his respect for, and encouragement of, learning. He made great efforts to rule fairly and ensure just treatment for his people.

Skill 3.7 **Identify the ideas and effects of important individuals in classical Greek society, examining the diffusion of Greek culture, and analyze the contributions of Hellenistic and Roman culture**

Plato (427-347 B.C.) and **Aristotle** (384-322 B.C.) both contributed to the field of political science. Both believed that political order would result in the greatest stability. In fact, Aristotle studied under Plato. Both Plato and Aristotle studied the ideas of causality and the Prime Mover, but their conclusions were different. Aristotle, however, is considered to be "the father of political science" because of his development of systems of political order the true development, a scientific system to study justice and political order.

Aristotle's conception of government was based on a simple idea. The function of government was to provide for the general welfare of its people. A good government, and one that should be supported, was one that did so in the best way possible, with the least pressure on the people. Bad governments were those that subordinated the general welfare to that of the individuals who ruled. At no time should any function of any government be that of personal interest of any one individual, no matter who that individual was. This does not mean that Aristotle had no sympathy for the individual or individual happiness (something Plato has been accused of by those who read his *Republic,* which was the first important philosophical text to explore these issues). Rather, Aristotle believed that a society is greater than the sum of its parts or that "the good of the many outweighs the good of the few and also of the one".

Alexander the Great, a Macedonian general who conquered both Greece and Persia, eventually adding Egypt, Phoenician cities, and part of India, created an empire that was staggering in its geography and impact. **Hellenization** brought the Greek enlightened way of life to the peoples of the East while also bringing the exotic goods and customs of the East to Greece. Until this time, the peoples of East and West exchanged goods and customs in small ways but were generally suspicious of their enemies. Alexander changed all that, bringing both sides together under one banner and beginning an exchange of ideas, beliefs, and goods that would capture the imagination of rulers for years after his untimely death.

Skill 3.8   Demonstrate knowledge of polytheism in the ancient world, the development of monotheism in ancient Hebrew and Persian civilizations, and the origins and diffusion of Christianity in Roman society

The civilizations of the Sumerians, Amorites, Hittites, Assyrians, Chaldeans, and Persians controlled various areas of the land we call Mesopotamia. With few exceptions, tyrants and military leaders controlled the vast majority of aspects of society, including trade, religions, and the laws. Each Sumerian city-state (and there were a few) had its own god, with the city-state's leader doubling as the high priest of worship of that local god. Subsequent cultures had a handful of gods as well, although they had more of a national worship structure, with high priests centered in the capital city as advisors to the tyrant.

Judaism is the oldest of the Western world's three monotheistic religions. It grew out of the ancient religion of the Hebrews or Israelites. This early religion shared a number of common elements and primordial stories with neighboring peoples, especially the Mesopotamian and Babylonian cultures. Judaism's sacred writing, the Hebrew Scripture, is generally referred to as **Torah** or Tannakh. It consists of 24 books which are divided into three sections: Law (*Torah*), Prophets (*Nevi'im*), and Writings (*Ketuvim*).

The word and law of God were transmitted orally for many generations prior to the writing of the Hebrew Scripture. The *Mishna* is the collection of the oral tradition. The *Gemara* is a collection of commentary by the rabbis (teachers). The tradition of living interpretation and commentary continued through the centuries. *Halakah* is the tradition of interpretation of law, history and practice. *Kabbalah* is a body of Jewish mystical literature. *Kabbalah* arose from a movement in France in the eleventh century that discovered an esoteric system of symbolic interpretation of scripture.

Judaism is centered in belief in a single, all-powerful, all-seeing, and all-knowing God. God chose the Hebrew people from all the people of the earth and entered into a covenant with them. "I will be your God, and you will be my people." This covenant implies special privileges, but it also implies certain obligations of the people. The life of the people is to be structured around the promises and commandments of God. The Law provides the structure of religious practice and daily life. The Law is the guide for making ethical choices that reflect and demonstrate their unique character as the chosen people of God. Failure to act in accordance with God's law is a willful act, called sin. Sin destroys the proper relationship between the person and God. It is, however, possible to return from willful rebellion and restore the broken relationship. Judaism is also marked by a strong sense of communal identity and sin can be either individual or communal.

Christianity grew out of Judaism and its belief that God would send a Messiah ("anointed one") who would establish the Kingdom of God on earth. Jesus of Nazareth appeared in the early years of the first century CE, preaching repentance in preparation for the arrival of the Kingdom of God. His brief (about three years) ministry of teaching, preaching, healing and miracles gathered followers from among the common and the despised of his day, as well as non-Jews and the wealthy. This ministry was confined to the areas of Galilee and northwest Palestine. According to Christian writings, Jesus eschewed the separatism of Judaism and reached out to the poor, the sick, and the social outcasts. He preached a Kingdom of God not of this world, which ran contrary to Jewish expectation of a political Messiah who would establish an earthly kingdom.

As the movement grew, the teachings of Jesus were perceived as a danger to the political order by both the Jews and the Roman government. Jesus was handed over to the authorities by one of his closest followers, arrested, tried, and crucified. According to Christian belief, Jesus rose from the dead on the third day, appeared to his disciples and then ascended to heaven.

Christians believe that Jesus was the Son of God who died on the cross as an offering and sacrifice that saved humankind from sin. Those who believe in him will be saved. Christian scripture (**the Bible**) consists of two major parts: the Old Testament, which is an adoption of the Hebrew Scripture, and the New Testament, which consists of 27 books. As an outgrowth of Judaism, Christianity accepts many of the beliefs, though not the practices of Judaism. Fundamental beliefs of Christianity are: (1) there is one God who is the creator and redeemer of humankind; God is all-knowing, all-powerful, and all-present; (2) Jesus Christ is the unique Son of God who is the savior of humankind. The doctrine of the Trinity teaches that the one God has three natures through/by which God is active in the world: God the Father, the creator and governor of creation, is the judge of humankind, God the Son (Jesus) is God in the flesh, who came among humankind to save them from sin, and God the Holy Spirit is the invisible presence of God for believers to provide strength, faith and guidance.

Christian ethics are based on the **Ten Commandments** of the Old Testament and the teachings of Jesus, which include the "Golden Rule" ("Do unto others as you would have them do unto you") and a broadening of the application of the commandments.

COMPETENCY 4.0   **UNDERSTAND THE ORIGINS, IMPORTANT FEATURES, SIGNIFICANT DEVELOPMENTS, AND NOTABLE ACHIEVEMENTS OF AFRICAN, ASIAN, AND LATIN AMERICAN SOCIETIES FROM ANCIENT TIMES THROUGH THE SIXTEENTH CENTURY**

Skill 4.1   **Demonstrate knowledge of the emergence of the Mongol Empire, identify basic features of Mongol society, and analyze the significance of Mongol expansion across Asia**

The Mongol Empire, founded by Genghis Khan, included the majority of the territory from Southeast Asia to central Europe during the height of the empire. One of the primary military tactics of conquest was to annihilate any cities that refused to surrender.

Government was by decree on the basis of a code of laws developed by Genghis Khan. It is interesting that one of the tenets of this code was that the nobility and the commoners shared the same hardship. The society, and the opportunity to advance within the society, was based on a system of meritocracy. The carefully structured and controlled society was efficient and safe for the people. Religious tolerance was guaranteed. Theft and vandalism were strictly forbidden. Trade routes and an extensive postal system were created. linking the various parts of the empire. Taxes were quite onerous, but teachers, artists and lawyers were exempted from the taxes. Mongol rule, however, was absolute. The response to all resistance was collective punishment in the form of destruction of cities and slaughter of the inhabitants.

The lasting achievements of the Mongol Empire include:

- Reunification of China and expansion of its borders,
- Unification of the Central Asian Republics that later formed part of the USSR,
- Expansion of Europe's knowledge of the world.

Genghis Khan was known as a conqueror, and Kublai was known as a uniter. They both extended the borders of their empire, however; at its height, the Mongol Empire was the largest the world has ever seen, encompassing all of China, Russia, Persia, and central Asia. Following the Mongols were the Ming and Manchu Dynasties, both of which focused on isolation. As a result, China at the end of the eighteenth century knew very little of the outside world, and vice versa. Ming artists created beautiful porcelain pottery, but not much of it saw its way into the outside world until much later. The Manchus were known for their focus on farming and road-building, two practices that were instituted in greater numbers in order to try to keep up with expanding population. Confucianism, Taoism, and ancestor worship—the staples of Chinese society for hundreds of years— continued to flourish during all this time

Skill 4.2   Examine the importance of the Silk Road in the movement of goods and the diffusion of ideas among Asia, the Middle East, Africa, and Europe

The **Silk Road** was a network of routes connecting Asia and the Mediterranean, and passing through India and the Middle East. It is named after the silk trade but was also the route for trade in other materials such as livestock, wine and minerals. The network included overland routes as well as naval routes, extending over 8,000 miles.

The Silk Road grew out of more local trade networks that had been in use for thousands of years. The Macedonian conqueror **Alexander** contributed directly to the development of the Silk Road in the fourth century BC by pushing eastward and connecting Mediterranean Europe with the people of the Middle East. A short time later, in the second century BC, China sent the ambassador Zhang Qian westward to establish diplomatic and commercial ties with the civilizations of Central Asia. At the same time, the Persians had developed a system of Royal Roads throughout their region, allowing them to quickly pass information from city to city and facilitating trade. The routes opened by Alexander and Zhang Qian connected with this system of Persian roads, establishing the framework for a continuous trade route. When Rome conquered Egypt in 70 BC, Africa became a vital section of the Silk Road.

The Silk Road was not only a route for the exchange of goods. Religious, artistic and cultural ideas moved along the routes as well. Buddhism, which originated in Central Asia, moved outward along the Silk Road toward China, Korea and Japan, where it flourished. Likewise, Islam expanded into the west. European ideas were transmitted eastward, as well. Some deities recognized in the Japanese Shinto belief have nearly identical Greek counterparts, for example.

Technology moved along the Silk Road, too. Korean printing methods and Chinese mapmaking and shipbuilding skills were brought to the Mediterranean. Advances in mathematics and astronomy in Persia and Egypt were opened to the rest of the known world.

Portions of the route through Asia was perilous, with bands of marauders attacking travelers and looting shipments. The expansion of the Mongol Empire in the thirteenth and fourteenth centuries stabilized this region, strengthening the connection between east and west. It was during this time that **Marco Polo** became the first European to travel the Silk Road to China and to bring back a description of what he encountered. As the fifteenth century approached, the Mongol Empire crumbled, however, destabilizing the road once again. This, along with the increased Muslim control over the central portion of the Silk Road, prompted Europeans to seek other routes to the prosperous Asian trade. They began to look to the west, for a route by sea.

Skill 4.3 Identify migration patterns of Bantu-speaking peoples and analyze the significance of those migrations

Bantu-speaking people currently populate most of sub-Equatorial Africa. Their exact patterns of migration are not known for certain, but linguistic evidence suggests that they originated in west and north Africa some time in the second millennium BC moving eastward and southward.

The dominance of the Bantu language in Africa leads historians to believe that this was one of the largest migrations in human history. Evidence points to it beginning around 1000 BC and lasting until about 1100 AD, taking place in several waves.

Along with the spread of their language, the Bantu also introduced iron working and agricultural advances wherever they settled. Their superior technology and common language allowed their communities to thrive and supported further expansion.

The Bantu migration has shaped the present population of Africa, as well. The modern language of Swahili, which is spoken throughout most of southern Africa, is a Bantu language.

Skill 4.4 Demonstrate knowledge of the development and decline of major Sudanic kingdoms.

During the fourteenth and fifteenth centuries, the Muslim Empire experienced great expansion. The conquest of **Ghana** by Muslim Berbers in 1076 permitted rule to devolve to a series of lesser successor states. By the thirteenth century, the successor state of Kangaba established the Kingdom of Mali. This vast trading state extended from the Atlantic coast of Africa to beyond Gao on the Niger River in the east.

Much of the history of **Mali** was preserved by Islamic scholars because the Mali rulers converted to Islam and were responsible for the spread of Islam throughout Africa. The expansion of the Mali kingdom began from the city of Timbuktu and gradually moved downstream along the Niger River. This provided increasing control of the river and the cities along its banks, which were critical for both travel and trade. The Niger River was a central link in trade for both west and north African trade routes. The government of the Mali kingdom was held together by military power and trade. The kingdom was organized into a series of feudal states that were ruled by a king. Most of the kings used the surname "Mansa" (meaning, "sultan"). The most powerful and effective of the kings was Mansa Musa.

The religion and culture of the kingdom of Mali was a blend of Islamic faith and traditional African belief. The influence of the Islamic empire provided the basis of a large and very structured government which allowed the king to expand both territory and influence. The people, however, did not follow strict Islamic law. The king was thought of in traditional African fashion as a divine ruler removed from the people. A strong military, control of the Niger River and the trade that flourished along the river, enabled Mali to build a strong feudal empire.

Farther to the east, the king of the **Songhai** people had earlier converted to Islam in the eleventh century. Songhai was at one time a province of Mali. By the fifteenth century, Songhai was stronger than Mali and it emerged as the next great power in western Africa. Songhai was situated on the great bend of the Niger River. From the early fifteenth to the late sixteenth centuries, the Songhai Empire stood, one of the largest empires in the history of Africa. The first king Sonni Ali conquered many neighboring states, including the Mali Empire. This gave him control of the trade routes and cities like Timbuktu. He was succeeded by Askia Mohammad who initiated political reform and revitalization. He also created religious schools, built mosques, and opened his court to scholars and poets from all parts of the Muslim world.

During the same period, the **Zimbabwe** kingdom was built. "Great Zimbabwe" was the largest of about 300 stone structures in the area. This capital city and trading center of the Kingdom of Makaranga was built between the twelfth and fifteenth centuries. It was believed to have housed as many as 20,000 people. The structures are built entirely of stone, without mortar. The scanty evidence that is available suggests that the kingdom was a trading center that was believed to be part of a trading network that reached as far as China.

The area known today as the Republic of **Benin** was the site of an early African kingdom known as Dahomey. By the seventeenth century, the kingdom included a large part of West Africa. The kingdom was economically prosperous because of slave trading relations with Europeans, primarily the Dutch and Portuguese, who arrived in the fifteenth century. The coastal part of the kingdom was known as "the Slave Coast." This kingdom was known for a very distinct culture and some very unusual traditions. In 1729 the kingdom started a female army system. A law was passed stating that young women would be inspected at the age of 15. Those thought beautiful were sent to the Palace to become wives of the king. Those who were sick or were considered unattractive were executed. The rest were trained as soldiers for two years. Human sacrifice was practiced on holidays and special occasions. Slaves and prisoners of war were sacrificed to gods and ancestors.

The slave trade provided economic stability for the kingdom for almost three hundred years. The continuing need for human sacrifices caused a decrease in the number of slaves available for export. As many colonial countries declared the trade of slaves illegal, demand for slaves subsided steadily until 1885 when the last Portuguese slave ship left the coast. With the decline of the slave trade, the kingdom began a slow disintegration. The French took over in 1892.

The ancient empire of **Ghana** occupied an area that is now known as Northern Senegal and Southern Mauritania. There is no absolute certainty regarding the origin of this empire. Oral history dates the rise of the empire to the seventh century BCE. Most believe, however, that the date should be placed much later. Many believe the nomads who were herding animals on the fringes of the desert posed a threat to the early Soninke people, who were an agricultural community. In times of drought, it is believed the nomads raided the agricultural villages for water and places to pasture their herds. To protect themselves, it is believed that these farming communities formed a loose confederation that eventually became the empire of ancient Ghana.

The word "Ghana" means king or war chief. It is believed that the Arabs and Europeans took this reference to the king to be the name of the society. These rulers conquered neighboring communities and thus extended the boundaries of the growing empire. The purpose of expansion was to gain control of trade routes. By the fifth century (some say the seventh century) a kingdom had been established. This kingship was significantly different from most other kingships of the time. First, kingship was matrilineal. The sister of the king provided the heir to the throne. Second, the king ruled in conjunction with a People's Council chosen from all social strata.

The empire's economic vitality was determined by geographical location. It was situated midway between the desert, which was the major source of salt and the gold fields. This location along the trade routes of the camel caravans provided exceptional opportunity for economic development. The caravans brought copper, salt, dried fruit, clothing, manufactured goods, etc. For these goods, the people of Ghana traded kola nuts, leather goods, gold, hides, ivory and slaves. In addition, the empire collected taxes on every trade item that entered the boundaries of the empire.

With the revenue from the trade goods tax, the empire supported a government, an army that protected the trade routes and the borders, the maintenance of the capital, and primary market centers. But it was control of the gold fields that gave the empire political power and economic prosperity. The location of the gold fields was a carefully guarded secret. By the tenth century, Ghana was very rich and controlled an area about the size of the state of Texas. Demand for this gold sharply increased in the ninth and tenth centuries as the Islamic states of Northern Africa began to mint coins. As the gold trade expanded, so did the empire. The availability of local iron ore enabled the early people of the Ghana kingdom to make more efficient farm implements and effective weapons. But in the eleventh century the Berbers attacked the empire in an attempt to gain control of the gold fields and to purify Islam as it was practiced in Ghana. They eventually withdrew, but they left behind a greatly weakened empire. Later invasions and internal rebellions further weakened the empire and made the trade routes quite dangerous. The merchants moved east and the empire began to crumble. A serious drought compounded the disintegration of the empire through deterioration of the environment and overgrazing. By the middle of the thirteenth century, the empire was just a memory.

Skill 4.5   Demonstrate knowledge of the operation of major African trading networks and analyze the process of religious syncretism by which traditional African beliefs blended with new ideas from Islam and Christianity

Africa's primary trade commodities with the outside world were slaves, gold, spices and ivory. Trade caravans carried gold, spices and ivory from southern Africa across the Sahara Desert along a network of oases, providing an overland link to the Mediterranean. In the fifteenth century, the Chinese established a naval connection on the east coast of Africa and the Europeans began exporting slaves from along the west coast.

The slave trade provided economic stability for coastal kingdoms for almost three hundred years. As many colonial countries declared the trade of slaves illegal, demand for slaves subsided steadily until 1885 when the last Portuguese slave ship left the coast.

The slave trade was part of the **triangular trade system,** which linked England, Africa and the New World. Trade goods such as beads, cloth and weapons were shipped to the west coast of Africa where they were exchanged for slaves. Slaves were then transported to the West Indies and sold, with the profits used to purchase rum, sugar or molasses. This was then shipped back to England and the process started again.

Portuguese explorers visited the kingdoms of Africa beginning in the late fifteenth century. They captured some Africans to take with them back to Portugal and left behind Catholic missionaries to undertake the spread of Christianity. In 1491, the

King of Kongo was baptized and began the task of converting his people to Catholicism.

Kongo relied on a synthetic combination of Christianity and older traditional beliefs, a process called *syncretism*, to popularize Catholicism. Africans were sent to Portugal to be educated and then returned to open schools. With very few ordained clergy, Kongo's conversion to Christianity was overseen by laypeople who were not strictly versed in Catholic doctrine. As a result, a unique form of Christianity developed incorporating non-Christian beliefs.

A similar exchange of religious traditions took place in Ethiopia a thousand years prior to the coming of the Portuguese. In the fourth century, two Greek Christian brothers were taken in to the Ethiopian royal household after their ship was stranded while exploring the east coast of Africa. They converted the queen and several of the nobility, and with their involvement, Christianity became the official religion of Ethiopia. As would happen in the Kingdom of Kongo, Ethiopia followed its own path in shaping its Christian faith in accordance with its previous religious beliefs. This would eventually lead to a break with the Catholic Church in the seventeenth century with the establishment of the Ethiopian Orthodox Church and the expulsion of Jesuits and other Europeans.

Islam had spread from the Middle East across North Africa during the eighth century. Muslim Berbers conquered the powerful kingdom of Mali in 1076, introducing Islam to a wide area of Africa. As Mali's influence grew, so did Islam. African Islam did not adhere to the strict Muslim traditions and teachings, however. African kings, for instance, were still revered as having divine status, in direct conflict with traditional Islamic teaching. As Islam spread farther from its source, its traditions mingled with local ones, resulting in occasional religiously motivated invasions by northern Muslims to "purify" the faith.

Also Refer to Skill 4.4.

Skill 4.6   Compare early cultures of the Americas and analyze the rise and fall of the Olmec, Mayan, Aztec, and Inca empires

Those people who lived in **North America** had large concentrations of people and houses, but they didn't have the kind of large civilization centers like the cities elsewhere in the world. These people didn't have an exact system of writing, either. These were two technological advances that were found in many other places in the world, including, to varying degrees, South America. We know the most about the empires of South America, the Aztec, Inca, and Maya. People lived in South America before the advent of these empires, of course. One of the earliest people of record was the Olmecs, who left behind little to prove their existence except a series of huge carved figures.

The **Aztecs** dominated Mexico and Central America. They weren't the only people living in these areas, just the most powerful ones. The Aztecs had many enemies, some of whom were only too happy to help Hernan Cortes precipitate the downfall of the Aztec society. The Aztecs had access to large numbers of metals and jewels, and they used these metals to make weapons and these jewels to trade for items they didn't already possess. Actually, the Aztecs didn't do a whole lot of trading; rather, they conquered neighboring tribes and demanded tribute from them; this is the source of so much of the Aztec riches. They also believed in a handful of gods and believed that these gods demanded human sacrifice in order to continue to smile on the Aztecs. The center of Aztec society was the great city of Tenochtitlan, which was built on an island so as to be easier to defend and boasted a population of 300,000 at the time of the arrival of the conquistadors. Tenochtitlan was known for its canals and its pyramids, none of which survive today.

The **Inca** Empire stretched across a vast period of territory down the western coast of South America and was connected by a series of roads. A series of messengers ran along these roads, carrying news and instructions from the capital, Cusco, another large city similar to, but not as spectacular as, Tenochtitlan. The Incas are known for inventing the *quipu*, a string-based device that provided them with a method of keeping records. The Inca Empire, like the Aztec Empire, was very much a centralized state, with all income going to the state coffers and all trade going through the emperor as well. The Incas worshiped the dead, their ancestors, and nature and often took part in what we could consider strange rituals.

The most advanced Native American civilization was the **Maya**, who lived primarily in Central America. They were the only Native American civilization to develop writing, which consisted of a series of symbols that have yet to be deciphered. The Mayas also built huge pyramids and other stone figures and sculptures, mostly of the gods they worshiped. The Mayas are most famous, however, for their calendars and for their mathematics. The Mayan calendars were the most accurate on the planet until the 16th century. The Mayas also invented the idea of zero, which might sound like a small thing except that no other culture had thought of such a thing. Maya worship resembled the practices of the Aztec and Inca, although human sacrifices were rare. The Mayas also traded heavily with their neighbors.

Skill 4.7   **Recognize the geographical extent of the Ottoman Empire during the rule of Sleyman the Magnificent, the Safavid Empire during the reign of Shah Abbas I, and the Mughal Empire during the reigns of Babur and Akbar, and analyze the influence of these empires on legal, religious, and artistic developments across Southwest Asia**

The Ottoman Empire reached its greatest potential and acquired the vast majority of its eventual territory before and during the reign of **Suleyman the Magnificent**. From its tiny beginnings in what is now Turkey, the Empire stretched throughout the Mediterranean region, encompassing such previous empires as Egypt, Athens, and Carthage. The entire western and eastern strips of the Arabian Peninsula were Ottoman, with vast wealth coming from the important trading centers there. The Ottoman borders stretched into what is now Austria and Russia, nearly to Vienna and Kiev. Indeed, the vast majority of the Balkan lands alternately thrived and seethed under Ottoman rule.

This geographical element included more than just territory. Art and culture flourished under the reign of Suleyman, as evidenced by the thriving trade throughout the Empire and into Europe and Asia. Suleyman was as powerful and as well-known as any Western monarch, and he was feared by them all. Suleyman was known as a just ruler, striving for and often achieving a system of law that was the envy of many Western states.   Naturally, Islam spread throughout the Empire as it expanded. This, perhaps more than any other factor, was a main cause of the internecine wars known as the **Crusades.**

One of the main competitors of the Ottoman Empire in the Middle East was the Safavid Empire, which dominated what is now Iran and Iraq for many years. Baghdad, in particular, was a principal source of conflict, changing hands multiple times during the reign of Shah Abbas, the greatest of the Safavid monarchs. Though Abbas and the Safavids were determined to assert their authority on their surroundings, they succeeded in very little in the way of territorial acquisitions, outside much of Azerbaijan, Iran, and Iraq.

Coming into conflict with the Ottomans on the eastern flank was the **Mughal Empire**, one of India's greatest rulerships. The greatest of the Mughal rulers were Babur and Akbar, both of whom expanded the empire and its relevance and notoriety far beyond its roots. Despite India's history of Hinduism, the Mughals ruled as Muslims and expanded the reach and influence of that religion despite its relative newness compared to the ancient religions of India. (It should be said, however, that Akbar worked hard to assimilate Hundus with promises of reconciliation and proved adept, akin to Suleyman, at controlling various ethnic strife and keeping the empire together.) The Mughals would have come into conflict with various Middle Eastern empires, over territory, mostly. Like the Ottomans as well, the greater Mughal ruler succeeded at bringing together a succession of smaller kingdoms under one centralized whole.

COMPETENCY 5.0   UNDERSTAND THE IMPORTANCE OF THE BYZANTINE EMPIRE, THE ORIGINS AND EXPANSION OF ISLAM, CHARACTERISTICS OF EUROPEAN MEDIEVAL SOCIETY, AND THE SIGNIFICANCE OF THE RENAISSANCE AND THE REFORMATION

Skill 5.1   Analyze the relationship of the Byzantine Empire to the Roman Empire, examine the establishment of Christianity in Byzantium, recognize the role of Orthodox Christianity in Byzantine society, and demonstrate knowledge of the causes and consequences of the Western Schism

The **Byzantines** (Christians) made important contributions in art and the preservation of Greek and Roman achievements including architecture (especially in eastern Europe and Russia), the Code of Justinian and Roman law. Byzantium was known for its exquisite artwork (including the famous church Hagia Sophia), which the West was never recognized as having.

Bordering the east of Europe was the **Byzantine Empire**, which was the Eastern Roman Empire, after it was divided by Emperor Diocletian. Diocletian's successor, Emperor Constantine, renamed the capital of Byzantium **Contstantinople**, after himself. With the fall of Western Rome in 476 CE, the Byzantine emperors, starting with Justinian, attempted to regain the lost western territories. Due to ineffective rulers between the seventh and ninth centuries CE, any gains were completely lost, reverting the territorial limits to the eastern Balkans of Ancient Greece and Asia Minor. The late ninth through eleventh centuries were considered the Golden Age of Byzantium.

Although Constantine had earlier made Christianity the official state religion of Rome, it left an unresolved conflict between Christian and Classical (Greek and Roman) ideals for the Byzantines. There were points of contention between the Pope in Rome and the Patriarch of Constantinople including celibacy of priests, language of the Liturgy (Latin in the west, Greek in the east), religious doctrine, and other unreconciled issues. These issues led to the **Great Schism** which permanently split the Roman Catholic and Eastern Orthodox Churches.

Perhaps the most wide-ranging success of the Byzantine Empire was in the area of trade. Uniquely situated at the gateway to both West and East, Byzantium could control trade going in both directions. Indeed, the Eastern Empire was much more centralized and rigid in its enforcement of its policies than the feudal West. The **Byzantine Empire**, which the Eastern Empire became, was closer to the Middle East, and thus inherited the traditions of Mesopotamia and Persia. This was in stark contrast to the Western Empire, which inherited the traditions of Greece and Carthage.

Skill 5.2   **Analyze the role of Constantinople as a trading and religious center and examine the influence of the Byzantine Empire on Russia**

In a way that governments never could, Christianity unified Europe. Especially with the pope at the head of the religion, the peoples of Europe could correctly be called Christendom because they all had the same beliefs, the same worries, and the same tasks to perform in order to achieve the salvation that they so desperately sought. The Church was only too happy to capitalize on this power, which increased throughout the Middle Ages until it met a stalwart from Germany named Martin Luther.

Also refer to Skill 5.1 and Skill 5.4.

Skill 5.3   **Demonstrate knowledge of the origins and expansion of the Islamic Empire; the effects of Muslim trade with Asia, Africa, and Europe; and the contributions of Islamic scholars**

A few years after the death of the Emperor Justinian, **Mohammed** was born (570 CE) in a small Arabian town near the Red Sea. Before this time, Arabians played only an occasional role in history. Arabia was a vast desert of rock and sand, except for the coastal areas on the Red Sea. It was populated by nomadic wanderers called **Bedouin**, who lived in scattered tribes near oases where they watered their herds. Tribal leaders engaged in frequent war with one another. The family or tribe was the social and political unit, under the authority of the head of the family, within which there was cruelty, infanticide, and suppression of women. Their religion was a crude and superstitious paganism and idolatry. Although there was regular contact with Christians and Jews through trading interactions, the idea of monotheism was foreign. What vague unity there was within the religion was based upon common veneration of certain sanctuaries. The most important of these was a small square temple called **the Kaaba** (cube), located in the town of **Mecca**. Arabs came from all parts of the country in annual pilgrimages to Mecca during the sacred months when warfare was prohibited. For this reason, Mecca was considered the center of Arab religion.

In about 610, a prophet named **Mohammed** came to some prominence. He called his new religion **Islam** (submission [to the will of God]) and his followers were called **Moslems** – those who had surrendered themselves. His first converts were members of his family and his friends. As the new faith began to grow, it remained a secret society. But when they began to make their faith public, they met with opposition and persecution from the pagan Arabians who feared the new religion and the possible loss of the profitable trade with the pilgrims who came to the Kaaba every year.

Islam slowly gained ground, and the persecutions became more severe around Mecca. In 622, Mohammed and his close followers fled the city and found refuge in **Medina** to the North. His flight is called the **Hegira**. This event marks the beginning of the Moslem calendar. Mohammed took advantage of the ongoing feuds between Jews and Arabs in the city and became the rulers of Medina, making it the capital of a rapidly growing state.

In the years that followed, Islam changed significantly. It became a fighting religion and Mohammed became a political leader. The group survived by raiding caravans on the road to Mecca and plundering nearby Jewish tribes. This was a victorious religion that promised plunder and profit in this world and the blessings of paradise after death. It attracted many converts from the Bedouin tribes. By 630, Mohammed was strong enough to conquer Mecca and make it the religious center of Islam, toward which all Moslems turned to pray, and the *Kaaba* the most sacred **Mosque** or temple. Medina remained the political capital.

Mohammed left behind a collection of divine revelations (**surahs***)* he believed were delivered by the angel Gabriel. These were collected and published in a book called the **Koran** (reading), which has since been the holy scripture of Islam. The revelations were never dated or kept in any kind of chronological order. After the prophet's death they were organized by length (in diminishing order). The *Koran* contains Mohammed's teachings on moral and theological questions, his legislation on political matters, and his comments on current events.

These Moslem Arabians immediately launched an amazing series of conquests which, in time, extended the empire from the Indus to Spain. It has often been said that these conquests were motivated by religious fanaticism and the determination to force Islam upon the infidel. However, economic and political motives fueled the conquests.

Reading and writing in Arabic, the study of the Koran, arithmetic and other elementary subjects were taught to children in schools attached to the mosques. In larger and wealthier cities, the mosques offered more advanced education in literature, logic, philosophy, law, algebra, astronomy, medicine, science, theology and the tradition of Islam. Books were produced for the large reading public. The wealthy collected private libraries and public libraries arose in large cities.
The most popular subjects were theology and the law. But the more important field of study was philosophy. The works of the Greek and Hellenistic philosophers were translated into Arabic and interpreted with commentaries. These were later passed on to the Western Christian societies and schools in the twelfth and thirteenth centuries. The basis of Moslem philosophy was Aristotelian and Neo-platonic ideas, which were essentially transmitted without creative modification.

The Moslems were also interested in natural science. They translated the works on Galen and Hippocrates into Arabic and added the results of their own experience in medicine. Avicenna was regarded in Western Europe as one of the great masters of medicine. They also adopted the work of the Greeks in the other sciences and modified and supplemented them with their own discoveries. Much of their work in chemistry was focused on alchemy (the attempt to transmute base metals into gold). The **Muslim** culture outdistanced the Western world in the field of medicine, primarily because the people weren't constrained by the sort of superstitious fervor that had so embraced the West at this time. The Muslim doctor **Al-Razi** was one of the most well-known physicians in the world and was the author of a medical encyclopedia and a handbook for smallpox and measles.

Adopting the heritage of Greek mathematics, the Moslems also borrowed a system of numerals from India. This laid the foundation for modern arithmetic, geometry, trigonometry and algebra.

Moslem art and architecture tended to be mostly uniform in style, allowing for some regional modification. They borrowed from Byzantine, Persian and other sources. The floor plan of the mosques was generally based on Mohammed's house at Medina. The notable unique elements were the tall minarets from which the faithful were called to prayer. Interior decoration was the style now called arabesque. Mohammed had banned paintings or other images of living creatures. These continued to be absent from mosques, although they occasionally appeared in book illustration and secular contexts. But their skilled craftsmen produced the finest art in jewelry, ceramics, carpets, and carved ivory.

Skill 5.4   Demonstrate knowledge of the reasons for the split between Sunni and Shi'ah Muslims; analyze the relationships among Judaism, Christianity, and Islam; and analyze the effects of the Crusades on both the Islamic world and Europe.

Judaism was one of the earliest monotheistic religions and one of the oldest religions still being observed today. Judaism is characterized by a belief in one all-powerful God who created the universe and is still active. Jews place a great importance on tradition and the teachings of the Torah, a collection of texts that form a central holy book. There are currently approximately 15 million observers of Judaism worldwide.

Christianity developed as a Jewish sect during the first century AD and is based on the belief that Jesus of Nazareth, who was crucified about 30 AD, was the Messiah promised in the ancient Hebrew Scriptures. Three main branches of Christianity, the Roman Catholic, Eastern Orthodox, and Protestant denominations make up the largest portion of modern Christianity, accounting for over 2 billion followers worldwide. Christian sects differ widely in specific beliefs and practices, but all believe that Jesus was the Messiah sent by God to redeem the world, and in the existence of an afterlife. Christians follow the teachings of Jesus and his followers as spelled out in the Gospels and other books written by early Christians. These books, called the New Testament, are coupled with the ancient Hebrew Scriptures, called the Old Testament, to form the Christian Bible.

Islam is based on the teachings of the seventh century figure Muhammad, who claimed that the word of God was revealed to him, and that he was meant to perfect the teachings of Judaism and Christianity. Originally persecuted, Muhammad led a group of followers, called Muslims, to the area of Saudi Arabia that is now the city of Medina. From there, the religion spread throughout the east and into the Middle East, where it is still the dominant faith. Muslims follow the teachings of Muhammad as written in the Koran. Like Judaism and Christianity, Islam is monotheistic. There are currently approximately 1.4 billion Muslims throughout the world, making it the second largest religion practiced today.

The Muslim community split shortly after the death of the prophet Muhammad, in 632, over the question of who should succeed him as Caliph, or head of the Muslim community. The Shi'ah believe that Muhammad indicated that Ali should succeed him, but the Sunni discount this, claiming that Abu Bakr was the rightful successor to Muslim leadership. These groups solidified as separate sects of Islam after civil war broke out in 656 following the assassination of Uthman ibn Affan, the third Caliph to succeed Muhammad. Ali was elevated to Caliph and is recognized by the Shi'ah as the first true Caliph. The division between the two groups continues to the present day.

Within a century of the death of Muhammad, an Islamic nation had spread from Arabia to the west, including Egypt and the Middle East, to the region that is now Spain. The Franks repelled the Islamic invasion of Europe in 732 AD.

The conflict between the Christian west and the Islamic east continued to grow, culminating in the eleventh century with the first Crusade, a Christian military campaign to take control of Jerusalem and the Holy Land. Several more Crusades took place through the following centuries, as Jerusalem and other areas changed hands between Christian and Islamic control. While usually bloody and devastating, the Crusades did connect cultures and contribute to trade routes throughout the region.

The **Crusades** were a series of military campaigns beginning in the eleventh century against the encroaching Muslim empire, particularly in the holy land of Palestine and the city of Jerusalem.

The Christian Byzantine Empire was centered in Constantinople. The empire was under attack from Seljuk Turk forces, who had taken Palestine. The eastern emperor Alexius I called on his western counterpart, Pope Urban II, for assistance. Urban saw the situation as an opportunity to reunite Christendom, which was still in the throes of schism between the Eastern Orthodox and the Western Catholic sects, and to invest the papacy with religious authority.

In 1095, Urban called on all Christians to rally behind the campaign to drive the Turks out of the Holy Land. Participation in the crusade, Urban said, would count as full penance for sin in the eyes of the Church. A force of crusaders marched to Jerusalem and captured it, massacring the inhabitants. Along the way, several small Crusader states were established. A second unsuccessful crusade was led against Damascus in 1145.

In 1187, the Sultan of Egypt recaptured Jerusalem and a third Crusade was called for by Pope Gregory VIII. This Crusade was joined by the combined forces of France, England and the Holy Roman Empire, but fell short of its goal to recapture Jerusalem.

The fourth Crusade took place in 1202, under Pope Innocent III. The intention of the fourth Crusade was to enter the Holy Land through Egypt. The plan was changed and forces diverted to Constantinople.

Crusades continued into the thirteenth century as Jerusalem and other holy cities changed hands between Christian and Muslim forces. Several crusades took place within Europe, as well, such as the efforts to re-conquer portions of the Muslim-occupied Iberian Peninsula.

One result of the crusades was to establish and reinforce the political and military authority of the Catholic Church and the Roman Pope. The religious fervor spurred on by the Crusades would eventually culminate in such movements as the Inquisition in Spain and the expulsion of the Moors from Europe. The marches of the crusaders also opened new routes between Europe and the East along which culture, learning and trade could travel.

Skill 5.5 **Recognize basic features of the manorial system and feudalism in medieval Europe, analyze the role and political effects of Christianity in European medieval society, demonstrate knowledge of how increasing trade led to the growth of towns and cities in late medieval Europe, and examining the crisis of the fourteenth century that precipitated the end of the European Middle Ages**

As trade and travel increased, more cities sprang up and began to grow in the west. Craft workers in the cities developed their skills to a high degree, eventually organizing guilds to protect the quality of the work and to regulate the buying and selling of their products. City government developed and flourished, centered on strong town councils, and a mercantile class began to grow and exert its influence. The city-states of Italy, which were to figure so importantly in the coming Renaissance, began to flourish.

During the Middle Ages, the system of **feudalism** became a dominant feature of the economic and social system in Europe. Feudalism began as a way to ensure that a king or nobleman could raise an army when needed. In exchange for the promise of loyalty and military service, *lords* would grant a section of land, called a *fief*, to a *vassal*, as those who took this oath of loyalty were called. The vassal was then entitled to work the land and benefit from its proceeds or to grant it in turn as a fief to another.

At the bottom of this ladder were peasants who actually worked the land. At the top was the King, to whom all lands might legally belong. The King could ensure loyalty among his advisors by giving them use of large sections of land which they in turn could grant as fiefs.

Monorails, Manorials, which also arose during the Middle Ages, are similar to feudalism in structure, but consisted of self-contained manors that were often owned outright by a nobleman. Some manors were granted conditionally to their lords and some were linked to the military service and oaths of loyalty found in feudalism, meaning that the two terms overlap somewhat.

Manors usually consisted of a large house for the lord and his family, surrounded by fields and a small village which supported the activities of the manor. The lord of the manor was expected to provide certain services for the villagers and laborers associated with the manor, including the support of a church.

Land is a finite resource, however, and as population grew during the middle centuries of the Middle Ages, the manorial/feudal system became less and less effective as a system of economic organization. The end of the system was sealed by the outbreak and spread of the Black Death, which killed over one-third of the total population of Europe. Those who survived and were skilled in any job or occupation were in demand. Many serfs and peasants found freedom and, for that time, a decidedly improved standard of living.

The **High Middle Ages** refers to the period in Europe between the Early and Late Middle Ages, spanning approximately the 11th, 12th and 13th centuries. The period is noted for a rapid increase in population which contributed to dramatic changes in society, culture, and political organization.

During this period, the concept of the nation state took hold as populations became more stable and people began to think of themselves as belonging to a larger group of ethnically similar cultures. In Italy, the independent nation states such as Venice, Pisa and Florence were established, providing a basis for the Renaissance. The concept of inherited nobility gained wide acceptance and knighthood and chivalry developed as virtuous codes of conduct.

The crusades took place during the High Middle Ages, further strengthening the importance of these orders of knights and solidifying the strength of the western Church throughout Europe. As the power and influence of the Church grew, it contributed to the growth of art and architecture, particularly in the development of the great gothic cathedrals, most of which were constructed during this era.

The routes opened by crusaders marching to Jerusalem paved the way for an increase in trade, and contributed to the growth of many cities based on this trade. A merchant class developed and began to exert its influence on political and economic affairs.

Crucial advances in thinking and technology occurred during the High Middle Ages. Improvements in shipbuilding and clock-making led to advances in navigation and cartography, setting the stage for the Age of Exploration. The field of printing, while not yet to the stage that Gutenberg was to take it in the fifteenth century, expanded the availability of texts, serving a growing educated class of people. The philosophy of Scholasticism, which emphasized empiricism and opposed mysticism in Christian education, was espoused by Thomas Aquinas.

The population increase that had brought these significant developments to Europe in the High Middle Ages was suddenly reversed in the mid fourteenth century by the Black Plague, which decimated the region. As the concept of the nation state arose, so did the idea of national borders and national sovereignty. This led to numerous wars, which in turn had a deleterious effects on the economy. These events are now used to mark the period of transition between the High Middle Ages and the Late Middle Ages.

Skill 5.6 **Recognize the social, economic, and political changes that contributed to the rise of Florence and shaped the ideas of Machiavelli, recognize the main characteristics of Renaissance humanism, and identify the artistic and scientific achievements of major Renaissance figures**

The word **Renaissance** literally means "rebirth", and signaled the rekindling of interest in the glory of ancient classical Greek and Roman civilizations. It was the period in human history marking the start of many ideas and innovations leading to our modern age.

The Renaissance began in Italy with many of its ideas starting in **Florence**, controlled by the infamous Medici family. Education, especially for some of the merchants, required reading, writing, math, the study of law, and the writings of classical Greek and Roman writers.

A combination of a renewed fascination with the classical world and new infusion of money into the hands of those so fascinated brought on the Renaissance. In the areas of art, literature, music, and science, the world changed for the better.

Most famous are the Renaissance artists, first and foremost Leonardo, Michelangelo, and Raphael, but also Titian, Donatello, and Rembrandt. All of these men pioneered a new method of painting and sculpture—that of portraying real events and real people as they really looked, not as the artists imagined them to be. One need look no further than Michelangelo's *David* to illustrate this.

Literature was a focus as well during the Renaissance. Humanists Petrarch, Boccaccio, Erasmus, and Sir Thomas More advanced the idea of being interested in life here on earth and the opportunities it can bring, rather than constantly focusing on heaven and its rewards. The monumental works of Shakespeare, Dante, and Cervantes found their origins in these ideas as well as the ones that drove the painters and sculptors. All of these works, of course, owe much of their existence to the invention of the printing press, which occurred during the Renaissance.

The Renaissance changed music as well. No longer just a religious experience, music could be fun and composed for its own sake, to be enjoyed in fuller and more humanistic ways than in the Middle Ages. Musicians worked for themselves, rather than for the churches, as before, and so could command good money for their work, increasing their prestige.

Science advanced considerably during the Renaissance, especially in the area of physics and astronomy. Copernicus, Kepler, and Galileo led a Scientific Revolution in proving that the earth was round and certainly not perfect, a profound revelation to those who clung to medieval ideals of a geocentric, church-centered existence.

All of these things encouraged people to see the world in a new way, more real, more realized, and more realistic than ever before. Contributions of the Italian Renaissance period were made n:

art - the more important artists were **Giotto** and his development of perspective in paintings; **Leonardo da Vinci,** an artist but also a scientist and inventor; **Michelangelo,** a sculptor, painter, and architect; and others including **Raphael**, **Donatello**, **Titian**, and **Tintoretto.**

political philosophy - the writings of **Machiavelli.**

literature - the writings of **Petrarch** and **Boccaccio.**

science – Galileo.

medicine - the work of Brussels-born **Andrea Vesalius** earned him the title of "father of anatomy" and had a profound influence on the Spaniard **Michael Servetus** and the Englishman **William Harvey.**

In Germany, Gutenberg's invention of the **printing press** with movable type facilitated the rapid spread of Renaissance ideas, writings and innovations, thus ensuring the enlightenment of most of Western Europe. Contributions were also made by Durer and Holbein in art and by Paracelsus in science and medicine.

The effects of the Renaissance in the Low Countries can be seen in the literature and philosophy of **Erasmus** and the art of **van Eyck** and **Breughel the Elder.** **Rabelais** and **de Montaigne** in France also contributed to literature and philosophy. In Spain, the art of **El Greco** and **de Morales** flourished, as did the writings of **Cervantes** and **De Vega**. In England, **Sir Thomas More** and **Sir Francis Bacon** wrote and taught philosophy and were inspired by **Vesalius**. **William Harvey** made important contributions in medicine. The greatest talent was found in literature and drama and given to mankind by **Chaucer, Spenser, Marlowe, Jonson,** and the incomparable **Shakespeare.**

The Renaissance ushered in a time of curiosity, learning, and incredible energy, sparking the desire for trade to procure these new, exotic products and to find better, faster, cheaper trade routes to get to them. The work of geographers, astronomers and mapmakers made important contributions and many studied and applied the work of such men as Hipparchus of Greece, Ptolemy of Egypt, Tycho Brahe of Denmark, and Fra Mauro of Italy.

Skill 5.7   **Identify major figures of the Protestant Reformation, analyze the effects of the Reformation on Europe, comparing the Reformation on the Continent and the English Reformation, and demonstrate knowledge of major features of the Counter-Reformation**

The **Reformation** period consisted of two phases: the **Protestant Revolution** and the **Catholic Reformation**. The Protestant Revolution came about because of religious, political, and economic reasons. The religious reasons stemmed from abuses in the Catholic Church including fraudulent clergy with their scandalous immoral lifestyles; the sale of religious offices, indulgences, and dispensations; different theologies within the Church; and frauds involving sacred relics.

The political reasons for the Protestant Revolution involved the increase in the power of rulers who were considered "absolute monarchs", who desired all power and control, especially over the Church. The growth of "nationalism" or patriotic pride in one's own country was another contributing factor.

Economic reasons included the greed of ruling monarchs to possess and control all lands and wealth of the Church, the deep animosity against the burdensome papal taxation, the rise of the affluent middle class and its clash with medieval Church ideals, and the increase of an active system of "intense" capitalism.

The Protestant Revolution began in Germany with the revolt of Martin Luther against Church abuses. It spread to Switzerland where it was led by Calvin. It began in England with the efforts of King Henry VIII to have his marriage to Catherine of Aragon annulled so he could wed another and have a male heir. The results were the increasing support given not only by the people but also by nobles and some rulers, and of course, the attempts of the Church to stop it.

The Catholic Reformation was undertaken by the Church to "clean up its act" and to slow or stop the Protestant Revolution. The major efforts to this end were supplied by the Council of Trent and the Jesuits. Six major results of the Reformation included:

- Religious freedom,
- Religious tolerance,
- More opportunities for education,
- Power and control of rulers limited,
- Increase in religious wars, and
- An increase in fanaticism and persecution.

Skill 5.8 **Recognize the importance of Gutenberg's printing press to the spread of ideas in Europe**

The system of movable type used in a printing press was invented by **Johannes Gutenberg** in the mid fifteenth century. The Koreans and Chinese had movable type prior to this, but Gutenberg's method of casting identical characters and using them in a press, along with the use of oil-based inks, was a significant advancement of the technology, which allowed for the production of consistent, high-quality printing.

The importance of the Gutenberg system to the growth of ideas throughout Europe was critical. One of the first major printing projects that Gutenberg undertook was an edition of the Bible. Bibles up to that point had only been hand-copied in manuscript form, taking a year or more to be produced. The great expense of a hand-copied Bible meant that only clergy and wealthy individuals had direct access to the text. Gutenberg's Bibles were also very expensive, but far less than a manuscript. As the technology improved and printing advanced throughout Europe, printed religious texts became more widespread, setting the stage for the Protestant Revolt of Martin Luther in the early sixteenth century. Luther used printing to create and disseminate copies his *95 theses*, fueling the Reformation.

Gutenberg's method of printing found its way to the city of Venice, in Italy, which was poised to become one of the centers of scientific and artistic advancement during the Renaissance. Venetian printers soon dominated the craft, producing literary and scientific books that were distributed throughout Europe. The ease with which ideas could be shared through printing allowed writers and scientists scattered across the map to collaborate and build upon each other's work.

SUBAREA III.   WORLD HISTORY 1500 TO THE PRESENT

COMPETENCY 6.0   UNDERSTAND THE IMPORTANCE OF THE AGE OF
                  DISCOVERY AND EXPANSION, THE EFFECTS OF THE
                  SCIENTIFIC REVOLUTION AND THE
                  ENLIGHTENMENT, AND MAJOR DEVELOPMENTS OF
                  THE AGE OF REVOLUTIONS AND REBELLIONS

Skill 6.1   Identify the roles of major explorers and conquistadors and
             recognize how improved technology contributed to world
             exploration.

The advances made during the Renaissance in the areas of astronomy,
cartography and shipbuilding opened the possibility of distant travel by sea. As
cities grew and trade increased, Europe's monarchs began looking toward new
lands to fuel growth.

In the East, Islam was beginning to spread not only outward from the Middle East,
but also through the travels of the Chinese explorer **Zheng He,** a Chinese admiral
of the Muslim faith who made several naval journeys throughout Southeast Asia
and the Indian Ocean, reaching the coast of Africa. He established diplomatic ties
between the Ming dynasty and these coastal nations, promoting Chinese trade and
the Muslim faith. As Islam spread, Christian nations also wished to find routes that
bypassed areas of Islamic control. The Age of Exploration was underway.

Portugal led the first wave of exploration by sea in the early fifteenth century, under
Prince Henry the Navigator. Using ships that borrowed technology from Arab
sailing vessels, the Portuguese discovered new islands in the Atlantic and opened
sea routes to the west coast of Africa. Over the next several decades, Portuguese
explorers pushed farther south along the African coast until, in 1498, **Vasco De
Gama** became the first to navigate the Cape of Good Hope at the southern tip of
Africa, opening a new sea route to India.

Portugal's control over the African coast troubled the Spanish, who devised a plan
to bypass the route entirely by sailing west, around the globe, to the profitable
trade lands of Asia. In 1492, Spain sent **Christopher Columbus** to explore this
possible new route. Columbus did not reach Asia, but landed in the New World of
the Americas. Spain would continue to explore - and conquer - Central America,
where they found large numbers of natives and a steady supply of gold.
Meanwhile, Portuguese explorers surveyed the east coast of South America,
where present day Brazil is located. In 1520, **Ferdinand Magellan**, exploring for
Spain, found a passage around the southern tip of South America, opening the
Pacific Ocean as a westward connection between Europe and Asia.

Spain and Portugal dominated new world exploration, but northern Europeans were not idle. In 1497 the British sent **John Cabot** to the east coast of North America. Cabot was looking for the same thing Columbus was, a passage to Asia. He did not find one, but his voyage opened the door for further exploration and colonization of North America. French-sponsored explorers Cartier and Verrazano soon followed, establishing footholds in the new world. In the early seventeenth century, Frenchman **Samuel de Champlain** established the site of Quebec City and explored the Atlantic coast of North America.

By the seventeenth century, advances in sailing technology led to the mapping of almost all the world's coastlines and the age of exploration by sea drew to a close, but the impact of these new discoveries on the economy of Europe was enormous. As trade increased, so did the influence of the merchant class. As Atlantic trade and colonization increased, the economic center of Europe shifted from the Mediterranean to the Atlantic coast countries. The opening of North and South America to colonization and expansion from Europe increased demand for European goods, and eventually led to the founding of several new nations.

The eighteenth century witnessed great strides in the science of navigation, allowing for a new level of precision in mapmaking and the establishment of trade routes. The great British navigator **James Cook** employed his skill by plying the South Pacific and opened routes to the Hawaiian Islands, Australia and New Zealand.

Skill 6.2   Demonstrate knowledge of the Columbian Exchange, analyze its global economic and cultural effects, and demonstrate knowledge of the causes, extent, and consequences of the trans-Atlantic slave trade

The **Columbian Exchange** refers to the great exchange of plants, animals and peoples that took place between Europe and the New World following Columbus' voyage in 1492. New World foods such as the tomato, potato, corn and chocolate were returned to Europe where they became essential. Tobacco was not known in Europe before the Columbian Exchange.

From Europe, such important things as horses and cattle were introduced to the New World. Coffee and bananas were brought to Central and South America, where they thrived. Wheat was introduced. There was also an exchange of disease that brought ruin to some New World communities through **smallpox** and **influenza**.

These epidemics resulted in a shortage of labor to work the agricultural plantations established by the Europeans, and prompted, in the sixteenth century, a spike in the importation of slaves from Africa to fill the need.

The Portuguese, who were the first to explore the west and central African coasts, dominated the **Atlantic slave trade**. They relied on the coastal kingdoms to supply them with slaves, who were often either prisoners from military raids or kidnapped from rival kingdoms. A regular trade developed as the New World flourished, with the eventual transportation of approximately 10 million African slaves across he Atlantic, mostly to Brazil and the Caribbean.

The economic growth of the New World would not have been possible without slave labor. Slavery brought with it social problems as societies began to wrestle with the moral issue of enslaving other human beings. Slave revolts were successful in some places such as Haiti in 1804, where former slaves formed an independent country.

Following the **Haitian Revolution**, the British began a concerted effort to end the slave trade to the European colonies in the New World. Through diplomacy and military intervention, the slave trade was ended in the 1850's. This did not end slavery itself, however. The issue of slavery was a key part of the American Civil War, which started shortly after the end of the slave trade.

The slave trade also enriched the African kingdoms that supplied the slaves and its end had serious economic and political repercussions in Africa as formerly powerful kingdoms had to adapt to other areas of trade. Those that could not adapt, disintegrated.

Skill 6.3   **Recognize the scientific contributions of Copernicus, Galileo, Kepler, and Newton and examine how these ideas changed the European worldview**

A Polish astronomer, **Nicolaus Copernicus**, began the Scientific Revolution. He crystallized a lifetime of observations into a book that was published about the time of his death; in this book, Copernicus argued that the sun, not the Earth, was the center of a solar system and that other planets revolved around the sun, not the Earth. This flew in the face of established (read: Church-mandated) doctrine. The Church still wielded tremendous power at this time, including the power to banish people or sentence them to prison or even death.

The Danish astronomer **Tycho Brahe** was the first to catalog his observations of the night sky, of which he made thousands. Building on Brahe's data, German scientist **Johannes Kepler** instituted his theory of planetary movement, embodied in his famous Laws of Planetary Movement. Using Brahe's data, Kepler also confirmed Copernicus's observations and argument that the Earth revolved around the sun.

The most famous defender of this idea was **Galileo Galilei**, an Italian scientist who conducted many famous experiments in the pursuit of science. He is most well-known for his defense of the heliocentric (sun-centered) idea. He wrote a book comparing the two theories, but most readers could tell easily that he favored the new one. He was convinced of this mainly because of what he had seen with his own eyes. He had used the relatively new invention of the telescope to see four moons of Jupiter. They certainly did not revolve around the Earth, so why should everything else? His ideas were not at all favored with the Church, which continued to assert its authority in this and many other matters. The Church was still powerful enough at this time, especially in Italy, to order Galileo to be placed under house arrest.

Galileo died under house arrest, but his ideas didn't die with him. Picking up the baton was an English scientist named **Isaac Newton**, who became perhaps the most famous scientist of all. He is known as the discoverer of gravity and a pioneering voice in the study of optics (light), calculus, and physics.
More than any other scientist, Newton argued for (and proved) the idea of a mechanistic view of the world: You can see how the world works and prove how the world works through observation; if you can see these things with your own eyes, they must be so. Up to this time, people believed what other people told them; this is how the Church was able to keep control of people's lives for so long. Newton, following in the footsteps of Copernicus and Galileo, changed all that.

Skill 6.4   **Identify major Enlightenment ideas from the writings of Locke, Voltaire, and Rousseau; analyze their relationship to European politics and society; and demonstrate knowledge of the spread of Enlightenment ideas**

The **Enlightenment**, a period of intense self-study focused on ethics and logic. More so than at any time before, scientists and philosophers questioned cherished truths, widely held beliefs, and their own sanity in an attempt to discover why the world worked—from within. "I think, therefore I am" was one of the famous sayings of that or any day, uttered by Rene Descartes, a French scientist-philosopher whose dedication to logic and the rigid rules of observation was a blueprint for the thinkers who came after him.

One of the giants of the era was England's **David Hume**, a pioneer of the doctrine of empiricism (believing things only when you've seen the proof for yourself). Hume was a prime believer in the value of skepticism; in other words, he was naturally suspicious of things that other people told him to be true and constantly set out to discover the truth for himself. These two related ideas influenced many great thinkers after Hume, and his writings (of which there are many) continue to inspire philosophers to this day.

The Enlightenment thinker who might be the most famous is **Immanuel Kant** of Germany. He was both a philosopher and a scientist and he took a definite scientific view of the world. He wrote the movement's most famous essay, "Answering the Question: What Is Enlightenment?" and he answered his famous question with the motto "Dare to Know."

For Kant, the human being was a rational being capable of hugely creative thought and intense self-evaluation. He encouraged all to examine themselves and the world around them. He believed that the source of morality lay not in nature of in the grace of God but in the human soul itself. He believed that man believed in God for practical, not religious or mystical, reasons.

During the Enlightenment, the idea of the **social contract** confirmed the belief that government existed because people wanted it to, that the people had an agreement with the government that they would submit to as long as it protected them and didn't encroach on their basic human rights. This idea was first made famous by the Frenchman Jean-Jacques Rousseau but was also adopted by England's John Locke and America's Thomas Jefferson.

Thomas Hobbes' (1588-1679) *Leviathan* (1651) was actually written as a reaction to the disorders caused by the English civil wars that had culminated with the execution of King Charles I. Hobbes perceived people as rational beings, but unlike Locke and Jefferson, he had no faith in their abilities to live in harmony with one another without a government. The trouble was, as Hobbes saw it, people were selfish and the strong would take from the weak. However, because they were rational, the weak would in turn band together against the strong. For Hobbes, the state of nature became a chaotic state in which every person becomes the enemy of every other. It became a war of all against all, with terrible consequences for all.

John Locke (1632-1704) was an important thinker on the nature of democracy. He regarded the mind of man at birth as a tabula rasa, a blank slate upon which experience imprints knowledge and behavior. He did not believe in the idea of intuition or theories of innate knowledge. Locke also believed that all men are born good, independent and equal and that their actions would determine their fate. In his most important work, *Two Treatises of Civil Government* (1690), Locke attacked the theory of the divine right of kings and the nature of the state as conceived by Thomas Hobbes. Locke argued that sovereignty did not reside in the state, but with the people. The state is supreme, but only if it is bound by civil and what he called "**natural**" law. Many of Locke's political ideas, such as those relating to natural rights, property rights, the duty of the government to protect those rights and the rule of the majority, were embodied in the Constitution of the United States. He further held that revolution was not only a right, but also an obligation and advocated for a system of checks and balances in which government is comprised of three branches, the legislative being more powerful than either the executive or the judicial. He also believed in the separation of church and state. As is apparent, all of these ideas were to be incorporated in the Constitution of the United States. As such, Locke is considered in many ways the true founding father of our Constitution and of our government system. He remains one of history's most influential political thinkers to this day.

Jean-Jacques Rousseau (1712-1778) was one of the most famous and influential political theorists before the French Revolution. His most important and most studied work is **The Social Contract** (1762). He was concerned with what should be the proper form of society and government. However, unlike Hobbes, Rousseau did not view the state of nature as one of absolute chaos.

As Rousseau saw it, the problem was that the natural harmony of the state of nature was due to people's intuitive goodness and not to their actual reason. Reason only developed once a civilized society was established. Intuitive goodness was easily overwhelmed, however, by arguments for institutions of social control, which likened rulers to father figures and extolled the virtues of obedience to such figures. To a remarkable extent, strong leaders have, in Rousseau's judgment, already succeeded not only in extracting obedience from the citizens that they ruled, but also more importantly, have managed to justify such obedience as necessary.

Rousseau's most direct influence was during the **French Revolution** (1789-1815*). Declaration of the Rights of Man and the Citizen* (1789) explicitly recognized the sovereignty of the general will as expressed in the law. In contrast to the American **Declaration of Independence***,* it contains explicit mention of the obligations and duties of the citizen, such as assenting to taxes in support of the military or police forces for the common good. In modern times, ideas such as Rousseau's have often been used to justify the ideas of authoritarian and totalitarian systems.

Skill 6.5 **Demonstrate knowledge of the policies of Japan's Tokugawa rulers and China's Qing rulers, analyze the effects of population growth on the two societies between the seventeenth century and mid-nineteenth century, and examine Chinese and Japanese interaction with westerners during this period**

Tokugawa Ieyasu came to power in Japan in 1600 by defeating a coalition that sought political power in Japan. His rise to power marks the beginning of the Tokugawa shogunate, which held power as military rulers in Japan until 1868. In the sixteenth century, Japan had absorbed a great deal of European influence. The Portuguese had arrived in 1543 and **Francis Xavier**, a Jesuit priest, brought a mission to Japan in 1549. By 1600 there were about 300,000 Christians, including a number of the military aristocracy. Hideyoshi began to suppress Christianity as a foreign threat in 1587, and banished the Portuguese missionaries. The Tokugawa shoguns persecuted Christianity more extensively by executing thousands of Christians and driving the Church underground. An uprising in 1637-38 culminated in a massive slaughter. After this event, foreigners were banned from the country, except for a small number of Dutch merchant traders who were strictly confined to an island.

This military dictatorship adopted the existing social class hierarchy that was in place in 1600. The warrior-caste of samurai was at the top of the hierarchy. Next were farmers, artisans, and traders. This very tightly controlled hierarchy eventually led to conflict. The peasants were taxed in fixed amounts. As monetary values changed, the lack of variation in the amount of the tax resulted in less support for the samurai who collected the taxes. There were a number of confrontations between the samurai, who were growing steadily poorer, and the peasants, who were growing steadily wealthier. None of these conflicts had significant results until the arrival of foreign power and influence.

A rebellion by the titular Emperor and several of the powerful nobles resulted in the Boshin War. The war ended in the Meiji Restoration and the overthrow of the Tokugawa shogunate. Foreign travel and books were banned, permitting a flourishing of local culture. Although the government was stable, the financial situation of the government was slowly declining, resulting in higher taxes. The tax increases caused riots among the farmers and peasants. A number of natural disasters caused years of famine and deepening financial difficulties. The merchant class claimed greater power and many samurai became financially dependent upon them. The second part of the Edo era was marked by corruption, decline of morality, and government incompetence.

The financial difficulties and the inability of the government to respond to numerous natural disasters and famine produced growing anti-government sentiment. Movements arose that tried to limit Western influence and to restore control of the government to the imperial line. Others wanted greater openness to Western ideas and technology.

The **Chinese Revolution** was a response to imperial rule under the Qing Dynasty. Numerous internal rebellions caused widespread oppression and death. Conflicts with foreign nations had tended to end with treaties that humiliated China and required the payment of reparations that amounted to massive cost. In addition, there were popular feelings that political power should be restored from the Manchus to the Han Chinese.

There was some attempt at reform, but it was undercut by the conservative supporters of the dynasty. The failures in modernization and liberalization and the violent repression of dissidents moved the reformers toward revolution.

The most popular of the numerous revolutionary groups was led by Sun Yat-sen. His movement was supported by Chinese who were living outside China and by students in Japan. He won the support of regional military officers. Sun's political philosophy consisted of "three principles of the people":

   • Nationalism, which called for ousting of the Manchus and putting an end to foreign hegemony

   • Democracy, to establish a popularly elected government

   • People's livelihood, or socialism, which was designed to help the common people by equalizing the ownership of land and the tools of production.

Revolution began with the discontented army units. This was called the Wuchang Uprising. The uprising spread to other parts of China. The Qing Court put it down within 50 days. During this time, however, a number of other provinces declared independence of the Qing Dynasty. A month later Sun Yat-sen was elected the first Provisional President of the new Republic of China. Yuan Shikai, who had control of the Army tried to prevent civil war and possible intervention by foreign governments. He claimed power in Beijing. Sun agreed to unite China under a government headed by Yuan, who became the second provisional president of the Chinese republic.

Yuan quickly gathered more power than was controlled by the Parliament. He revised the constitution and became a dictator. In the national elections of 1912, Sung Jiaoren led the new Nationalist Party in winning the majority of seats in the parliament. A month later, Yuan had Sung assassinated. This increased Yuan's unpopularity. Several leadership missteps of a dictatorial nature aroused greater discontent. A second revolution began in 1913. This resulted in the flight to Japan of Sun and his followers.

While Yuan pursued an imperialistic policy, Sun gathered more followers. Yuan alienated the parliament and the military. When WWI broke out, Japan issued the "Twenty-one Demands," and Yuan agreed to many of them, further alienating the people of China. Several southern provinces declared independence. In 1916, Yuan stepped down as emperor.

A period of struggle between rival warlords followed. By the end of WWI, Duan Qirui had emerged as the most powerful Chinese leader.
He declared war on Germany and Austria-Hungary in 1917 in the hope of getting loans from Japan. His disregard for the constitution led Sun Yat-sen and others to establish a new government and the Constitutional Protection Army. Sun established a military government. The Constitutional Protection War continued through 1918. The result was a divided China, divided along the north-south border.

By 1921, Sun had become president of a unified group of southern provinces. He was unable to obtain assistance from Western nations, and turned to the Soviet Union in 1920. The Soviets supported both Sun and the newly established Communist Party in China. This set off a power struggle between the Communists and the Nationalists. In 1923, Sun and a Soviet representative promised Soviet support for the re-unification of China. The Soviet advisers sent Chiang Kai-shek to Moscow to be trained in propaganda and mass mobilization. Sun died in1925. Chiang Kai-shek was commander of the National Revolutionary Army, and began to take back the Northern provinces from the warlords. By 1928 all of China was under his control, and his government was recognized internationally.

Skill 6.6 **Demonstrate knowledge of absolutism through a comparison of the rules of Louis XIV, Peter the Great, and Tokugawa Ieyasu**

Louis XIV acceded to the throne shortly before his fifth birthday. His mother and the First Minister, Mazarin, controlled the government until Mazarin's death in 1661, at which time Louis XIV declared that he would rule the country. He has been referred to alternately as Louis the Great, the Great Monarch and The Sun King. During his reign, France attained cultural dominance, as well as military and political superiority. Louis XIV created a centralized government that he ruled with absolute power. He is often considered the archetype of an absolute monarch. He is quoted as claiming "I am the State." However, many scholars believe this statement was falsely attributed to him by political opponents. It did, however, summarize the absolute power he held.

Mazarin was hated and distrusted in most political circles because he was not French born. The absolute rule exercised by Anne (his mother) and Mazarin was very unpopular among the people. At about the time the Thirty Years' War ended (1648), the *Fronde*, a civil war broke out in France. Mazarin continued the policies of his predecessors in trying to expand the power of the Crown at the expense of the nobles. He tried to impose a tax on the members of the Parliament, but they refused to pay the tax and ordered all of his previous financial edicts burned. Mazarin responded by arresting several members of the Parliament. The result was insurrection and rioting in Paris. The royal family fled. When the war ended the French army was available to aid and protect the royal family. By January 1649, the conflict was temporarily ended with the Peace of Rueil.

The second *Fronde* broke out in 1650. This was a revolt of the nobility and the clergy against the crown. During these times of rebellion, the Queen sold jewels to feed her family. Louis XIV emerged from these years of internal rebellion with a strong distrust of both the nobility and the common people.

. To be sure, Louis XIV and his advisors moved France to economic strength and political power and influence in Europe. But the claim of absolute power by divine right, combined with his distrust of others, led to unique actions to maintain power and to control any who might instigate rebellion against him. One of his tactics to control the nobility was to require them to remain at the Palace of Versailles, where he could watch them and prevent them from plotting unrest in their communities. He spent lavishly on parties and distractions to keep the nobility occupied and to strengthen his control over them. He was determined to undercut the power and influence of the nobility. He tried to fill high offices with commoners or members of the new aristocracy because he believed that if commoners got out of hand, they could be dismissed. He knew he could not mitigate the influence of great nobles. By forcing the powerful nobles to remain at court he effectively reduced their power and influence. By appointing commoners and new aristocracy to government functions, he increased his control over both the functions and those who held them. He controlled the nobles to such an extent that he was able to ensure that there would never be another *Fronde*.

Louis XIV also tried to control the Church. He called an assembly of the clergy in 1681. By the time the assembly ended, he had won acceptance of the Declaration of the Clergy of France, by which the power of the Pope was greatly reduced and his power was greatly enhanced. This Declaration was never accepted by the Pope.

Perhaps the great mistake of Louis XIV's reign was his attitude toward Protestantism and his handling of the Huguenots. In 1685 he revoked the Edict of Nantes. This resulted in the departure from the country of these French Protestants, who were among the wealthiest and most industrious people in the nation. He also alienated the Protestant countries of Europe, particularly England.

Peter the Great of Russia was named Tsar in 1682, when he was ten years old, with his mother, Sophia, as regent. During his reign, Peter suppressed revolt and dissent with violence, eventually being named Emperor of Russia. Peter was a reformer who brought Western culture to Russia and traveled to Europe to learn about the newest military technology. Peter also laid the foundations of a legislative body by creating a Governing Senate made up of his appointees, and introduced a system of ranking based on merit and service rather than heredity.

Also refer to Skill 6.5.

Skill 6.7   **Identify the causes and analyze the results of revolutions in England (1640–1689), the United States (1776), France (1789), Haiti (1791), and Latin America (1808–1825), and the emergence of constitutional government**

The period from the 1700s to the 1800s was characterized in Western countries by opposing political ideas of democracy and nationalism. This resulted in strong nationalistic feelings and people of common cultures asserting their belief in the right to have a part in their government.

The **American Revolution** resulted in the successful efforts of the English colonists in America to win their freedom from Great Britain. After more than one hundred years of mostly self-government, the colonists resented the increased British meddling and control, they declared their freedom, won the Revolutionary War with aid from France, and formed a new independent nation.

The **French Revolution** was the revolt of the middle and lower classes against the gross political and economic excesses of the rulers and the supporting nobility. It ended with the establishment of the First in a series of French Republics. Conditions leading to revolt included extreme taxation, inflation, lack of food, and the total disregard for the impossible, degrading, and unacceptable condition of the people on the part of the rulers, nobility, and the Church.

The American Revolution and the French Revolution were similar yet different, liberating their people from unwanted government interference and installing a different kind of government. They were both fought for the liberty of the common people, and they both were built on writings and ideas that embraced such an outcome, yet that is where the similarities end. Both Revolutions proved that people could expect more from their government and that such rights as self-determination were worth fighting—and dying—for. Several important differences need to be emphasized:

The British colonists were striking back against unwanted taxation and other sorts of government interference. The French people were starving and, in many cases, destitute and were striking back against an autocratic regime that cared more for high fashion and courtly love than bread and circuses.
The American Revolution involved a years-long campaign of often bloody battles, skirmishes, and stalemates. The French Revolution was bloody to a degree but was mainly an overthrow of society and its outdated traditions.

The American Revolution resulted in a representative government, which marketed itself as a beacon of democracy for the rest of the world. The French Revolution resulted in a consulship, a generalship, and then an emperor—probably not what the perpetrators of the Revolution had in mind when they first struck back at the king and queen. Still, both Revolutions are viewed as turning points in history, as times when the governed stood up to the governors and said, "Enough."

New Granada (northern South America) – In 1808, Venezuela proclaimed its Independence from Spain and sent Andrés Bello, Luis López Mendez, and Simón Bolívar to Great Britain on a diplomatic mission: a plan to foment full independence from Spain for all the colonies from the New World. On returning to Venezuela on June 3, 1811, he enlisted under the command of Francisco de Miranda, who acted as dictator of Venezuela, fighting with him until he was defeated and imprisoned by royalist forces. Simón traveled to Cartagena and wrote the Cartagena manifesto: he argued for the cooperation of all the different kingdoms of New Granada. He was persuasive and successful and he continued leading the revolutionary cause, invading Venezuela, taking the city of Merida and the capital, Caracas. There he was proclaimed "el Libertador" (The Liberator). He was defeated by the Royalists, in 1814 and found asylum in Nueva Granada where he intervened and assisted in freeing Bogotá after being appointed commander in chief of the forces of the federal republic. After falling out with province leaders, he sought refuge in Jamaica and there wrote the "Letter from Jamaica," a document on the current struggle and purpose of Latin American independence. He returned to Venezuela in 1817 with assistance from newly independent Haiti and continued fighting.

On August 7, 1819, Bolívar defeated the Spanish at the battle of Boyacá and founded "la Gran Colombia" (The Great Colombia) at the Angostura congress: it represented the now present-day areas of Venezuela, Colombia, Panama and Ecuador. He was named president. His military hand: Antonio José de Sucre, Francisco Antonio Zea and Francisco Paula Santander, all kept fighting for a stronger and more independent state. Northern South America was completely liberated from all Spanish and royalist authority on May 22, 1822, when Antonio José de Sucre defeated the Spanish at Pichincha, in Ecuador. He began talks with the "Knight of the Andes," the liberator of southern South America, José de San Martín, to begin planning a total victory over the Spanish royalists. Eventually, Simón was made chief and defeated the Spanish in the battle of Junin on August 6, 1824 and the battle of Ayacucho on December 9, 1824. Spanish rule over South America no longer existed. On August 6, 1825, the Republic of Bolivia was created at the congress of upper Peru, which had been invoked by Antonio José de Sucre.

Peru and "el Río de la Plata" (southern South America) – In 1810, a momentous French invasion of Spain allowed for the wealthy residents of Argentina to seize power, asserting their own authority under King Fernando VII and deposing the viceroy. On July 9, 1816, the Argentine Declaration of Independence was signed. The connecting ties to the Spanish monarchy began their eventual separation. Royalist viceroy of Peru remained in the north. Revolutionary movements, created to sever any possibility of Spanish rule, were starting to formulate.

With the help of his longtime friend and Chilean patriot Bernard O'Higgins, enlisted support from the patriots residing in Chile and the Argentine government, raising an army, "el Ejército de los Andes" (The Army of the Andes). They crossed the Andes with success and defeated the Spanish on February 2, 1817, re-establishing a national government in Santiago and placing O'Higgins at the head as the Republic's first president. Chile was fully independent in April, 1818. After failing in negotiations with the Royalists in Peru upon Martin's suggestion that they themselves form an independent monarchy, Martín's forces began incursions into Peru and backed the remaining Spaniards into defeat, in 1821, as a result of blocking their last remaining seaport. José de San Martín was proclaimed the protector of Peru. In 1822, he abdicated his powers at the first invocation of the Peruvian congress, leaving power to Bolívar.

The economic growth of the New World would not have been possible without slave labor. Slavery brought social problems as well, however, as societies began to wrestle with the moral issue of enslaving other human beings. Slave revolts were successful in some places, such as Haiti in 1804, where former slaves formed an independent country. Following the **Haitian Revolution**, the British began a concerted effort to end the slave trade to the European colonies in the New World. Through diplomacy and military intervention, the slave trade was ended in the 1850's. This did not end slavery itself, however. The issue of slavery was a key part of the American Civil War, which started shortly after the end of the slave trade.

Skill 6.8 **Demonstrate knowledge of Napoleon's rise to power and defeat and analyze the consequences of these developments for Europe**

Napoleon was a dominating figure on the European landscape, shaping and reshaping the fabric of the Continent in ways that are still being explained. He rose from the ranks of a common soldier to become a powerful politician and eventually ruler of an empire. He was totally the product of his age, but he ushered in a new one as well.

First and foremost, he changed the geography of Europe. The borders of France swelled under his reign, as did the Grand Armee and its reputation. Napoleon brought to the battlefield brilliant tactics and sound military mind, in addition to a great daring to attempt the seemingly impossible and make it work. As with Alexander before him, Napoleon could snatch the grandest victory from the jaws of defeat. One need look no further than **Jena**, perhaps Napoleon's most stunning victory.

With a numerically inferior force, he crushed the Prussian army, inflicting on it a number of casualties five times as much as his own army suffered. On the same day, the Grand Armee inflicted an even greater defeat on the Prussian Army, crushing it completely with a much wider disparity in troop numbers. The result was a capitulation, effectively ending Prussia's influence in Europe for years to come.

His ability to move his troops with lightning speed, before and during battles, earned Napoleon a reputation for being an expert in mobile warfare, and indeed he was that, even when heavy cannons were involved. He was also a master of the use of cavalry on the battlefield, sending many a numerically superior force scurrying from the battlefield in flying defeat. This translated into new strategies and technologies on the battlefield, not only for France but also for the rest of Europe. Napoleon's tactics, successes, and failures continue to be studied for their effectiveness and their innovation.

His ambition eventually outstripped his fortune, however, and he effected a humiliating retreat from Russia, effectively ending his reign. Other battles followed, but the twin defeats of Russia and Trafalgar ended his hopes and dreams of being Master of Europe.

Napoleon was certainly a unifier of his own people and of the rest of Europe against him. In the early days of the Continental System, he ruled Europe (Russia excluded) and dreamed of a huge political state with himself at the head and the peoples of Europe under his banner, albeit reluctantly. As they began to chip away at this authority, however, they began to follow Britain's and Russia's leads and became more bold in their opposition. This eventually resulted in the kind of united force that opposed the French at **Waterloo**. Such union continued throughout the Congress of Vienna, the political end of the **Napoleonic Wars**, and lasted for a time until nationalism gripped Europe fully and fomented the Revolutions of 1848.

The transformation of Napoleon from a hero of the egalitarian French Revolution into an overarching monarch was a cautionary tale for both French people and the rest of Europe. The ideals that fired the revolution against the monarchy in France took root in other European countries, and Napoleon's assumption of absolute power proved a perfect example of how the common people should be given more of a check on governmental power. The emperor's ultimate defeat (twice, actually) was a victory for nationalists everywhere as well as the end of an era.

The major turning point for Latin America, already unhappy with Spanish restrictions on trade, agriculture, and the manufacture of goods, was Napoleon's move into Spain and Portugal. Napoleon's imprisonment of King Ferdinand VII made the local agents of the Spanish authorities feel that they were in fact agents of the French. Conservative and liberal locals joined forces, declared their loyalty to King Ferdinand, and formed committees (*juntas*). Between May of 1810 and July of 1811, the *juntas* in Argentina, Chile, Paraguay, Venezuela, Bolivia and Colombia all declared independence. Fighting erupted between Spanish authorities in Latin America and the members and followers of the *juntas*. In Mexico City another *junta* declared loyalty to Ferdinand and independence.

The United States' unintentional and accidental involvement in what was known as the **War of 1812** came about due to the political and economic struggles between France and Great Britain. Napoleon's goal was complete conquest and control of Europe, and especially of Great Britain. Although British troops were temporarily driven off the mainland of Europe, the navy still controlled the seas, across which France had to bring necessary products. America traded with both nations, especially with France and its colonies. The British decided to destroy the American trade with France, mainly for two reasons: (a) Products and goods from the US gave Napoleon what he needed to keep up his struggle with Britain. He and France was the enemy and it was felt that the Americans were aiding the Mother Country's enemy. (b) Britain felt threatened by the increasing strength and success of the US merchant fleet. They were becoming major competitors with the ship owners and merchants in Britain.

The British issued the **Orders in Council,** which was a series of measures prohibiting American ships from entering any French ports, not only in Europe but also in India and the West Indies. At the same time, Napoleon began efforts for a coastal blockade of the British Isles. He issued a series of Orders prohibiting all nations, including the United States, from trading with the British. He threatened seizure of every ship entering French ports after they stopped at any British port or colony, even threatening to seize every ship inspected by British cruisers or that paid any duties to their government. The British were stopping American ships and impressing American seamen to service on British ships, and the Americans were outraged.

The period of European peace after the defeat of Napoleon and the reliance upon the gold standard in that time is often referred to as "The First Era of Globalization." This period began to disintegrate with the crisis of the gold standard in the late 1920s and early 1930s.

COMPETENCY 7.0   **UNDERSTAND THE EFFECTS OF INDUSTRIALIZATION, THE RISE OF NATIONALISM, MAJOR CHARACTERISTICS OF IMPERIALISM, THE CAUSES AND GLOBAL EFFECTS OF WORLD WAR I, MAJOR DEVELOPMENTS OF THE INTERWAR PERIOD, AND THE CAUSES AND CONSEQUENCES OF WORLD WAR II**

Skill 7.1   **Analyze the process and effects of British, German, and Japanese industrializations**

The Industrial Revolution of the late eighteenth and early nineteenth century brought not only vast technological changes, but also drastically changed social and political structures. In Britain and Europe, centrally located factories replaced household-based industry. The standard of living was raised, leading to a population increase. This in turn led to the increased employment of children in industry until national laws were passed limiting child labor.

Cities were built to support the new centralized industries, bringing with them new political opportunities as well as the problems of urbanization, such as overcrowding and pollution. Early political groups appeared opposed to the rapid industrial growth, such as the **Luddites**. The Luddites were made up of people whose trades were threatened by mechanization, such as weavers who were replaced by machines that could be operated by relatively unskilled workers.

Bringing workers together into central factories also facilitated the organization of labor groups and trade unions that banded together to ensure adequate wages and working conditions. Workers held the threat of a strike in support of their demands, and sometimes conflicted with employers. Legislation was enacted to protect both industry and labor.

The German philosopher **Karl Marx** viewed industrialization and capitalism as an unsustainable system that undercut itself by placing value on capital rather than on the value of goods themselves. Along with his historical philosophy of class struggle, Marx predicted that capitalism would end and that only communism could replace it as a stable economic system. Marx's views grew in popularity after his death in the 1880s, and were espoused by the Russian revolutionaries who founded the Soviet Union in the early twentieth century.

Laissez-faire economics, or pure capitalism, is based on free markets without government interference in the marketplace. The role for government was to establish the framework for the functioning of the economy, determining things like standards of weights and measures, providing public goods, etc. Adam Smith, author of **The Wealth of Nations**, believed that free markets should exist without government interference because any interference limited the rights and liberties of the market participants, even though laissez-faire economics results in an unequal distribution of income. The economy, if left alone, would function as if an invisible hand guided it to an efficient allocation of resources.

Karl Marx viewed economics from a different perspective. He felt that labor was the value determining factor. Since it was labor that gave a commodity value, labor was entitled to the value of what it produced, or the surplus. The capitalist didn't do anything to earn the surplus. He appropriated it from labor and, therefore, exploited labor. This is the basis for Marxian economics. Marx goes on to apply the doctrine of historical necessity and the Hegelian triad to history and predicts a revolution based on the exploitation of labor. Marxian theories were the basis for the former Soviet and Eastern block economies.

Industrialization in Japan followed a deliberate course under the reforms of the Emperor Meiji in the second half of the nineteenth century. Meiji adopted a free market system based on American and British models and stimulated industrial growth by building several state sponsored factories. A common currency was adopted, and Japan rapidly became involved in mercantile trades, buying raw materials from other countries and producing finished items.

Because Japan was able to learn from the industrialization processes of the rest of the world, it was able to rapidly enter the world economy by borrowing from them directly.

Populism is the philosophy that is concerned with the common sense needs of average people. Populism often finds expression as a reaction against perceived oppression of the average people by the wealthy elite in society. The prevalent claim of populist movements is that they will put the people first. Populism is often connected with religious fundamentalism, racism, or nationalism. Populist movements claim to represent the majority of the people and call them to stand up to institutions or practices that seem detrimental to their well-being.

Populism flourished in the late nineteenth and early twentieth centuries. Several political parties were formed out of this philosophy, including the Greenback Party, the Populist Party, the Farmer-Labor Party, the Single Tax movement of Henry George, the Share Our Wealth movement of Huey Long, the Progressive Party, and the Union Party.

In the 1890s, the People's Party won the support of millions of farmers and other working people. This party challenged the social ills of the monopolists of the "Gilded Age."

The tremendous change that resulted from the Industrial Revolution led to a demand for reform that would control the power wielded by big corporations. The gap between the industrial moguls and the working people was growing. This disparity between rich and poor resulted in a public outcry for reform at the same time that there was an outcry for governmental reform that would end the political corruption and elitism of the day.

This fire was fueled by the writings of investigative journalists – the "muckrakers" – who published scathing exposes of political and business wrongdoing and corruption. The result was the rise of a group of politicians and reformers who supported a wide array of populist causes. The period 1900 to 1917 came to be known as the Progressive Era. Although these leaders came from many different backgrounds and were driven by different ideologies, they shared a common fundamental belief that government should be eradicating social ills and promoting the common good and the equality guaranteed by the Constitution.

The reforms initiated by these leaders and the spirit of **Progressivism** were far-reaching. Politically, many states enacted the initiative and the referendum. The adoption of the recall occurred in many states. Several states enacted legislation that would undermine the power of political machines. On a national level the two most significant political changes were (1) the ratification of the 17th Amendment, which required that all US Senators be chosen by popular election, and (2) the ratification of the 19th Amendment, which granted women the right to vote.

Skill 7.2   **Compare and contrasting the rise of the nation-state in Germany under Otto von Bismarck and in Japan under Emperor Meiji and analyze the rise of nationalism as seen in the ideas of Sun Yat-sen, Mustafa Kemal Atatürk, and Mohandas Gandhi**

Between the 1860s and the turn of the twentieth century, Japan and the German Confederacy underwent significant political reorganization that resulted in each becoming major world powers.

In Japan, the **Emperor Meiji** ended the feudalistic state by placing land under his jurisdiction and established a central representative government, appointing hereditary nobility as regional governors. Meiji also embarked on a plan to modernize Japan's technology and economic system by inviting foreign consultants to assist in reorganization. In order to support the importance of the Imperial line, Meiji made Shinto the state religion and emphasized the traditional supernatural origins of the ruling family. Meiji had become Emperor of Japan at the age of 15 and ruled for 45 years, during which time Japan became a significant economic and political force.

In Europe at this time, the German states were organized in a loose confederacy under King Wilhelm I and dominated by Prussia. Through military and diplomatic strategies, **Otto von Bismarck** unified the German states against Austria and France, creating a powerful nation state with Wilhelm I as Emperor and Bismarck as Chancellor. Bismarck strongly supported the divine right of the monarchy, and while Wilhelm I was the nominal ruler, he was close to Bismarck and cooperated with the Chancellor. Bismarck undertook the "Germanization" of outlying peoples within the empire and sought to eradicate the influence of the Catholic Church.

Bismarck's rule saw the rise of German importance in Europe as a central power. When Wilhelm II became emperor upon the death of his father, he wished to exercise more autonomy than his father had and Bismarck fell from importance. The nation state he had helped create and the nationalism movement that it had signaled was to contribute directly to the origins of the First World War.

While Meiji and Bismarck sought to bring unity to their nations through political reorganization, in China **Sun Yat-sen** was trying to build a central government through revolution against regional warlords who held control under the Qing Dynasty. By organizing various movements into a unified effort, Sun's followers were able to gain a tenuous hold over a provisional central government. Sun did not live to see the unified China he envisioned, but in Mainland China he is widely viewed as a nationalistic forerunner to the Communist Revolution that followed. Sun is also revered in Taiwan as the father of modern China.

Mustafa Kemal Atatürk was a leader of the Turkish national movement in the years following the partition of the Ottoman Empire after World War I. Through military leadership Ataturk created a new Turkish nation and was placed at its head as the first President of Turkey. He is widely considered to have set Turkey on its path to becoming a modern state.

Mohandas Gandhi was an Indian lawyer educated in Britain. He became involved in the civil rights movement among Indians in South Africa in the 1890's and later returned to India to lead non-violent protests against British domination. Through peaceful demonstration and protest, Gandhi and his followers promoted a national view of an independent India, which gained independence from Britain following World War II. Gandhi's non-violent methods of social protest inspired civil rights leaders throughout the world.

Skill 7.3   Examine British, French, and Japanese imperialism in Africa and Asia and analyze the reactions of indigenous populations to foreign domination

In Europe, Italy and Germany each was totally united into one nation from many smaller states. There were revolutions in Austria and Hungary, the Franco-Prussian War, the dividing of Africa among the strong European nations, interference and intervention of Western nations in Asia, and the breakup of Turkish dominance in the Balkans.

France, Great Britain, Italy, Portugal, Spain, Germany, and Belgium controlled the entire African continent except Liberia and Ethiopia. In Asia and the Pacific Islands, only China, Japan, and present-day Thailand (Siam) kept their independence. The others were controlled by the strong European nations.

An additional reason for **European imperialism** was the harsh, urgent demand for the raw materials needed to fuel and feed the great Industrial Revolution. These resources were not available in the huge quantity so desperately needed, which necessitated (and rationalized) the partitioning of the continent of Africa and parts of Asia. In turn, these colonial areas would purchase the finished manufactured goods. Europe in the nineteenth century was a crowded place as populations were growing but resources were not. The peoples of many European countries were also agitating for rights as never before. To address these concerns, European powers began to look elsewhere for relief.

One of the main places for European imperialist expansion was Africa. Britain, France, Germany, and Belgium took over countries in Africa and claimed them as their own. The resources (including people) were then shipped back to the mainland and claimed as colonial gains. The Europeans set about "civilizing the savages," reasoning that their technological superiority gave them the right to rule and "educate" the peoples of Africa.

Southeast Asia was another area of European expansion at this time, mainly by France. So, too, was India, colonized by Great Britain. These two nations combined with Spain to occupy countries in Latin America. Spain also seized the rich lands of the Philippines.

As a result of all this activity, a whole new flood of goods, people, and ideas began to come back to Europe and a whole group of people began to travel to these colonies to oversee the colonization and to "help bring the people up" to the European level. European leaders could also assert their authority in the colonies as they were not able to back home.

This colonial expansion would come back to haunt the European imperialists in a very big way, as colonial skirmishes spilled over into alliances that dragged the European powers into World War I. Some of these colonial battles were still being fought as late as the start of World War II as well.

Skill 7.4 **Demonstrate knowledge of the causes of World War I; conditions on the war front for soldiers; major decisions made at the Paris Peace Conference; the political and economic destabilization of Europe resulting from the collapse of the great empires; and the effects of World War I on science, art, and social thinking**

In Europe, war broke out in 1914, eventually involving nearly 30 nations, and ended in 1918. One of the major causes of the war was the tremendous surge of nationalism during the 1800s and early 1900s. People of the same nationality or ethnic group sharing a common history, language or culture began uniting or demanding the right of unification, especially in the empires of Eastern Europe, such as Russian Ottoman and Austrian-Hungarian Empires. Getting stronger and more intense were the beliefs of these peoples in loyalty to common political, social, and economic goals, goals that began to take precedence over loyalty to the controlling nation or empire. Other causes included the increasing strength of military capabilities, massive colonization for raw materials needed for industrialization and manufacturing, and military and diplomatic alliances. The initial spark, which started the conflagration, was the assassination in Sarajevo of Austrian Archduke Francis Ferdinand and his wife.

In Europe, Italy and Germany were each totally united into one nation from many smaller states. A number of other events occurred, as well: revolutions in Austria and Hungary, the Franco-Prussian War, the dividing of Africa among the strong European nations, interference and intervention of Western nations in Asia, and the breakup of Turkish dominance in the Balkans.

France, Great Britain, Italy, Portugal, Spain, Germany, and Belgium controlled the entire African continent except for Liberia and Ethiopia. In Asia and the Pacific Islands, only China, Japan, and present-day Thailand (Siam) kept their independence. The others were controlled by the strong European nations.

Under the administration of Theodore Roosevelt, the US armed forces were built up, greatly increasing its strength. Roosevelt's foreign policy was summed up in the slogan of "speak softly and carry a big stick," backing up the efforts in diplomacy with a strong military. During the years before the outbreak of World War I, evidence of US emergence as a world power could be seen in a number of actions. Using the Monroe Doctrine of non-involvement of Europe in the affairs of the Western Hemisphere, President Roosevelt forced Italy, Germany, and Great Britain to remove their blockade of Venezuela; gained the rights to construct the Panama Canal by threatening force; assumed the finances of the Dominican Republic to stabilize it and prevent any intervention by Europeans; and under President Woodrow Wilson in 1916, US troops were sent to the Dominican Republic to keep order.

World War I saw the introduction of such warfare as use of tanks, airplanes, machine guns, submarines, poison gas, and flame-throwers. Fighting on the Western front was characterized by a series of trenches that were used throughout the war until 1918. US involvement in the war did not occur until 1916. When the war began in 1914, President Woodrow Wilson declared that the US was neutral and most Americans were opposed to any involvement. In 1916, Wilson was reelected to a second term based on his efforts at keeping America out of the war. For a few months after, he put forth most of his efforts to stopping the war but German submarines began unlimited warfare against American merchant shipping.

Skill 7.5   Analyze the causes and results of the Russian Revolution through Stalin's First Five-Year Plan, examine the rise of fascism in Europe and Asia, and recognize how the totalitarian governments of Russia, Germany, and Italy differed from traditional authoritarian governments

Until the early years of the twentieth century **Russia** was ruled by a succession of Czars. The Czars ruled as autocrats or at times as despots. Society was essentially feudalistic and was structured in three levels. At the top of the feudal system was the Czar. The second level was composed of the rich nobles who held government positions and owned vast tracts of land. The third level of the society was composed of the remaining people who lived in poverty as peasants or serfs. There were several unsuccessful attempts by the peasants to revolt during the nineteenth century, but they were quickly suppressed. The revolutions of 1905 and 1917, however, were quite different.

The causes of the 1905 Revolution were:

- Discontent with the social structure
- Discontent with the living conditions of the peasants
- Discontent with working conditions despite industrialization
- The general discontent was aggravated by the Russo-Japanese War (1904-1905) with inflation, rising prices, etc. Peasants who had been able to eke out a living began to starve.
- Many of the fighting troops were killed in battles Russia lost to Japan because of poor leadership, lack of training, and inferior weaponry.
- Czar Nicholas II refused to end the war despite setbacks
- In January 1905 Port Arthur fell.

A trade union leader, Father Gapon, organized a protest to demand an end to the war, industrial reform, more civil liberties, and a constituent assembly. Over 150,000 peasants joined a demonstration outside the Czar's Winter Palace. Before the demonstrators even spoke, the palace guard opened fire on the crowd. This destroyed the people's trust in the Czar. Illegal trade unions and political parties formed and organized strikes to gain power. The strikes eventually brought the Russian economy to a halt. This led Czar Nicholas II to sign the October Manifesto, which created a constitutional monarchy, extended some civil rights, and gave Parliament limited legislative power. In a very short period of time, the Czar disbanded the parliament and violated the promised civil liberties. This violation contributed to the foment of the 1917 Revolution.

The causes of the 1917 Revolution were:

- The violation of the October Manifesto.
- Defeats on the battlefields during WWI caused discontent, loss of life, and a popular desire to withdraw from the war.
- The Czar continued to appoint unqualified people to government posts and handle the situation with general incompetence.
- The Czar took the advice of his wife Alexandra, who was strongly influenced by Rasputin. This caused increased discontent among all levels of the social structure.
- WWI had caused another surge in prices and scarcity of many items. Most of the peasants could not afford to buy bread.

Workers in Petrograd went on strike in 1917 over the need for food. The Czar again ordered troops to suppress the strike. This time, however, the troops sided with the workers. The revolution then took a unique direction. The parliament created a provisional government to rule the country. The military and the workers also created their own governments called soviets (popularly elected local councils). The parliament was composed of nobles who soon lost control of the country when they failed to comply with the wishes of the populace, resulting ins chaos.

The most significant differences between the 1905 and 1917 revolutions were the formation of political parties and their use of propaganda; in addition, the nobles and the military supported the latter revolution.

Skill 7.6   Recognize major features of Nazi ideology, demonstrate knowledge of political control and resistance in Nazi Germany, and examine how Nazi beliefs and policies led to the Holocaust

The effects of the Depression were very strong throughout Europe, which was still rebuilding after the devastation of World War I. Germany was especially hard hit, as US reconstruction loans dried up. Unemployment skyrocketed in Germany, leaving millions out of work.

During the Depression in Germany, large numbers of urban workers found themselves unemployed and dissatisfied with the government. Communist and Fascist paramilitary organizations arose, promising dramatic action and economic restructuring. These organizations found a receptive audience among the disgruntled German workers. It was out of this climate that the **Nazi Party** emerged.

After a failed attempt at a coup, many of the Nazi leaders, including **Adolf Hitler**, were jailed. Upon his release, Hitler was able to take leadership again and built the fascist Nazi party into a political organization with seats in the German parliament. Hitler was eventually named Chancellor of Germany, from which position he implemented his policies of military expansion and aggression, which culminated in the Second World War.

The most well known genocide of the twentieth century is the **Holocaust** of Jews before and during World War II. Much of this took place in Germany, although the practice increased throughout German-occupied countries throughout the war. German authorities capitalized on hundreds of years of distrust of Jewish people and invented what they saw as "the Final Solution of the Jewish Question": extermination of the Jewish people. Germans in charge of this "Final Solution" constructed a vast, complicated system of transport systems and concentration camps, where Jews were imprisoned, forced to work, and killed in increasingly large numbers.

This Holocaust was known especially for its efficiency and record keeping, which was extensive. Thousands of pages of documents describe in excruciating detail how thorough and determined Nazi authorities were in pursuing their goals. The number of Jews killed during the Holocaust is generally said to be 6 million. This figure includes people from all over Europe. The Holocaust didn't kill just Jews. Gypsies, communists, homosexuals, Jehovah's Witnesses, Catholics, psychiatric patients, and even common criminals were systematically incarcerated and, in many cases, killed for being "enemies of the state." There were more than 40 concentration camps in Nazi-controlled lands during World War II. Although some camps were not death camps, the most famous concentration camps, including Auschwitz, were such.

The Holocaust ended with Germany's defeat in World War II. The liberating troops of the West and East uncovered the concentration camps and the killing that the Nazis wrought. Much of the meticulous record keeping was intact, preserving for all the world the horrors that these people had perpetrated.

Skill 7.7   Demonstrate knowledge of the aggression and conflict leading to World War II in Europe and Asia, Allied and Axis strategy and the major battles of the war and their outcomes

The extreme form of patriotism called nationalism that had been the chief cause of World War I grew even stronger after the war ended in 1918. The political, social, and economic unrest fueled nationalism and it became an effective tool enabling dictators to gain and maintain power from the 1930s to the end of World War II in 1945. In the Soviet Union, **Joseph Stalin** succeeded in gaining political control and establishing a strong and harsh dictatorship.

Benito Mussolini and the Fascist party, promising prosperity and order in Italy, gained national support and set up a strong government. In Japan, although the ruler was considered Emperor **Hirohito,** actual control and administration of government came under military officers. In Germany, the results of war, harsh treaty terms, loss of territory, great economic chaos and collapse all enabled **Adolf Hitler** and his Nazi party to gain complete power and control.

Germany, Italy, and Japan initiated a policy of aggressive territorial expansion, with Japan being the first to conquer. In 1931, the Japanese forces seized control of Manchuria, a part of China containing rich natural resources, and in 1937 began an attack on China, occupying most of its eastern part by 1938. Italy invaded Ethiopia in Africa in 1935, and controlled it totally by 1936. The Soviet Union did not invade or take over any territory but participated actively, along with Italy and Germany, in the Spanish Civil War, using it as a proving ground to test tactics and weapons and setting the stage for World War II.

In Germany, almost immediately after taking power, in direct violation of the World War I peace treaty, Hitler began a buildup of the armed forces. He sent troops into the Rhineland in 1936, invaded Austria in 1938 and united it with Germany, seized control of the Sudetenland in 1938 (part of western Czechoslovakia and containing mostly Germans), the rest of Czechoslovakia in March 1939 and on September 1, 1939, began World War II in Europe by invading Poland. In 1940, Germany invaded and controlled Norway, Denmark, Belgium, Luxembourg, the Netherlands, and France.

After the war began in Europe, US **President Franklin D. Roosevelt** announced that the United States was neutral. Most Americans, although hoping for an Allied victory, wanted the US to stay out of the war. President Roosevelt and his supporters, called "interventionists," favored all aid except war to the Allied nations fighting Axis aggression. They were fearful that an Axis victory would seriously threaten and endanger all democracies. On the other hand, the "isolationists" were against any US aid being given to the warring nations, accusing President Roosevelt of leading the US into a war that it was very much unprepared to fight. Roosevelt's plan was to defeat the Axis nations by sending the Allied nations the equipment needed to fight: ships, aircraft, tanks, and other war materials.

In Asia, the US had opposed Japan's invasion of Southeast Asia, an effort to gain Japanese control of that region's rich resources. Consequently, the US stopped important exports to Japan, whose industries depended heavily on petroleum, scrap metal, and other raw materials. Later Roosevelt refused the Japanese withdrawal of its funds from American banks. General Tojo became the Japanese premier in October 1941 and quickly realized that the US Navy was powerful enough to block Japanese expansion into Asia.

Deciding to cripple the Pacific Fleet, the Japanese aircraft, without warning, bombed the Fleet December 7, 1941, while at anchor in **Pearl Harbor** in Hawaii. It was an initial success, destroying many aircraft and disabling much of the US Pacific Fleet. In the end, though, it was a costly mistake as it quickly motivated the Americans to prepare for and wage war.

Military strategy in the European theater of war as developed by **Roosevelt, Churchill, and Stalin** was to concentrate on Germany's defeat first, then Japan's. The strategy was first undertaken in North Africa, pushing Germans and Italians off the continent, in the summer of 1942 and ending successfully in May 1943. Before the war, Hitler and Stalin had signed a non-aggression pact in 1939, which Hitler violated in 1941 by invading the Soviet Union. The German defeat at Stalingrad, which marked a turning point in the war, was brought about by a combination of entrapment by Soviet troops and the horrendous winter conditions: German troops froze to death or died of starvation. All of this occurred at the same time the Allies were driving the Germans out of North Africa.

The liberation of Italy began in July 1943 and ended May 2, 1945. The third part of the strategy was **D-Day,** with the Allied invasion of France at Normandy on June 6, 1944. At the same time, starting in January 1943, the Soviets began pushing the German troops back into Europe and they were greatly assisted by supplies from Britain and the United States. By April 1945, Allies occupied positions beyond the Rhine and the Soviets moved on to Berlin, surrounding it by April 25. Germany surrendered May 7 and the war in Europe was finally over.

Meanwhile, in the Pacific, in the six months after the attack on Pearl Harbor, Japanese forces moved across Southeast Asia and the western Pacific Ocean. By August 1942, the Japanese Empire was at its largest, extending northeast to Alaska's Aleutian Islands, west to Burma, and south to what is now Indonesia. Invaded and controlled areas included Hong Kong, Guam, Wake Island, Thailand, part of Malaysia, Singapore, the Philippines, and bombed Darwin on the north coast of Australia.

The raid of **General Doolittle**'s bombers on Japanese cities and the American naval victory at Midway along with the fighting in the Battle of the Coral Sea helped turn the tide against Japan. Island hopping by US Seabees and Marines and the grueling bloody battles resulted in gradually pushing the Japanese back towards Japan.

After victory was attained in Europe, concentrated efforts were made to secure Japan's surrender, but it but it wasn't until the US dropped two **atomic bombs** on the cities of Hiroshima and Nagasaki that the war in the Pacific finally end. Japan formally surrendered on September 2, 1945, aboard the US battleship Missouri, which was anchored in Tokyo Bay.

Before war in Europe had ended, the Allies had agreed on a military occupation of Germany, with it being divided into four zones, each one occupied by Great Britain, France, the Soviet Union, and the United States and the four powers jointly administering Berlin. After the war, the Allies agreed that Germany's armed forces would be abolished, the Nazi Party outlawed, and the territory east of the Oder and Neisse Rivers forfeited. Nazi leaders were accused of war crimes and brought to trial. After Japan's defeat, the Allies began a military occupation directed by American General Douglas MacArthur, who introduced a number of reforms that eventually rid Japan of its military institutions, transforming it into a democracy. A constitution was drawn up in 1947 transferring all political rights from the emperor to the people, granting women the right to vote, and denying Japan the right to declare war. War crimes trials of 25 war leaders and government officials were also conducted. The US did not sign a peace treaty until 1951. The treaty permitted Japan to re-arm but required it to forfeit its overseas empire.

The years between WWI and WWII produced significant advancement in **aircraft technology**. But the pace of aircraft development and production was dramatically increased during WWII. Major developments included (1) flight-based weapon delivery systems, (2) the long-range bomber, (3) the first jet fighter, (4) the first cruise missile, and (5) the first ballistic missile. Although they had been invented, the cruise and ballistic missiles were not widely used during the war. Glider planes were heavily used in WWII because they were silent upon approach. Another significant development was the broad use of paratrooper units. Finally, hospital planes came into use to extract the seriously wounded from the front and transport them to hospitals for treatment.

Weapons and technology in other areas also improved rapidly during the war. These advances were critical in determining the outcome of the war. Radar, electronic computers, nuclear weapons, and new tank designs were employed for the first time were. More new inventions were registered for patents than ever before. Most of these new ideas were designed either to kill or prevent being killed.

The war began with essentially the same weaponry that had been used in WWI. The aircraft carrier joined the battleship; the Higgins boat, a primary landing craft, was invented; light tanks were developed to meet the needs of a changing battlefield; other armored vehicles were developed. **Submarines** were also perfected during this period.

Numerous other weapons were also developed or invented to meet the needs of battle during WWII: the bazooka, the rocket propelled grenade, anti-tank weapons, assault rifles, the tank destroyer, mine-clearing Flail tanks, Flame tanks, submersible tanks; cruise missiles, rocket artillery and air launched rockets, guided weapons, torpedoes, self-guiding weapons and napalm.

The atomic bomb, probably the most profound military development of the war years, was also developed and used for the first time during WWII. This invention made it possible for a single plane to carry a single bomb that was sufficiently powerful to destroy an entire city. It was believed that possession of the bomb would serve as a deterrent to any nation because it would make aggression against a nation with a bomb tantamount to mass suicide. Two nuclear bombs were dropped in 1945 on the cities of Nagasaki and Hiroshima. They caused the immediate deaths of 100,000 to 200,000 people and resulted in far more deaths over time. The decision to deploy a nuclear bomb was, and still is, a controversial decision. Those who opposed the use of the atom bomb argued that it was an unnecessary act of mass killing, particularly of non-combatants. Proponents argued that it ended the war sooner, thus resulting in fewer casualties on both sides. The development and use of nuclear weapons marked the beginning of a new age in warfare that created greater distance from the act of killing and eliminated the ability to minimize the effect of war on non-combatants.

The introduction and possession of nuclear weapons by the United States quickly led to the development of similar weapons by other nations, proliferation of the most destructive weapons ever created, and massive fear of the effects of the use of these weapons, including radiation poisoning and acid rain, and led to the Cold War.

Skill 7.8   Examine major military and diplomatic negotiations during World War II and demonstrate knowledge of Allied policies for the postwar period.

After a major world war came efforts to prevent war from occurring again throughout the world. Preliminary work began in 1943 when the US, Great Britain, the Soviet Union, and China sent representatives to Moscow where they agreed to set up an international organization that would work to promote peace around the world. In 1944, the four Allied powers met again and made the decision to name the organization the **United Nations**. In 1945, a charter for the U. N. was drawn up and signed, taking effect in October of that year.

The **Yalta Conference** took place in Yalta in February 1945 between the Allied leaders Winston Churchill, Franklin Roosevelt and Joseph Stalin. With the defeat of Nazi Germany within sight, the three allies met to determine the shape of post-war Europe. Germany was to be divided into four zones of occupation, as was the capital city of Berlin. Germany was also to undergo demilitarization and to make reparations for the war. Poland was to remain under control of Soviet Russia. Roosevelt also received a promise from Stalin that the Soviet Union would join the new United Nations. Following the surrender of Germany in May 1945, the Allies called the Potsdam Conference in July between Clement Attlee, Harry Truman and Stalin.

The Potsdam Conference addressed the administration of post-war Germany and provided for the forced migration of millions of Germans from previously occupied regions.

After 1945, social and economic chaos continued in Western Europe, especially in Germany. Secretary of State George C. Marshall came to realize that the US had greatly serious problems and to assist in the recovery, he proposed a program known as the European Recovery Program or **the Marshall Plan**. Although the Soviet Union withdrew from any participation, the US continued to assist Europe in regaining economic stability. In Germany, the situation was critical with the US Army shouldering the staggering burden of relieving the serious problems of the German economy. In February 1948, Britain and the US combined their two zones, with France joining in June.

Major consequences of the war included horrendous death and destruction, millions of displaced persons, a stronger foothold for Communism, and resulting Cold War tensions as a result of nuclear buildup. World War II ended more lives and caused more devastation than any other war. Besides the losses of millions of military personnel, the devastation and destruction directly affected civilians, reducing cities, houses, and factories to ruin and rubble and totally wrecking communication and transportation systems. Millions of civilian deaths, especially in China and the Soviet Union, were the results of famine.

More than 12 million people were uprooted by war's end, with no place to live. Included were prisoners of war, those that survived Nazi concentration camps and slave labor camps, orphans, and people who escaped war-torn areas and invading armies. Changing national boundary lines also caused the mass movement of displaced persons.

COMPETENCY 8.0   UNDERSTAND DECOLONIZATION OF AFRICA AND ASIA, THE ORIGINS AND COURSE OF THE COLD WAR, MAJOR WORLD DEVELOPMENTS SINCE THE 1960S, AND THE IMPORTANCE OF GLOBALIZATION IN THE CONTEMPORARY WORLD

Skill 8.1   Analyze revolutionary movements in India, China, and Ghana

China underwent several revolutionary movements during the twentieth century. Sun Yat-sen, considered the father of modern China, led a rebellion against the emperor, leading the Nationalist Party to power. He served as President until his death in 1925. **Chiang Kai-shek,** a leading general and supporter of Sun Yat-sen, became the leader of the Nationalist Party following Sun's death. Chiang's military efforts helped to unify China. Chiang resisted the growing support for the communist movement throughout the country. Both the communists and the Chiang government resisted Japanese aggression during World War II. Following the war, the struggle for control of China continued between the communists and the Nationalist government. A new leader of the Communist Party ultimately emerged, **Mao Zedong**. Mao was a founder of the Chinese Community Party. Unlike other communist revolutions, which focused on the industrial workers in urban areas, Mao and the Chinese Communist built support in the peasant population. Mao's control of the Chinese Communist Party emerged during the long march. In 1949 the Chinese Communists defeated the Nationalist government and assumed control of the People's Republic of China. Chiang Kai-shek and the Nationalist Government were exiled to Taiwan. The United States and its allies continued to recognize the Taiwan government as the legitimate government of China until the 1970s. Chiang Kai-shek ruled Taiwan until his death in 1975, helping to build a successful economy in Taiwan.

Mao ruled China until his death in 1976, although in his latter years he relinquished control due to health reasons. Mao adopted many of the practices of the Soviet Communist model, including nationalization of industries and collective farming. The Great Leap Forward, introduced in the late 1950s, was designed to build industrialization and advance the economy. During the 1960s China began the Cultural Revolution to renew the values of the original revolution, which was very brutal and bloody.

Mohandas Karamchand (Mahatma) Gandhi, the father of independent India, led a movement for India's freedom of British colonial rule following World War II. Gandhi, a Hindu, believed in peaceful nonviolent resistance as a means to independence. His leadership ultimately led to India's independence in 1947. India was partitioned into India and Pakistan. Gandhi was assassinated in 1948.

Another leader of the India independence movement was **Jawaharlal Nehru**. Both Gandhi and Nehru were leaders in the India Congress Party. Nehru became the first prime minister of independent India and served until his death in 1964. His daughter Indira Gandhi was elected prime minister in 1966.

Like Southern Asia, most of Africa was under the colonial control of European powers. Through the leadership of **Kwame Nkrumah**, Ghana, formerly the Gold Coast, was able to win its independence from Great Britain in 1957. Ghana was the first sub-Saharan nation to win independence. Nkrumah studied in both the United States and Great Britain and then returned to Ghana, where he worked for the independence of the country. His leadership of the nonviolent independence movement led to his election to parliament and to Prime Minister of Ghana prior to independence. Following independence, Nkrumah was elected President and remained in that position until a military coup overthrew the government and sent him into exile.

Skill 8.2 Demonstrate knowledge of the formation of the state of Israel and analyze the impact of that development on the Middle East

Israel was established by Great Britain in 1948 as a nation for the Jews from all over the world. People of Jewish faith had lived in Palestine since ancient times along with people of other faiths, but they did not have a designated Jewish nation. In the wake of the Holocaust after World War II, Great Britain designated one of its colonies, Palestine, to be a homeland for the Jews. The Jews that had fled to Europe migrated to Israel and many more Jews joined them from all over the world. This migration and settlement has become an area of great conflict in the region, since the Palestinian Arabs living in Palestine had been displaced by the Jews. The conflict has yet to be resolved. The official language for Israel is Hebrew and Israeli customs come from a variety of cultures, as do the Israeli people. Other customs celebrate different aspects of the Jewish faith. The people of Israel have in a short time been able to build a strong economy that depends on farming and industry.

The **Middle East** is defined by its name and its geographic position. It is in the middle of the globe, a position that enables it to exert tremendous influence on not only the trade that passes through its realm of influence but also on the political relations between its countries and those of different parts of the world. From the beginnings of civilization, the Middle East has been a destination—for attackers, for adventure-seekers, for those starving for food and in need of a progressively more technologically advanced series of other resources, from iron to oil. Now, as then, the countries of the Middle East play an important role in the economics of the world.

Religious conflict goes back to the beginnings of Islam, in the seventh century. Muslims claimed Jerusalem, capital of the ancient civilization of Israel, as a holy city, in the same way that Jews and Christians did. Muslims seized control of Palestine and Jerusalem and held it for a great many years, prompting Christian armies from Europe to mount the Crusades in a series of attempts to "regain the Holy Land." For hundreds of years after Christendom's failure, these lands were ruled by Muslim leaders and armies.

Skill 8.3   Examine major developments in the arms race

The development of the atomic bomb was probably the most profound military development of the war years. This invention made it possible for a single plane to carry a single bomb that was sufficiently powerful to destroy an entire city. It was believed that possession of the bomb would serve as a deterrent to any nation because it would make aggression against a nation with a bomb tantamount to mass suicide. Two nuclear bombs were dropped in 1945 on the cities of Nagasaki and Hiroshima. They caused the immediate deaths of 100,000 to 200,000 people and far more deaths over time. This was (and still is) a controversial decision. Those who opposed the use of the atom bomb argued that the bombing of Nagasaki and Hiroshima was an unnecessary act of mass killing, particularly of non-combatants. Proponents argued that it ended the war sooner, thus resulting in fewer casualties on both sides. The development and use of nuclear weapons marked the beginning of a new age in warfare that created greater distance from the act of killing and eliminated the ability to minimize the effect of war on non-combatants.

The introduction and possession of nuclear weapons by the United States quickly led to the development of similar weapons by other nations, proliferation of the most destructive weapons ever created, massive fear of the effects of the use of these weapons, including radiation poisoning and acid rain, and led to the Cold War.

The major thrust of US foreign policy from the end of World War II to 1990 was the post-war struggle between non-Communist nations, led by the United States, and the Soviet Union and the Communist nations who were its allies. The buildup was referred to as a **Cold War** because its conflicts did not lead to major combat or a "hot war." Both the Soviet Union and the United States embarked on an arsenal buildup of atomic and hydrogen bombs as well as other nuclear weapons. Both nations had the capability of destroying each other but because of the continuous threat of nuclear war and accidents, extreme caution was practiced on both sides. Concerns over mutual assured destruction led the United States and the Soviet Union to begin discussions to limit stockpiles of nuclear weapons. This resulted in two separate, landmark agreements that survive in various forms to this day.

The talks were given the unimaginative yet entirely descriptive name of **Strategic Arms Limitation Talks,** often abbreviated as the acronym **SALT**. They began in 1969. The first round of talks continued, off and on, for three years in Vienna and Helsinki. The first agreement between both countries was signed by US President Richard Nixon and Soviet leader Leonid Brezhnev in 1972. This was the **Anti-Ballistic Missile Treaty**, which limited both strategic offensive and strategic defensive weapons. The result was a renewed focus on nuclear weapons and their destructive power.

This treaty led to a second round of talks, SALT II, which continued for another seven years and resulted in yet more curtailment of nuclear arms buildup. This agreement was signed by Brezhnev again, who was still the Soviet leader, and by US President Jimmy Carter.

As a result of these treaties, both the US and the USSR significantly curtailed spending on manufacturing nuclear weapons. Neither side ever used any of the bombs or missiles made, but the threat of nuclear attack and mutual assured destruction were ever-present, especially in the 1950s and 1960s. The SALT talks and subsequent treaties helped people in both countries to breathe a sigh of relief.

Skill 8.4   Analyze efforts in the pursuit of freedom

The South African Anti-Apartheid Movement

The **anti-apartheid** movement in **South Africa** began with a large handful of people performing passive protests, such as handing out **leaflets**. It progressed to more active protests like boycotting economic goods and then to extremely violent actions like **selective sabotage**. These acts were in increasing response to the continued stubbornness of the South African government and to a rise in the number of violent acts by apartheid adherents, including a number of shootings.

The anti-apartheid movement (or the AAM, as it came to be known) was an organization that gathered strength over time, gaining powerful friends from around the world. Such determined individuals as Tennyson Makiwane and Abdul Minty were instrumental in the founding of the organization and of the Congress movement, whose most prominent member was the **African National Congress.**

As more of the international community became aware of the plight of Black Africans in South Africa, calls for the abolition of apartheid grew. Time and again, international leaders (including South African black activists) addressed the United Nations or otherwise pleaded their case to the court of world opinion. Of particular interest to many in the international community was the South African government's appalling treatment of political prisoners such as the famous **Nelson Mandela.**

South Africa's continued refusal to eliminate its law-enforced segregation resulted in economic sanctions from countries around the world. These sanctions varied in their severity and enforcement. Britain, as the former colonial power most interested in the situation, initially resisted such actions but eventually joined the world chorus as well. The eventual result was the repudiation—legal and otherwise—of apartheid in South Africa.

The Fall of the Berlin Wall

The **Berlin Wall** was long a symbol of the Cold War disparity between West and East, between opportunity and rigidity. It was built in 1961 and improved on for more 20 years. Ironically, it was dismantled, in 1989, much more quickly than it was put up.

The Wall was built at the height of the Cold War, when the Communist government of East Germany decided to divide its capital as thoroughly as the victors of World War II had decided to divide the entire country. Nearly overnight, a long wall sprung up, dividing East from West. Initially just a barbed wire fence, the Berlin Wall evolved over two decades into a staggering defensive fortification, a symbol of Communist Germany's determination to keep its people from leaving its borders.

The Wall thrived as a symbol of division between East and West for a full two decades, as thousands attempted escape and a few hundred were shot dead in the process. The tide began to turn away from repression, however.

Beginning with the **Solidarity** movement in **Poland**, the countries of the Communist bloc, including the Soviet Union itself, moved toward *glasnost*, or openness. In the latter half of the 1980s, Communist Hungary relaxed its border restrictions with non-Communist Austria. Czechoslovakia, whose Communist government wasn't long for the world, explored a similar relaxation of restrictions. Germans took the hint and began demonstrating against the Berlin Wall and the repression it represented.

Tensions that had been simmering for years spilled over into public demonstrations and the Communism that ruled East Germany disappeared rather quickly. In a disorganized fashion, the leader of the Communist Party resigned, instructions were given to allow a host of border crossings, and then authority over border crossing checkpoints disappeared altogether. Before the Germans knew it, the wall dividing their capital city was being torn down by their own countrymen and by soldiers who had so recently been employed to enforce its maintenance.

The freedom movement that resulted in the dismantling of the Berlin Wall was peaceful for the most part, unless the lives of those lost while trying to escape are taken into account. The events of 1989, though, were tumultuous and momentous indeed. The result was not only an undivided Berlin but, in the end, a unified Germany.

Tiananmen Square Protest Movement

One freedom movement that did not have a happy ending for most of its participants was the gathering of thousands of students and intellectuals in China's **Tiananmen Square** in the spring and summer of 1989. Emboldened by the fall of Communism elsewhere and the government's increasing trend toward capitalism and openness in business practices, at least, students began to speak out for certain freedoms that they believed were denied. They began to gather in Tiananmen Square, one of Beijing's largest and most historic public places.

The students stayed there for weeks, their numbers growing all the time. Their numbers swelled to thousands at the height of the protest and some even crafted a miniature Statue of Liberty to represent the kind of freedoms that they were missing.

The government's initial response was to ignore the protests, but that eventually became impossible, as world attention focused on the gatherings and their implications. A split developed among the **Chinese Communist Party** leadership and eventually the hard-liners prevailed. The decision was made to declare martial law and clear the Square by force.

Troops were brought in from outside the city because government leaders feared that the local soldiers would be sympathetic to the protesters' pleas and plight. In a crackdown captured on audio and videotape worldwide, Chinese troops began forcibly removing the protesters. Many protesters were driven out of the Square. Others were assaulted and many more were killed. To this day, the death toll varies from a handful to hundreds, depending on who is doing the calculating.

It wasn't just students, either. Many adults gathered to speak out against the government's policy of one-party rule and a "closed society." They were rewarded for their efforts with the blunt edge of batons and guns. Tanks and armored personnel carriers were called into the Square to help disperse the protesters. One of the most famous images of the crackdown was of one man carrying a briefcase standing in front of a column of tanks, attempting to prevent further bloodshed.

China since then has adopted some of the freedoms that those protesters were striving for, but many more go wanting still. The Chinese government to this day refers to the crackdown as an "incident" and refuses to divulge how many people died.

Skill 8.5   Identify causes of ethnic conflicts and analyze the rise of new nationalisms

The genocides in **Bosnia-Herzegovina** and **Rwanda** were two sides of the same story, one of the oldest in the world, that of one ethnic group trying to eliminate another solely because of its ethnicity. The disparity between the number of people killed in these two modern **genocides** in no way reflects any difference in ferocity with which these people were murdered.

The Bosnian Genocide, as it is usually called, took place during the Bosnian War, which lasted from 1992 to 1995. It was part of a larger conflict that stemmed from the breakup of Yugoslavia, which was itself a confederation of ethnic societies held together by not much more than an iron fist. Bosnia-Herzegovina and Serbia were once and again their own countries and their ethnic conflict stretched back for ages. With modern weapons, however, the "ethnic cleansing" that the Serbs practiced on their Bosnian neighbors reached new heights of efficiency.

The worst group of mass murders on record is that at **Srebenica** in 1992, when, international observers estimate, Serbs murdered more than 8,000 Bosnians. The people of Bosnia-Herzegovina say that Srebenica was just one of many such instances of genocide. Some reports have deaths numbering in the hundreds of thousands, with millions forced to flee their homes.

Serbia also maintained detainment camps during this war that practiced cruel and unusual punishment of prisoners. Photos of some of these detainees made the rounds in international circles during the war, strengthening Bosnia's case against Serb oppression.

As more and more details of the Serb atrocities leaked out, the international outcry over such events grew stronger and stronger. United Nations forces were eventually sent to restore order.

In the end, Serbia was made to stop its "cleansing." The reason given for such atrocities was multi-faceted, but they were all facets of the same basic cause: one ethnic group determined to stamp out another.

The same was true in **Rwanda**, where Hutus systematically murdered close to a million Tutsis. This staggering number included fellow Hutus who were sympathetic to the Tutsi cause. Most shocking of all, this genocide took place in about 100 days, in the spring and summer of 1994. Perhaps world opinion was too much divided over how to respond to the Serbian problem; perhaps no one cared "because it's only Africa." Whatever the reason, it took other nations of the world a relatively long time to respond to such savagery.

The Rwandan Genocide was more a matter of geography and economics, as Hutus coveted land owned and worked by Tutsis. Then, as now, Rwanda was also a densely populated country, but only in certain areas. The ownership of much of those areas was in dispute, a dispute that spanned centuries of cohabitation and colonization.

International opinion eventually focused on Rwanda, however, and the killings were brought to a halt—not before the aforementioned million people died, however. Again, the impetus for the killings was competing ethnicities.

Another tremendously oppressive ethnic conflict is taking place in the **Darfur** region of **Sudan**. An organized campaign of Janjaweed militia has been persecuting members of ethnic groups Fur, Zaghawa and Massalit, among others. Some estimates put the death toll higher than 2 million and the number of displaced people higher than 4 million. The killing goes on in Darfur, with little repercussion from the outside world.

The African genocides fly in the face of Pan-Africanism, the belief that all Africans are one and that they should expand their solidarity under that maxim. The philosophy is a rather old one that has seen new life in recent decades, most notably in Ethiopia and South Africa. Many social scientists argue that if this doctrine were followed, such genocides as those in Rwanda and Sudan would not take place. These social scientists would argue that Africans should respect the lives, intentions, and ethnicities of their fellow Africans.

The same sort of cultural nationalism can be found in the doctrine of Pan-Arabism, which is the call for Arab peoples to unite as Arabs and put political, ethnic, and religious differences behind them in favor of a unity based on joint heritage and shared tradition. This doctrine was in force much more prominently in the early days of Islam and saw its zenith during the Crusades. Even then, though, divides in the Muslim world were deep for many Arabs. Those rifts have widened over the centuries and many social scientists question whether Pan-Arabism would gain many adherents in the modern, fragmented world. Indeed, many would argue that Pan-Africanism is more likely to succeed than Pan-Arabism, simply because of geography.

Skill 8.6 **Compare and contrast the reforms of Soviet leaders from Khrushchev to Gorbachev, demonstrate knowledge of events leading to the end of the Cold War, and analyze the geopolitical consequences of the breakup of the Soviet Union**

Following World War II, tensions developed between the United States and the Soviet Union, which led to the growth of militarism between the two countries, creating the Cold War. **Joseph Stalin** ruled the Soviet Union from the time of Lenin's death in 1924 until his death in 1953. Stalin ruled the country with an iron fist. **Nikita Khrushchev** served at General Secretary of the Community Party from 1953 to 1964. He led efforts to de-Stalinize the Soviet Union, criticizing the brutality of Stalin, who was responsible for the death or imprisonment of millions of Soviet citizens who he believed opposed his rule. Several of the satellite countries--Hungary and Poland--attempted to gain independence from the Soviet Union during Khrushchev's term and he was forced to use military force to maintain control. Khrushchev created the Warsaw Pact to counteract the creation of the North Atlantic Treaty Organization (NATO) and he also increased military armaments and the growth of the military industry. His efforts to install missiles in Cuba led to the **Cuban Missile Crisis** in 1962. He was forced to retire in 1964.

Leonid Brezhnev succeeded Khrushchev as General Secretary of the Communist Party. Eastern European satellite governments were demanding greater autonomy. Brezhnev was forced to use military force to control the independence movement in Czechoslovakia in 1968. Relations with China continued to deteriorate. At the same time the United States was developing relations with the People's Republic of China, which forced Brezhnev to reach out and begin a dialogue with the United States. This dialogue ultimately led to the **Strategic Arms Limitation Treaty**, a peace settlement for Vietnam, the détente policy of coexistence between the United States and the Soviet Union and a decline of Cold War tensions. Brezhnev died of a heart attack in 1982.

Brezhnev was succeeded by Yuri Andropov. Poor health led to his death in 1984. Andropov was succeeded by Konstantin Chernenko, who died the following year. **Mikhail Gorbachev** succeeded to the Party leadership. Gorbachev was a reformer who worked to create a democratic system and a market economy and who attempted to improve the productivity of the economy by introducing a number of reforms. A greater openness to ideas (**glasnost**) was encouraged, leading to greater freedoms within the country. Perestroika attempted to introduce democratic reforms throughout the country, including free-market practices. Greater dialogue between the United States and the Soviet Union resulted in agreements to reduce nuclear arms. He encouraged greater autonomy of satellite countries, which led to the ultimate independence of eastern Europe and the reunification of Germany. In 1991 Gorbachev resigned after achieving a restructuring of the political system. The Soviet Union ceased to exist and **Boris Yeltsin** was elected President of a new Russia.

Other countries grew out of the collapse of the Soviet Union, declaring their independence. Many of the countries continue to build both government systems and economies. Eastern European states continue to struggle economically. Additionally, various ethnic conflicts have fostered tension in the region.

Skill 8.7 **Analyze terrorism as a form of warfare in the twentieth century and recognize the effects of terrorism on the modern world**

Modern global terrorism can trace its roots to 1967 when Israel defeated Arab forces in Palestine. Palestinian fighters, realizing they could not win a military battle against Israel, turned to urban terror tactics to attack Israel's population centers. Taking advantage of modern communications and technology, radical Palestinian organizations undertook a series of airline hijackings, bombings and kidnappings to draw attention to their demands and to terrorize and demoralize their enemies, specifically Israel. In 1972, at the **Olympic Games in Munich,** radical Palestinians kidnapped nine Israeli athletes who were all killed in a subsequent gun battle. Supported by some Arab states and criminal organizations, the radical Palestinians developed a network of connections through which their techniques and training could flow to other parts of the world.

Terrorist activity continued throughout the 1970s. In 1979, the Soviet Union invaded Afghanistan and an Islamic revolution took place in Iran, two events that were to provide opportunities for terrorist tactics to advance as radical organizations gained valuable military experience and state support from the leadership in Iran.

During the 1980s, the use of suicide bombers became an effective technique that struck deeply. Anti-Israeli sentiments grew, as well as anti-US feelings over America's support of Israel. Radical terrorists began to choose western targets, as in the bombing of the **US Marine barracks** in Lebanon in 1983 and the 1988 bombing of a Pan Am airliner over Scotland.

With the withdrawal of the Soviet Union from Afghanistan, and its subsequent collapse, the region of Afghanistan became a safe haven for radical groups to organize and train followers in terror tactics. The Taliban, a strict religious sect, took control in Afghanistan and harbored these groups, including Al-Qaeda. **Al-Qaeda** is led by Saudi millionaire Osama Bin Laden and claims opposition to US military presence in Saudi Arabia and elsewhere in the Middle East. In 1993, Al-Qaeda operatives struck at the United States in 1993 by bombing the World Trade Center in New York City. On September 11, 2001, Al-Qaeda followers hijacked four commercial airliners, flying two of them into the World Trade Center towers, and one into the Pentagon in Washington, D.C. The fourth airliner crashed in Pennsylvania. It was the largest single terrorist attack the world had seen, killing thousands of people. The United States reacted by launching an attack on Afghanistan, driving Bin Laden and his followers into the hills.

Since that attack the prospect of global terrorism has become a reality in the modern world, driving much of the world's foreign policy toward Middle Eastern states, as well as domestic security policies.

Skill 8.8   Examine the rise of women as major world leaders

Historians could come up with a list of famous women who were world leaders from times past, but that list would be rather short. Famous names like Hatshepsut, Cleopatra, and Queen Elizabeth I would no doubt top the list. They, however, were leaders of major states from centuries ago. Women have been elected to roles as heads of state only in the twentieth century, with the most obvious examples being **Golda Meir, Indira Gandhi, and Margaret Thatcher.**

Golda Meir was the first female prime minister of the modern state of Israel. A founder of the State of Israel itself, she served in various capacities in the Israeli Cabinet until becoming prime minister in 1969. She served for five years and was an inspiration to her people and to women around the world.

Meir grew up in the United States and emigrated to Palestine in 1921. Almost immediately, she began working on founding a Jewish state. She joined the Histradrut, the Gernal Federation of Labour, which assumed many of the functions of a shadow government within British-run Palestine. When the tide of world opinion turned in favor of a re-establishment of a Jewish state in the Middle East after World War II, Meir was one of a select group of people who took part in the planning and implementation of that dream. She served as the country's first Foreign Minister, under Prime Minister David Ben-Gurion, but retired because of a bout with lymphoma.

Meir came out of retirement at her party's urging and became the country's fourth (and first female) prime minister. Israel at that time had just won the Six Day War but was struggling with its neighbors, Egypt especially, over borders and influence in the Middle East. She was leader of Israel when the Munich Olympics and the Yom Kippur War took place, and she provided iron leadership for people throughout these crises and the events that followed. She resigned in 1974 and died of cancer four years later. She continues to be an inspiration to women in Israel and elsewhere for having done what many people still consider to be "a man's job."

Another strong female prime minister was **Indira Gandhi**, the first female leader of modern **India**. She was the daughter of and the campaign manager for Jawaharlal Nehru, the first Prime Minister of the newly partitioned India. She had also created the **Vanara Sena** movement, which encouraged young boys and girls to take part in the independence movement that eventually prevailed over British colonialism.

In 1960, Gandhi (who was no relation to Mohandas Gandhi) became president of the Indian National Congress, one of the country's most powerful political organizations. When her father died in 1964 she became Minister for Information and Broadcasting and proved a powerful spokeswoman for peace and calm in the wake of the Indo-Pakistani War of 1965.

After this war ended and the current prime minister died suddenly, Gandhi became a candidate for Prime Minister. Stressing her bloodline and her experience, she won, rather easily as it turned out, becoming the country's fifth (and first female) prime minister.

Like Golda Meir before her, Indira Gandhi oversaw the development of a nuclear program. She also gave her people considerable strength in what is still a dispute over **Kashmir**, which both India and Pakistan claim.

Gandhi was also a leader of the Green Revolution, a massive effort to overhaul the nation's agricultural programs to avoid chronic food shortages. Under her leadership, the country went from being a victim of famine to being a food exporter.

After these successes, she moved to consolidate authority in the national government, initiating laws that stripped the country's various states of some of their responsibilities. Some of these moves proved very unpopular and ultimately resulted in her being tossed out of office in the 1977 election. She was back in power just three years later, however, when no national coalition could be formed and a new election was called. She won convincingly and returned to the head of government.

Her second tour of duty proved to be all about civil unrest, as troubles in the Punjab region and continued struggles with Pakistan threatened to overwhelm her agenda. In an effort to quell sectarian violence, she urged her troops to storm a Sikh temple, killing many pilgrims in the process. In response, she was assassinated, in 1984.

The most recognizable and familiar female head of state of the twentieth century is **Margaret Thatcher**, who was three times elected Prime Minister of the **United Kingdom**. The Tory leader rose up through the ranks to become party leader and then won three general elections in a row.

A shopkeeper's daughter, she worked her way through school and then became a research chemist and developed some notoriety for her work on soft frozen ice cream. She later became a lawyer and then ran for Parliament, losing more than once before finally securing a seat. She eventually served in the Cabinet and then became Conservative Party leader. In 1979, she became leader of the government.

She quickly cemented her reputation as a force to be reckoned with. After a particularly tough speech denouncing the Soviet Union, a Russian newspaper termed Thatcher the "**Iron Lady**." The nickname stuck and she embraced it.

Thatcher found a great friend in US President Ronald Reagan. The two agreed on political philosophy and also enjoyed each other's company. They stood together against the Soviet Union and its Cold War concerns, on many occasions angering peace activists by installing US cruise missiles on British soil and working together to bomb Libya in retaliation for the **bombing** of an airliner over **Lockerbie, Scotland**.

Thatcher was also Prime Minister during some of the most intense of "**The Troubles**," the struggle between Ireland and the U.K. over administration of Northern Ireland. This conflict had been going on for a great many years and the 1980s saw a much higher number of events surrounding the issue of independence.

She was also the U.K. leader who committed her country's armed forces to war to restore ownership of the **Falkland Islands**, which had been seized by nearby Argentina. This conflict was definitely an example of one country significantly overmatching another.

Her tenure was marked by civil unrest as well, including a long and divisive miners strike and a larger number of demonstrations against South Africa's apartheid policy. Her final years in office focused on welfare reform and the handover of Hong Kong to China.

Thatcher's political career ended when she and her party couldn't survive a no-confidence vote. She resigned as both Prime Minister and Conservative Party leader and retired to private life. She continues to be known as one of the most formidable politicians of the twentieth century.

Skill 8.9   **Analyze the cultural and intellectual integration of countries in the world economy through the development of television, satellites, and computers and recognize global economic and political connections.**

The most recent example of technology contributing to globalization is the development of the **Internet**. Instant communication between people millions of miles apart is possible just by plugging in a computer and connecting to the Net. The Internet is an extension of the telephone and cell phone revolutions; all three are developments that have brought faraway places closer together. All three allow people to communicate no matter the distance. This communication can facilitate friendly chatter and, of course, trade. A huge number of businesses use cell phones and the Internet to do business these days, and also use computers to track goods and receipts quickly and efficiently.

Globalization has also brought financial and cultural exchange on a worldwide scale. A large number of businesses have investments in countries around the world. Financial transactions are conducted using a variety of currencies. The cultures of the countries of the world are increasingly viewed by people elsewhere in the world through the wonders of television and the Internet. Not only goods are exchanged but also belief systems, customs, and practices.

Today, the world is primarily divided by political/administrative interests into state sovereignties. A particular region is recognized as controlled by a particular government, including its territory, population and natural resources. The only area of the earth's surface that today is not defined by state or national sovereignty is Antarctica.

Alliances are developed among nations on the basis of political philosophy, economic concerns, cultural similarities, religious interests, or for military defense. Some of the most notable alliances today are:

- The United Nations
- The North Atlantic Treaty Organization
- The Caribbean Community
- The Common Market
- The Council of Arab Economic Unity
- The European Union

GATT, NAFTA, WTO and EU are all forms of trade liberalization. The GATT or General Agreements on Tariffs and Trade was founded in 1947 and today, as the World Trade Organization or WTO, has 147 member nations. It is based on three principles. The first is Most Favored National status for all members. This means trade based on comparative advantage without tariffs or trade barriers. The second principle is elimination of quotas and the third is reduction of trade barriers through multilateral trade negotiations. The WTO is the successor to the GATT and came into being in 1995. Its objective is to promote free trade. As such it administers trade agreements, settles disputes, and provides a forum for trade discussions and negotiations. The North American Free Trade Agreement or NAFTA and the EU are both forms of regional economic integration, a method of economic integration based on trade liberalization by region. NAFTA represents the lowest form or first step in the regional trade integration process. A free trade area consists for two or more countries that abolish tariffs and other trade barriers among themselves but maintain their own trade barriers against the rest of the world.

A free trade area allows for specialization and trade on the basis of comparative advantage within the area. The next stage in the integration process is a customs union, which is a free trade area that has common external tariffs against non-members. The third stage is a common market, which is a customs union with free factor mobility within the area. Factors migrate where they find the best payment within the area. The fourth state is economic union where the common market members have common or coordinated economic and social policies. The final stage is monetary union where the area has a common currency. This is what Europe is working toward. They have a common market with elements of the fourth and fifth stages of integration.

The WTO does not change or blur the significance of political borders and territorial sovereignty in the same way that economic integration does, although the WTO is a way of settling trade disputes that arise from the different integration agreements. In the advanced stages of economic integration the political borders remain, but economic and social policies are common or coordinated and in monetary union, there is one common currency. Each nation is its own independent entity but they give up some sovereignty in the interest of having a successful union.

Trade agreements proliferate in the world today. The Smoot Hawley Tariffs and the rounds of retaliation in the 1930s are what laid the basis for what today are the WTO and the European Union (EU). The GATT and the beginnings of what is now the EU came into being as organizations trying to undo the effects of the Great Depression and the world war. Free trade without trade barriers results in the most efficient use of resources, with higher consumption, employment and income levels for all participants. This is why there are so many free trade agreements being negotiated in today's world.

There are many positive aspects of space exploration that one could discuss. The following is just a short list; Scientists have increased knowledge about earth's atmosphere. Satellites have provided improvements in communications and weather information. **Sputnik 1** launched on October 4, 1957 by the USSR., was the first satellite in orbit. **Explorer 1,** launched on January 31, 1958 by the US, was the first American satellite in orbit.

SUBAREA IV.   **US HISTORY TO 1914**

COMPETENCY 9.0   **UNDERSTAND EUROPEAN SETTLEMENT OF NORTH AMERICA; THE CAUSES, MAJOR EVENTS, AND OUTCOMES OF THE AMERICAN REVOLUTION; AND THE DEVELOPMENT OF THE US CONSTITUTION**

Skill 9.1   **Demonstrate knowledge of Native American cultures prior to European contact and analyze the effects of European settlement on Native Americans and on Europeans**

Native American tribes lived throughout what we now call the United States in varying degrees of togetherness. They adopted different customs, pursued different avenues of agriculture and food gathering, and made slightly different weapons. They fought among themselves and with other peoples.

Perhaps the most famous of the Native American tribes is the **Algonquians**. We know so much about this tribe because they were one of the first to interact with the newly arrived English settlers in Plymouth and elsewhere. Another group of tribes who lived in the Northeast were the **Iroquois**, who were fierce fighters but also forward thinkers. They lived in long houses and wore clothes made of buckskin. They, too, were expert farmers, growing the "Three Sisters" (corn, squash, and beans). Five of the Iroquois tribes formed a Confederacy, which was a shared form of government.

Living in the Southeast were the **Seminoles** and **Creeks**, a huge collection of people who lived in chickees (open, bark-covered houses) and wore clothes made from plant fibers. They were expert planters and hunters and were proficient at paddling dugout canoes, which they made. The **Cherokee** also lived in the Southeast. They were one of the most advanced tribes, living in domed houses and wearing deerskin and rabbit fur. They also played a game called lacrosse, which survives to this day in countries around the world.

In the middle of the continent lived the Plains tribes, such as the **Sioux, Cheyenne, Blackfeet, Comanche, and Pawnee**. Famous Plains people include Crazy Horse and Sitting Bull, authors of the Custer Disaster; Sacagawea, leader of the Lewis & Clark expedition; and Chief Joseph, the famous Nez Perce leader.

Dotting the deserts of the Southwest were a handful of tribes, including the famous **Pueblo**, who lived in houses that bear their tribe's name, wore clothes made of wool and woven cotton, farmed crops in the middle of desert land, created exquisite pottery and Kachina dolls, and had one of the most complex religions of all the tribes. The Pueblos chose their own chiefs. This was perhaps one of the oldest representative governments in the world.

Another well-known Southwestern tribe were the **Apache**, with their famous leader **Geronimo**. The Apache lived in homes called wickiups, which were made of bark, grass, and branches. The **Navajo**, also residents of the Southwest, lived in hogans (round homes built with forked sticks) and wore clothes of rabbit skin.

In the Northwest were the **Inuit**, who lived in tents made from animal skins or, in some cases, igloos. They wore clothes made of animal skins, usually seal or caribou. They were excellent fishermen and hunters and crafted efficient kayaks and umiaks to take them through waterways and harpoons with which to hunt animals. The Inuit are perhaps best known for the great carvings that they left behind. Among these are ivory figures and tall totem poles.

The Indian Removal Act of 1830 authorized the government to negotiate treaties with Native Americans to provide land west of the Mississippi River in exchange for lands east of the river. This policy resulted in the relocation of more than 100,000 Native Americans. Theoretically, the treaties were expected to result in voluntary relocation of the native people. In fact, however, many of the native chiefs were forced to sign the treaties.

One of the worst examples of "removal" was the Treaty of New Echota, which was signed by a faction of the Cherokees rather than the actual leaders of the tribe. When the leaders attempted to remain on their ancestral lands, the treaty was enforced by President Martin Van Buren. The removal of the Cherokees came to be known as "The Trail of Tears" and resulted in the deaths of more than 4000 Cherokees, mostly due to disease.

During the nineteenth century the nation expanded westward. This expansion and settlement of new territory forced the Native Americans to continue to move farther west. The Native Americans were gradually giving up their homelands, their sacred sites, and the burial grounds of their ancestors. Some of the American Indians chose to move west. Many, however, were relocated by force.

Numerous conflicts, often called the "Indian Wars," broke out between the US Army and many different native tribes. Many treaties were signed with the various tribes, but most were broken by the government for a variety of reasons. Two of the most notable battles were the Battle of Little Bighorn in 1876, in which native people defeated General Custer and his forces, and the massacre of Native Americans in 1890 at Wounded Knee. In 1876, the US government ordered all surviving Native Americans to move to reservations. This forced migration of the Native Americans to lands that were deemed marginal, combined with the near-extermination of the buffalo, caused a downturn in Prairie Culture that relied on the horse for hunting, trading, and traveling.

In the late nineteenth century, the avid reformers of the day instituted a practice of trying to "civilize" Indian children by educating them in Indian Boarding Schools. The children were forbidden to speak their native languages, they were forced to convert to Christianity, and generally made to give up all aspects of their native culture and identity. There are numerous reports of abuse of the Indian children at these schools.

During World War I, a large number of Native Americans were drafted into military service. Most served heroically. This fact, combined with a growing desire to see the native peoples effectively merged into mainstream society, led to the enactment of The Indian Citizenship Act of 1924, by which Native Americans were granted US citizenship.

Until recent years, the policy of the federal government was to segregate and marginalize Native Americans. Their religion, arts, and culture have been largely ignored until recent years. Safely restricted to reservations in the "Indian territory," various attempts were made to strip them of their inherited culture, just as they were stripped of their ancestral lands. Life on the reservations has been difficult for most Native Americans. The policies of extermination and relocation, as well as the introduction of disease among them significantly decimated their numbers by the end of the nineteenth century.

Skill 9.2 Demonstrate knowledge of Virginia's development, the settlement of New England, and the development of the mid-Atlantic colonies

The **New England** colonies consisted of Massachusetts, Rhode Island, Connecticut, and New Hampshire. Life in these colonies was centered on the towns. Any farming was done by each family on its own plot of land but a short summer growing season and limited amount of good soil gave rise to other economic activities such as manufacturing, fishing, shipbuilding, and trade. The vast majority of the settlers shared similar origins, coming from England and Scotland. Towns were carefully planned and laid out the same way. The form of government was the town meeting where all adult males met to make the laws. The legislative body, the General Court, consisted of an upper and lower house.

The **Middle or Middle Atlantic** colonies included New York, New Jersey, Pennsylvania, Delaware, and Maryland. New York and New Jersey were at one time the Dutch colony of New Netherland, and Delaware at one time was New Sweden. These five colonies, from their beginnings were considered melting pots, with settlers from many different nations and backgrounds. The main economic activity was farming with settlers scattered over the countryside who cultivated rather large farms. The Indians were not as much of a threat as in New England so they did not have to settle in small farming villages. The soil was very fertile, the land was gently rolling, and a milder climate provided a longer growing season. These farms produced a large surplus of food, not only for the colonists themselves but also for sale.

This colonial region became known as the breadbasket of the New World and the New York and Philadelphia seaports were constantly filled with ships being loaded with meat, flour, and other foodstuffs for the West Indies and England.

The **Southern** colonies were Virginia, North and South Carolina, and Georgia. Virginia was the first permanent successful English colony and Georgia was the last. The year 1619 was a very important year in the history of Virginia and the United States with three very significant events. First, sixty women were sent to Virginia to marry and establish families; second, twenty Africans, the first of thousands, arrived; and third, most importantly, the Virginia colonists were granted the right to self-government and they began by electing their own representatives to the House of Burgesses, their own legislative body.

The major economic activity in this region was farming. Here too the soil was very fertile and the climate was very mild with an even longer growing season. The large plantations, which required large numbers of slaves, were found in the coastal or tidewater areas. Although the wealthy slave-owning planters set the pattern of life in this region, most of the people lived inland away from coastal areas. They were small farmers and very few, it any, owned slaves.

The settlers in these four colonies came from diverse backgrounds and cultures. Virginia was colonized mostly by people from England, while Georgia was started as a haven for debtors from English prisons. Pioneers from Virginia settled in North Carolina while South Carolina welcomed people from England and Scotland, French Protestants, Germans, and emigrants from islands in the West Indies. Products from farms and plantations included rice, tobacco, indigo, cotton, some corn and wheat. Other economic activities included lumber and naval stores (tar, pitch, rosin, and turpentine) from the pine forests and fur trade on the frontier. Cities such as Savannah and Charleston were important seaports and trading centers.

On the other hand, life inland on the frontier had marked differences. All facets of daily living--clothing, food, home, economic and social activities--were connected to what was needed to sustain life and survive in the wilderness. Practically everything was produced by the colonists themselves. They were self-sufficient and extremely individualistic and independent. There were little, if any, levels of society or class distinctions as they considered themselves to be the equal to all others, regardless of station in life. The roots of equality, independence, individual rights and freedoms were extremely strong and well developed. People were not judged by their fancy dress, expensive house, eloquent language, or titles following their names.

Slavery in the English colonies began in 1619 when 20 Africans arrived in the colony of Virginia at Jamestown. From then on, slavery had a foothold, especially in the agricultural South, where a large amount of slave labor was needed for the extensive plantations. Free men refused to work for wages on the plantations when land was available for settling on the frontier. Therefore, slave labor was the only recourse left. If it had been profitable to use slaves in New England and the Middle Colonies, then without doubt slavery would have been more widespread. Slavery, however, was only profitable in the South, and not in the other two colonial regions.

Skill 9.3   Examine the reasons for French settlement of Quebec and compare the differences between French, Spanish, and British colonial societies in North America

The part of North America claimed by France was called New France and consisted of the land west of the Appalachian Mountains. This area of claims and settlement included the St. Lawrence Valley, the Great Lakes, the Mississippi Valley, and the entire region of land westward to the Rockies. They established the permanent settlements of **Montreal** and New Orleans, thus giving them control of the two major gateways into the heart of North America, the vast, rich interior. The St. Lawrence River, the Great Lakes, and the Mississippi River along with its tributaries made it possible for the French explorers and traders to roam at will, virtually unhindered in exploring, trapping, trading, and furthering the interests of France.

Most of the French settlements were in Canada along the St. Lawrence River. Only scattered forts and trading posts were found in the upper Mississippi Valley and Great Lakes region. The rulers of France originally intended New France to have vast estates owned by nobles and worked by peasants with the peasants living on the estates in compact farming villages--the New World version of the Old World's medieval system of feudalism. However, it didn't work out that way. Each of the nobles wanted his estate to be on the river for ease of transportation. The peasants working the estates wanted the prime waterfront location, also. The result of all this real estate squabbling was that New France's settled areas wound up mostly as a string of farmhouses stretching from Quebec to Montreal along the St. Lawrence and Richelieu Rivers.

In the non-settled areas in the interior were the **French fur traders.** They made friends with the friendly tribes of Indians, spending the winters with them getting the furs needed for trade. In the spring, they would return to Montreal in time to take advantage of trading their furs for the products brought by the cargo ships from France, which usually arrived at about the same time. Most of the wealth for New France and its Mother Country was from the fur trade, which provided a livelihood for many, many people. Manufacturers and workmen back in France, ship-owners and merchants, as well as the fur traders and their Indian allies all benefited. However, the freedom of roaming and trapping in the interior was a strong enticement for the younger, stronger men and resulted in the French focusing on areas other than those settled along the St. Lawrence.

Into the eighteenth century, the rivalry with the British was getting stronger and stronger. New France was united under a single government and enjoyed the support of many Indian allies. The French traders were very diligent in not destroying the forests and driving away game upon which the Indians depended for life. It was difficult for the French to defend all of their settlements as they were scattered over half of the continent. However, by the early 1750s, in Western Europe, France was the most powerful nation. Its armies were superior to all others and its navy was giving the British stiff competition for control of the seas. The stage was set for confrontation in both Europe and America.

Spanish settlement had its beginnings in the Caribbean with the establishment of colonies on Hispaniola (at Santo Domingo, which became the capital of the West Indies), Puerto Rico, and Cuba. There were a number of reasons for Spanish involvement in the Americas, including:

• the spirit of adventure
• the desire for land
• expansion of Spanish power, influence, and empire
• the desire for great wealth
• expansion of Roman Catholic influence and conversion of native peoples

Skill 9.4 Demonstrate knowledge of the development of mercantilism and the trans-Atlantic trade

The trans-African slave trade refers to the movement of black African slaves over trade routes through the deserts of northern Africa to slave trading posts on the eastern and northern coasts of the continent. From these posts, slaves were transported to markets in Muslim cities such as Morocco, Cairo, Algiers and Tripoli. The practice began sometime in the ninth century and continued into the early years of the twentieth century, predating and outlasting the trans-Atlantic slave trade by Europeans.

The slaves themselves were sometimes captured by Arab traders on raiding missions or were enslaved by other black groups as a result of war and subsequently traded into the slave market. These people came largely from sub-Saharan Africa and, once captured, were moved across the deserts by caravan routes. These routes stretched from oasis to oasis, from the interior to the coastal trading posts.

Slaves were exchanged for a variety of goods, including gold, horses, dye, jewels and cloth. They were sold mainly to become servants or to join harems if they were female. Some male slaves were castrated and served as eunuchs who acted as guards for the harems of wealthy Muslims.

Arabs dominated the sea routes of the Red Sea and the Indian Ocean during the Middle Ages and the slave trade expanded to bring laborers from posts on the eastern coast of Africa to the agricultural areas of India.

Little primary evidence remains of the Arab slave trade in Africa and exact figures on the number of Africans who were sold into slavery are unknown. The trade was significant, however, not only in the widespread area it affected but in the number of people upon which slavery was inflicted.

Skill 9.5 Analyze Anglo-French imperial competition in North America, identify important features of the French-Indian War, and evaluate the impact of the war on the British colonies

The first permanent settlement in what is now the United States was in 1565 at St. Augustine, Florida. A later permanent settlement in the southwestern United States was in 1609 at Santa Fe, New Mexico. At the peak of Spanish power, the area in the United States claimed, settled, and controlled by Spain included Florida and all land west of the Mississippi River--quite a piece of choice real estate. Of course, France and England also lay claim to the same areas. Nonetheless, ranches and missions were built and the Indians who came in contact with the Spaniards were introduced to animals, plants, and seeds from the Old World that they had never seen before. Animals brought in included horses, cattle, donkeys, pigs, sheep, goats and poultry.

Spain's control over her New World colonies lasted more than 300 years, longer than that of England or France. To this day, Spanish influence remains in names of places, art, architecture, music, literature, law, and cuisine. The Spanish settlements in North America were not commercial enterprises but were meant to protect and defend trade and wealth from Spanish colonies in Mexico and South America. The Russians, who were hunting seals, came down the Pacific coast, the English moved into Florida and west into and beyond the Appalachians, and the French traders and trappers were making their way from Louisiana and other parts of New France into Spanish territory. The Spanish never realized or understood that self-sustaining economic development and colonial trade was so important. Consequently, the Spanish settlements in the US never really prospered.

Before 1763, when England was rapidly on the way to becoming the most powerful of the three major Western European powers, its thirteen colonies, located between the Atlantic and the Appalachians, physically occupied the least amount of land. Moreover, it is interesting that even before the Spanish Armada was defeated, two Englishmen, Sir Humphrey Gilbert and his half-brother Sir Walter Raleigh were unsuccessful in their attempts to build successful permanent colonies in the New World. Nonetheless, the thirteen English colonies were successful and, by the time they had gained their independence from Britain, were more than able to govern themselves. They had a rich historical heritage of law, tradition, and documents leading the way to constitutional government conducted according to laws and customs. The settlers in the British colonies highly valued individual freedom, democratic government, and achievement through hard work.

The English colonies, with only a few exceptions, were considered commercial ventures to make a profit for the crown or the company or whoever financed their beginnings. One colony was strictly a philanthropic enterprise and three others were founded primarily for religious reasons but the other nine were started for economic reasons. Settlers in these unique colonies came for different reasons:

a) religious freedom;
b) political freedom;
c) economic prosperity; and
d) land ownership.

The colonies were divided generally into the three regions of **New England**, **Middle Atlantic,** and **Southern**. The culture of each was distinct and affected attitudes, ideas towards politics, religion, and economic activities. The geography of each region also contributed to its unique characteristics.

The **New England colonies** consisted of Massachusetts, Rhode Island, Connecticut, and New Hampshire. Life in these colonies was centered on the towns. What farming was done was by each family on its own plot of land but a short summer growing season and limited amount of good soil gave rise to other economic activities such as manufacturing, fishing, shipbuilding, and trade. The vast majority of the settlers shared similar origins, coming from England and Scotland. Towns were carefully planned and laid out the same way. The form of government was the town meeting where all adult males met to make the laws. The legislative body, the General Court, consisted of an Upper and Lower House.

The **Middle or Middle Atlantic colonies** included New York, New Jersey, Pennsylvania, Delaware, and Maryland. New York and New Jersey were at one time the Dutch colony of New Netherlands and Delaware at one time was New Sweden. These five colonies, from their beginnings, were considered melting pots with settlers from many different nations and backgrounds. The main economic activity was farming with settlers, scattered over the countryside, cultivating rather large farms. The Indians were not as much of a threat as in New England so the colonists did not have to contain themselves in small farming villages. The soil was very fertile, the land was gently rolling, and a milder climate provided a longer growing season.

These farms produced a large surplus of food, not only for the colonists themselves but also for sale. This colonial region became known as the breadbasket of the New World, and the New York and Philadelphia seaports were constantly filled with ships being loaded with meat, flour, and other foodstuffs for the West Indies and England. Other economic activities included shipbuilding, iron mines, and production of paper, glass, and textiles. The legislative body in Pennsylvania was unicameral or consisted of one house. In the other four colonies, the legislative body had two houses. Also, units of local government were in counties and towns.

The **Southern colonies** were Virginia, North and South Carolina, and Georgia. Virginia was the first permanent successful English colony and Georgia was the last. The year 1619 was a very important year in the history of Virginia and the United States with three very significant events: 1) sixty women were sent to Virginia to marry and establish families; 2) twenty Africans, the first of thousands, arrived; and most importantly, 3) Virginia colonists were granted the right to self-government and they began by electing their own representatives to the House of Burgesses, their own legislative body.

The major economic activity in this region was farming. Here the soil was very fertile and the climate was very mild with an even longer growing season. The large plantations eventually requiring large numbers of slaves were found in the coastal or tidewater areas. Although the wealthy slave-owning planters set the pattern of life in this region, most of the people lived inland away from coastal areas. They were small farmers and very few, it any, owned slaves.

The settlers in these four colonies came from diverse backgrounds and cultures. Virginia was colonized mostly by people from England while Georgia was started as a haven for debtors from English prisons. Pioneers from Virginia settled in North Carolina while South Carolina welcomed people from England and Scotland, French Protestants, Germans, and emigrants from islands in the West Indies. Products from farms and plantations included rice, tobacco, indigo, cotton, some corn and wheat. Other economic activities included lumber and naval stores (tar, pitch, rosin, and turpentine) from the pine forests and fur trade on the frontier. Cities such as Savannah and Charleston were important seaports and trading centers.

The daily life of the colonists differed greatly between the coastal settlements and the inland or interior. The Southern planters and the people living in the coastal cities and towns had a way of life similar to that in towns in England. The influence was seen and heard in how people dressed and talked. The architectural styles of houses and public buildings, and the social divisions or levels of society mimicked that of England. Both the planters and city dwellers enjoyed an active social life and had strong emotional ties to England.

On the other hand, life inland on the frontier had marked differences. All facets of daily living--clothing, food, housing, economic and social activities--were connected to what was needed to sustain life and survive in the wilderness. Practically everything was produced by the colonists themselves. They were self-sufficient and extremely individualistic and independent. There were little, if any, levels of society or class distinctions as they considered themselves to be the equal to all others, regardless of station in life. The roots of equality, independence, individual rights and freedoms were strong and well developed. People were not judged by their fancy dress, expensive house, eloquent language, or titles following their names.

The colonies had from 1607 to 1763 to develop, refine, practice, experiment, and experience life in a rugged, uncivilized land. The Mother Country had virtually left them on their own all that time. When in 1763, Britain decided she needed to regulate and "mother" the "little ones," to her surprise she had a losing fight on her hands.

By the 1750s in Europe, Spain was out of the picture, no longer the most powerful nation, or even a contender. The remaining rivalry was between Britain and France. For nearly 25 years, between 1689 and 1748, a series of armed conflicts involving these two powers had been taking place. These conflicts had spilled over into North America. The War of the League of Augsburg in Europe, 1689 to 1697, had been King William's War. The War of the Spanish Succession, 1702 to 1713, had been Queen Anne's War. The War of the Austrian Succession, 1740 to 1748, was called King George's War in the colonies. The two nations fought for possession of colonies, especially in Asia and North America, and for control of the seas, but none of these conflicts was decisive.

The final conflict, which decided once and for all who was the most powerful, began in North America in 1754, in the Ohio River Valley. It was known in America as the **French and Indian War** and in Europe as the Seven Years' War, since it began there in 1756. In America, both sides had advantages and disadvantages. The British colonies were well established and consolidated in a smaller area. British colonists outnumbered French colonists 23 to 1. Except for a small area in Canada, French settlements were scattered over a much larger area (roughly half of the continent) and were smaller. However, the French settlements were united under one government and were quick to act and cooperate when necessary. In addition, the French had many more Indian allies than the British. The British colonies had separate, individual governments and very seldom cooperated, even when needed. In Europe, at that time, France was the more powerful of the two nations.

The French depended on the St. Lawrence River for transporting supplies, soldiers, and messages--the link between New France and the Mother Country. Tied into this waterway system were the connecting links of the Great Lakes, Mississippi River and its tributaries, along which were scattered French forts, trading posts, and small settlements.

In 1758, once the British captured Louisburg on Cape Breton Island, New France was doomed. Louisburg gave the British navy a base of operations, which prevented French reinforcements and supplies getting to their troops. Other forts fell to the British: Frontenac, Duquesne, Crown Point, Ticonderoga, Niagara, those in the upper Ohio Valley, and, most importantly, Quebec and, finally, Montreal. Spain entered the war in 1762 to aid France but it was too late. British victories occurred all around the world: in India, in the Mediterranean, and in Europe.

In 1763 in Paris, Spain, France, and Britain met to draw up the Treaty of Paris. Great Britain got most of India and all of North America east of the Mississippi River, except for New Orleans. Britain received from Spain control of Florida and returned to Spain Cuba and the islands of the Philippines, taken during the war. France lost nearly all of its possessions in America. India and was allowed to keep four islands: Guadeloupe, Martinique, Haiti on Hispaniola, and Miquelon and St. Pierre. France gave Spain New Orleans and the vast territory of Louisiana, west of the Mississippi River. Britain was now without question the most powerful nation.

Skill 9.6 **Demonstrate knowledge of the Middle Passage and the institution of slavery in North America, recognize contributions of African Americans to colonial society, and analyze the emergence of distinct African American societies**

Slavery in the English colonies began in 1619 when 20 Africans arrived in the colony of Virginia at Jamestown. From then on, slavery had a foothold, especially in the agricultural South, where a large amount of slave labor was needed for the extensive plantations. Free men refused to work for wages on the plantations when land was available for settling on the frontier. Therefore, slave labor was the only recourse left. If it had been profitable to use slaves in New England and the Middle Colonies, then without doubt slavery would have been more widespread. Slavery was profitable in the South, but not in the other two colonial regions.

It is interesting that the West was involved in the controversy as well as the North and South. By 1860, the country was made up of these three major regions. The people in all three sections or regions had a number of beliefs and institutions in common. Of course, there were major differences and each region had its own unique characteristics. The basic problem was their development along very different lines.

The section of the North was industrial with towns and factories growing and increasing at a very fast rate. The South had become agricultural, eventually becoming increasingly dependent on a single crop--cotton. In the West, restless pioneers moved into new frontiers seeking land, wealth, and opportunity. Many were from the South and were slave owners, bringing their slaves with them. Between these three different parts of the country, the views differed widely on such matters as tariffs, public lands, internal improvements at federal expense, banking and currency, and the issue of slavery.

This period of US history was a period of compromises, breakdowns of those compromises, desperate attempts to restore and retain harmony among the three sections, short-lived intervals of uneasy balance of interests, and ever-increasing conflict.

At the Constitutional Convention, one of the slavery compromises concerned counting slaves for deciding the number of representatives for the House and the amount of taxes to be paid. Southerners pushed for counting the slaves for representation but not for taxes. The Northerners pushed for the opposite. The resulting compromise, sometimes referred to as the "three-fifths compromise," was that both groups agreed that three-fifths of the slaves would be counted for both taxes and representation.

The other compromise over slavery was part of the disputes over how much regulation the central government would control over commercial activities such as trade with other nations and the slave trade. It was agreed that Congress would regulate commerce with other nations, including taxing imports. Southerners were worried about taxing slaves and the possibility of Congress prohibiting the slave trade altogether. The agreement reached allowed the states to continue importation of slaves for the next 20 years until 1808, at which time Congress would make the decision as to the future of the slave trade.   During the 20-year period, no more than $10 per person could be levied on slaves coming into the country.

These two "slavery" compromises were a necessary concession to have Southern support and approval for the new document and new government. Many Americans felt that the system of slavery would eventually die out in the US, but by 1808, cotton was becoming increasingly important in the primarily agricultural South and the institution of slavery had become firmly entrenched in Southern culture. It is also evident that as early as the Constitutional Convention, active anti-slavery feelings and opinions were very strong, leading to extremely active groups and societies.

Democracy is loosely defined as "rule by the people," either directly or through representatives. Associated with the idea of democracy is freedom, equality, and opportunity. The basic concept of democracy existed in the 13 English colonies with the practice of independent self-government. The right of qualified persons to vote, hold office and actively participate in their government is sometimes referred to as "political" democracy. "Social" and "economic" democracy pertain to the idea that all have the opportunity to get an education, choose their own careers, and live as free people; each person is deemed to be equal to all others in the eyes of the law.

These three concepts of democracy were basic reasons why people came to the New World. The practices of these concepts continued through the colonial and revolutionary periods and were extremely influential in shaping the new central government under the Constitution. As the nation extended its borders into the lands west of the Mississippi, thousands of settlers streamed into the country. They brought with them ideas and concepts and adapted them to the development of the unique characteristics of the region.   Equality for everyone, as stated in the Declaration of Independence, did not yet apply to minority groups, black Americans or American Indians. Voting rights and the right to hold public office were restricted in varying degrees in each state. All of these factors decidedly affected the political, economic, and social life of the country and these were focused in the attitudes towards slavery in three sections of the country.

The first serious clash between North and South occurred during 1819-1820 when James Monroe was in office as President and it concerned admitting Missouri as a state. In 1819, the US consisted of 21 states: 11 free states and 10 slave states. The Missouri Territory allowed slavery and if admitted would cause an imbalance in the number of US Senators. Alabama had already been admitted as a slave state and that had balanced the Senate, with the North and South each having 22 senators. The first Missouri Compromise resolved the conflict by approving the admission of Maine as a free state along with Missouri as a slave state. The balance of power in the Senate continued with the same number of free and slave states.

An additional provision of this compromise was that with the admission of Missouri, slavery would not be allowed in the rest of the Louisiana Purchase territory north of latitude 36 degrees 30'. This was acceptable to the Southern Congressmen since it was not profitable to grow cotton on land north of this latitude line anyway. It was thought that the crisis had been resolved but in the next year, it was discovered that in its state constitution, Missouri discriminated against free blacks. Anti-slavery supporters in Congress went into an uproar, determined to exclude Missouri from the Union. Henry Clay, known as the Great Compromiser, then proposed a second **Missouri Compromise**, which was acceptable to everyone.

Skill 9.7 Demonstrate knowledge of the origins and significance of the Great Awakening and recognize the diversity of religious experience in the English colonies

Religion has always been a factor in American life. Many early settlers came to America in search of religious freedom. Religion, particularly Christianity, was an essential element of the value and belief structure shared by the Founding Fathers. Yet the Constitution prescribes a separation of Church and State. Religion is a basis for the actions of believers, no matter which religion is practiced or embraced. Because religion determines values and ethics, it influences the actions of individuals and groups to work to change conditions that are perceived to be wrong.

The **First Great Awakening** was a religious movement within American Protantism in the 1730s and 1740s. This was primarily a movement among Puritans seeking a return to strict interpretation of morality and values as well as emphasizing the importance and power of personal religious or spiritual experience. Many historians believe the First Great Awakening unified the people of the original colonies and supported the independence of the colonists.

Also refer to Skill 10.8 for further discussion.

Skill 9.8   Demonstrate knowledge of the causes, major events, developments, and key figures of the American Revolution

The **War for Independence** occurred due to a number of changes, the two most important ones being economic and political. By the end of the French and Indian War in 1763, Britain's American colonies were 13 out of a total of 33 scattered around the earth. Like all other countries, Britain strove for a strong economy and a favorable balance of trade. To have that delicate balance a nation needs wealth, self-sufficiency, and a powerful army and navy. The overseas colonies would provide raw materials for the industries in the Mother Country, be a market for the finished products by buying them and assist the Mother Country in becoming powerful and strong (as in the case of Great Britain). A strong merchant fleet would be a school for training the Royal Navy and provide bases of operation for the Royal Navy.

The foregoing explained the major reason for British encouragement and support of colonization, especially in North America. So between 1607 and 1763, at various times for various reasons, the British Parliament enacted different laws to assist the government in getting and keeping this trade balance. One series of laws required that most of the manufacturing be done only in England, such as prohibition of exporting any wool or woolen cloth from the colonies, no manufacture of beaver hats or iron products. The colonists weren't concerned, as they had no money and no highly skilled labor to set up any industries, anyway. The **Navigation Acts** of 1651 put restrictions on shipping and trade within the British Empire by requiring that only British ships could carry cargo. This increased the strength of the British merchant fleet and greatly benefited the American colonists. Since they were British citizens, they could have their own vessels, building and operating them as well. By the end of the war in 1763, the shipyards in the colonies were building one third of the merchant ships under the British flag. There were quite a number of wealthy, American, colonial merchants.

The Navigation Act of 1660 restricted the shipment and sale of colonial products to England only. In 1663 another Navigation Act stipulated that the colonies had to buy manufactured products only from England and that any European goods going to the colonies had to go to England first. These acts were a protection from enemy ships and pirates and from competition from European rivals.

The New England and Middle Atlantic colonies at first felt threatened by these laws as they had started manufacturing many of the products being produced in Britain. They soon found new markets for their goods and began what was known as a **triangular trade**. Colonial vessels started the first part of the triangle by sailing for Africa loaded with kegs of rum from colonial distilleries. On Africa's West Coast, the rum was traded for either gold or slaves. The second part of the triangle was from Africa to the West Indies where slaves were traded for molasses, sugar, or money. The third part of the triangle was home, bringing sugar or molasses (to make more rum), gold, and silver.

The major concern of the British government was that the trade violated the 1733 Molasses Act. Planters had wanted the colonists to buy all of their molasses in the British West Indies but these islands could give the traders only about one-eighth the amount of molasses needed for distilling the rum. The colonists were forced to buy the rest of what they needed from the French, Dutch, and Spanish islands, thus evading the law by not paying the high duty on the molasses bought from these islands. If Britain had enforced the Molasses Act, economic and financial chaos and ruin would have occurred. Nevertheless, for this act and all the other mercantile laws, the government followed the policy of "salutary neglect," deliberately failing to enforce the laws.

In 1763, after the war, Britain needed funds to finance the war debt, defend the empire, and govern the 33 colonies scattered around the earth. It was decided to adopt a new colonial policy and pass laws to raise revenue. It was reasoned that the colonists were subjects of the king and since the king and his ministers had spent a great deal of money defending and protecting them (this was especially true of the American colonists), it was only right and fair that the colonists should help pay the costs of their defense. The earlier laws passed had been for the purposes of regulating production and trade, which generally put money into colonial pockets. These new laws would take some of that rather hard-earned money out of the colonists' pockets and it would be done, in colonial eyes, unjustly and illegally.

Before 1763, except for trade and supplying raw materials, the colonies had been left pretty much to themselves. England looked on them merely as part of an economic or commercial empire. Little consideration was given as to how they were to conduct their daily affairs, so the colonists became very independent, self-reliant, and extremely skillful at handling those daily affairs. This, in turn, gave rise to leadership, initiative, achievement, and vast experience. In fact, there was a far greater degree of independence and self-government in the British colonies in America than could be found in Britain or the major countries on the Continent or any other colonies anywhere. There were a number of reasons for this:

1. The religious and scriptural teachings of previous centuries put forth the worth of the individual and equality in God's sight. Keep in mind that freedom of worship and from religious persecution were major reasons to live in the New World.

2. European Protestants, especially Calvinists, believed and taught the idea that government originates from those governed, that rulers are required to protect individual rights and that the governed have the right and privilege to choose their rulers.

3. Trading companies put into practice the principle that their members had the right to make the decisions and shape the policies affecting their lives.

4. The colonists believed and supported the idea that a person's property should not be taken without his consent, based on that treasured English document, the Magna Carta, and English common law.

5. From about 1700 to 1750, population increases in America came about through immigration and generations of descendants of the original settlers. The immigrants were mainly Scots-Irish who hated the English, Germans who cared nothing about England, and black slaves who knew nothing about England. The descendants of the original settlers had never been out of America at any time.

6. In America, as new towns and counties were formed, there began the practice of representation in government. Representatives to the colonial legislative assemblies were elected from the district in which they lived, chosen by qualified property-owning male voters, and represented the interests of the political district from which they were elected. One thing to remember: each of the 13 colonies had a royal governor appointed by the king to represent his interests in the colonies. Nevertheless, the colonial legislative assemblies controlled the purse strings, having the power to vote on all issues involving money to be spent by the colonial governments.

Thomas Paine (1737-1809), the great American political theorist, wrote "these are the times that try men's souls" in his 16-part pamphlet *The Crisis*. Paine's authoring of *Common Sense* was an important step in spreading information to the American colonists about their need for independence from Great Britain.

Contrary to this was the governmental set-up in England. Members of Parliament were not elected to represent their own districts. They were considered representative of classes, not individuals. If some members of a professional or commercial class or some landed interests were able to elect representatives, then those classes or special interests were represented. It had nothing at all to do with numbers or territories. Some large population centers had no direct representation at all, yet the people there considered themselves represented by men elected from their particular class or interest somewhere else. Consequently, it was extremely difficult for the English to understand why the American merchants and landowners claimed they were not represented because they themselves did not vote for a Member of Parliament.

The colonists' protest of "no taxation without representation" was meaningless to the English. Parliament represented the entire nation, was completely unlimited in legislation, and had become supreme; and the colonists were incensed at the English attitude, which assumed that of course everyone had representation. The colonists considered their colonial legislative assemblies equal to Parliament, which was totally unacceptable in England. Two different systems held sway: the older traditional British system in the Mother Country and new ideas and different ways of doing things in America. In a new country, a new environment has little or no tradition, institutions or vested interests. New ideas and traditions grew extremely fast, pushing aside what was left of the old ideas and old traditions. By 1763, Britain had changed its perception of its American colonies, deeming them now a "territorial" empire. The stage was set and the conditions were right for a showdown.

In 1763, Parliament decided to have a standing army in North America to reinforce British control. In 1765, the **Quartering Act** was passed requiring the colonists to provide supplies and living quarters for the British troops. In addition, efforts by the British were made to keep the peace by establishing good relations with the Indians. Consequently, a proclamation was issued which prohibited the American colonists from making any settlements west of the Appalachians until provided for through treaties with the Indians.

The Sugar Act of 1764 required collection of taxes on any molasses that was brought into the colonies. It also gave British officials free license to conduct searches of the premises of anyone suspected of violating the law. The colonists were taxed on newspapers, legal documents, and other printed matter under the **Stamp Act of 1765.** Although a stamp tax was already in use in England, the colonists would have none of it, which caused an uproar of rioting and mob violence, after which Parliament repealed the tax.
Of course, great exultation, jubilance, and wild joy resulted when news of the repeal reached America. However, what no one noticed was the small, quiet Declaratory Act attached to the repeal. This act plainly and unequivocally stated that Parliament still had the right to make all laws for the colonies. It denied their right to be taxed only by their own colonial legislatures--a very crucial, important piece of legislation which was virtually overlooked and unnoticed at the time. Other acts leading up to armed conflict included the **Townshend Acts** passed in 1767 taxing lead, paint, paper, and tea brought into the colonies. This increased anger and tension and resulted in the British sending troops to New York City and Boston.

In Boston, mob violence provoked retaliation by the troops thus bringing about the deaths of five people and the wounding of eight others. The so-called Boston Massacre shocked Americans and British alike. Subsequently, in 1770, Parliament voted to repeal all the provisions of the Townshend Acts with the exception of the tea tax. In 1773, the tax on tea sold by the British East India Company was substantially reduced, fueling colonial anger once more. This gave the company an unfair trade advantage and forcibly reminded the colonists of the British right to tax them. Merchants refused to sell the tea; colonists refused to buy and drink it; and a shipload of it was dumped into Boston Harbor, a most violent Tea Party.

In 1774, the passage of the Quebec Act extended the limits of that Canadian colony's boundary southward to include territory located north of the Ohio River. However, the punishment for Boston's Tea Party came in the same year with the **Intolerable Acts**. Boston's port was closed; the royal governor of the colony of Massachusetts was given increased power, and the colonists were compelled to house and feed the British soldiers. The propaganda activities of the patriot organizations **Sons of Liberty** and **Committees of Correspondence** kept the opposition and resistance before everyone. Delegates from twelve colonies met in Philadelphia on September 5, 1774, in the First Continental Congress. They definitely opposed acts of lawlessness and wanted some form of peaceful settlement with Britain. They maintained American loyalty to the Mother Country and affirmed Parliament's power over colonial foreign affairs.

They insisted on repeal of the Intolerable Acts and demanded ending all trade with Britain until this took place. The reply from King George III, the last king of America, was an insistence of colonial submission to British rule or be crushed. With the start of the Revolutionary War April 19, 1775, the Second Continental Congress began meeting in Philadelphia on May 10 of that year to conduct the business of war and government for the next six years.

The British had been extremely lax and totally inconsistent in enforcement of the mercantile or trade laws passed in the years before 1754. The government itself was not particularly stable so actions against the colonies occurred in anger and their attitude was one of a moral superiority; they believed that they knew how to manage America better than the Americans did themselves. This of course points to a lack of sufficient knowledge of conditions and opinions in America. The colonists had been left on their own for nearly 150 years and by the time the Revolutionary War began, they were quite adept at self-government and were adequately able to handle the affairs of their daily lives. The Americans equated ownership of land or property with the right to vote. Property was considered the foundation of life and liberty and, in the colonial mind and tradition, these went together.

Therefore when an indirect tax on tea was made, the British felt that since it wasn't a direct tax, there should be no objection to it. The colonists viewed any tax, direct or indirect, as an attack on their property. They felt that as a representative body, the British Parliament should protect British citizens, including the colonists, from arbitrary taxation. Since they felt they were not represented, Parliament, in their eyes, gave them no protection. And so war ensued. On August 23, 1775, George III declared that the colonies were in rebellion and warned them to stop or else.

By 1776, the colonists and their representatives in the Second Continental Congress realized that things were past the point of no return. The Declaration of Independence was drafted and declared July 4, 1776. George Washington labored against tremendous odds to wage a victorious war. The turning point in the Americans' favor occurred in 1777 with the American victory at **Saratoga**. This victory was the deciding factor for the French to align themselves with the Americans against the British. With the aid of Admiral deGrasse and French warships blocking the entrance to Chesapeake Bay, British General Cornwallis (who was trapped at Yorktown, Virginia) surrendered in 1781 and the war was over. The Treaty of Paris officially ending the war was signed in 1783.

Skill 9.9   **Analyze the strengths and weaknesses of the Articles of Confederation, demonstrate knowledge of key features of the Constitution and major arguments of the Federalists and Anti-Federalists during the debate on ratification, and recognize the role of the Bill of Rights as a protector of individual and state rights**

Articles of Confederation - This was the first political system under which the newly independent colonies tried to organize themselves. It was drafted after the Declaration of Independence was passed by the Continental Congress on November 15, 1777, ratified by the thirteen states, and took effect on March 1, 1781.

The newly independent states were unwilling to give too much power to a national government. They were already fighting Great Britain. They did not want to replace one harsh ruler with another. After many debates, the form of the Articles was accepted. Each state agreed to send delegates to the Congress and each state had one vote in the Congress. The Articles gave Congress the power to declare war, appoint military officers, and coin money. The Congress was also responsible for foreign affairs. The Articles of Confederation limited the powers of Congress by giving the states final authority. Although Congress could pass laws, at least nine of the thirteen states had to approve a law before it went into effect. Congress could not pass any laws regarding taxes. To get money, Congress had to ask each state for it as no state could be forced to pay.

Thus, the Articles created a loose alliance among the thirteen states. The national government was weak, in part, because it didn't have a strong chief executive to carry out laws passed by the legislature. This weak national government might have worked if the states were able to get along with each other. However, many different disputes arose and there was no way of settling them. Thus, the delegates met again to try to fix the Articles; instead, they ended up scrapping them and created a new Constitution that learned from these earlier mistakes.

Ratification of the US Constitution was by no means a foregone conclusion. The representative government had powerful enemies, especially those who had seen firsthand the failure of the Articles of Confederation. The strong central government had powerful enemies, including some of the guiding lights of the American Revolution.

Those who wanted to see a strong central government were called **Federalists** because they wanted to see a federal government reign supreme; among the leaders of the Federalists were Alexander Hamilton and John Jay. These two, along with James Madison, wrote a series of letters to New York newspapers, urging that that state ratify the Constitution. These became known as the *Federalist Papers.*
In the Anti-Federalist camp were Thomas Jefferson and Patrick Henry. These men and many others like them were worried that a strong national government would descend into the kind of tyranny that they had just worked so hard to abolish. In the same way that they took their name from their foes, they wrote a series of arguments against the Constitution called the **Anti-Federalist Papers.**

In the end, both sides got most of what they wanted. The Federalists got their strong national government, which was held in place by the famous "checks and balances." The Anti-Federalists got the Bill of Rights, the first ten Amendments to the Constitution and a series of laws that protect some of the most basic of human rights. The states that were in doubt for ratification of the Constitution signed on when the Bill of Rights was promised.

COMPETENCY 10.0 UNDERSTAND THE GROWTH AND EXPANSION OF THE UNITED STATES FROM 1789 THROUGH THE MID-NINETEENTH CENTURY

Skill 10.1 Recognize important features of the presidencies of George Washington, John Adams, and Thomas Jefferson

During the colonial period, political parties, as the term is now understood, did not exist. Issues that divided the people were centered around the relations of the colonies to the mother country. There was initially little difference of opinion on these issues. About the middle of the eighteenth century, after England began to develop a harsher colonial policy, two factions arose in America. One favored the attitude of home government and the other declined to obey and demanded a constantly increasing level of self-government. The former came to be known as **Tories**, the latter as **Whigs**. During the course of the American Revolution a large number of Tories left the country either to return to England or move to Canada.

From the beginning of the Confederation, there were differences of opinion about the new government. One faction favored a loose confederacy in which the individual state would retain all powers of sovereignty except the absolute minimum required for the limited cooperation of all the states. (This approach was tried under the Articles of Confederation.) The other faction, which steadily gained influence, demanded that the central government be granted all the essential powers of sovereignty and that what should be left to the states was only the powers of local self-government. The inadequacy of the Confederation demonstrated that the latter were promoting a more effective point of view.

The first real party organization developed soon after the inauguration of Washington as President. His cabinet included people of both factions. Hamilton was the leader of the **Nationalists** – the **Federalist Party** – and Jefferson was the spokesman for the Anti-Federalists, later known as **Republicans, Democratic-Republicans**, and finally **Democrats**.

George Washington (1789-1797) faced a number of challenges during his two terms as President. There were boundary disputes with Spain over the Southeast and wars with the Indians on the western frontier. The French Revolution and the ensuing war between France and England created great turmoil within the new nation. Thomas Jefferson, Secretary of State, was pro-French and believed the US should enter the fray. Alexander Hamilton, Secretary of the Treasury, was pro-British and wanted to support England. Washington took a neutral course, believing the US was not strong enough to be engaged in a war. Washington did not interfere with the powers of the Congress in establishing foreign policy. Two political parties were beginning to form by the end of his first term. In his farewell address he encouraged Americans to put an end to regional differences and exuberant party spirit. He also warned the nation against long-term alliances with foreign nations.

John Adams, of the Federalist Party, was elected President in 1796. When he assumed office, the war between England and France was in full swing. The British were seizing American ships that were engaging in trade with France. France, however, was refusing to receive the American envoy and had suspended economic relationships. The people were divided in their loyalties to either France or England. Adams focused on France and the diplomatic crisis known as the XYZ Affair. During his administration, Congress appropriated money to build three new frigates and additional ships, authorized the creation of a provisional army, and passed the Alien and Sedition Acts which were intended to drive foreign agents from the country and to maintain dominance over the Republican Party. When the war ended, Adams sent a peace mission to France. This angered the Republicans. The Election of 1800 pitted a unified and effective Republican Party against a divided and ineffective Federalist Party.

Thomas Jefferson won the election of 1800. Jefferson opposed a strong centralized government as a champion of States' Rights. He supported a strict interpretation of the Constitution. He reduced military expenditures, made budget cuts, and eliminated a tax on whiskey. At the same time, he reduced the national debt by one third. The Louisiana Purchase doubled the size of the nation. During his second term, the administration focused on keeping the US out of the Napoleonic Wars. Both the French and the British were seizing American ships and trying to deny the other access to trade with the US Jefferson's solution was to impose an embargo on all foreign commerce. The cost to the northeast was great and the embargo was both ineffective and unpopular.

Skill 10.2   Demonstrate knowledge of the importance of the Northwest Ordinances, identify major territorial, and analyze the causes and effects of westward expansion

In the United States, territorial expansion occurred in the move westward under the banner of "**Manifest Destiny,** the belief in the divinely given right of the nation to expand westward and incorporate more of the continent into the nation. This belief had been expressed, at the end of the Revolutionary War, in the demand that Britain cede all lands east of the Mississippi River to America. The goal of expanding westward was further confirmed with the **Northwest Ordinance** (1787) and the **Louisiana Purchase** (1803). Manifest Destiny was the justification for the Mexican-American War (1846-48), which resulted in the annexation of Texas and California, as well as much of the southwest. Due to the US involvement in the War with Mexico, the Spanish-American War, and support of the Latin American colonies of Spain in their revolt for independence, the Spanish colonies were successful in their fight for independence and self-government.

After the US purchased the Louisiana Territory, Jefferson appointed Captains Meriwether Lewis and William Clark to explore it, to find out exactly what had been bought. The Corps of Discovery went all the way to the Pacific Ocean, returning two years later with maps, journals, and artifacts. This led the way for future explorers to make available more knowledge about the territory and resulted in the Westward Movement and the later belief in the doctrine of Manifest Destiny. The US and Britain had shared the Oregon country. By the 1840s, with the increase in the free and slave populations and the demand of the settlers for control and government by the US, the conflict had to be resolved. In a treaty, signed in 1846, by both nations, a peaceful resolution occurred with Britain giving up its claims south of the 49th parallel.

The Red River cession was the next acquisition of land and came about as part of a treaty with Great Britain in 1818. It included parts of North and South Dakota and Minnesota. In 1819, Florida, both east and West, was ceded to the US by Spain along with parts of Alabama, Mississippi, and Louisiana. Texas was annexed in 1845, and after the war with Mexico in 1848, the government paid $15 million for what would become the states of California, Utah, and Nevada and parts of four other states.

In 1846, the Oregon Country was ceded to the US, which extended the western border to the Pacific Ocean. The northern US boundary was established at the 49th parallel. The states of Idaho, Oregon, and Washington were formed from this territory. In 1853, the Gadsden Purchase rounded out the present boundary of the 48 conterminous states with payment to Mexico of $10 million for land that makes up the present states of New Mexico and Arizona.

In the American southwest, the results were exactly the opposite. Spain had claimed this area since the 1540s, had spread northward from Mexico City, and in the 1700s had established missions, forts, villages, towns, and very large ranches. After the purchase of the Louisiana Territory in 1803, Americans began moving into Spanish territory. A few hundred American families in what is now Texas were allowed to live there but had to agree to become loyal subjects to Spain. In 1821, Mexico successfully revolted against Spanish rule, won independence, and chose to be more tolerant towards the American settlers and traders.

The Mexican government encouraged and allowed extensive trade and settlement, especially in Texas. Many of the new settlers were southerners and brought with them their slaves. Slavery was outlawed in Mexico and technically illegal in Texas, although the Mexican government much looked the other way.

Friction increased between land-hungry Americans swarming into western lands and the Mexican government, which controlled these lands. The clash was not only political but also cultural and economic. The Spanish influence permeated all parts of southwestern life: law, language, architecture, and customs. By this time, the doctrine of Manifest Destiny was in the hearts and on the lips of those seeking new areas of settlement and a new life. Americans were demanding US control of not only the Mexican Territory but also Oregon. Peaceful negotiations with Great Britain secured Oregon but it took two years of war to gain control of the southwestern US

In addition, the Mexican government owed debts to US citizens whose property was damaged or destroyed during its struggle for independence from Spain. By the time war broke out in 1845, Mexico had not paid its war debts. The government was weak, corrupt, ir'responsible, tom by revolutions, and not in decent financial shape. Mexico was also bitter over American expansion into Texas and the 1836 revolution, which resulted in Texas independence. In the 1844 Presidential election, the Democrats pushed for annexation of Texas and Oregon and after winning, they started the procedure to admit Texas to the Union.

When statehood occurred, diplomatic relations between the US and Mexico was ended. President Polk wanted US control of the entire southwest, from Texas to the Pacific Ocean. He sent a diplomatic mission with an offer to purchase New Mexico and Upper California but the Mexican government refused to even receive the diplomat. Consequently, in 1846, each nation claimed aggression on the part of the other and war was declared. The treaty signed in 1848 and a subsequent one in 1853 completed the southwestern boundary of the United States, reaching to the Pacific Ocean, as President Polk wished.

Skill 10.3   Demonstrate knowledge of the causes of the War of 1812 and analyze the significance of the war on the development of national identity

United States' unintentional and accidental involvement in what was known as the **War of 1812** came about due to the political and economic struggles between France and Great Britain. Napoleon's goal was complete conquest and control of Europe, including and especially Great Britain. Although British troops were temporarily driven off the mainland of Europe, the navy still controlled the seas, the seas across which France had to bring necessary products. America traded with both nations, especially with France and its colonies. The British decided to destroy the American trade with France, mainly for two reasons: (a) Products and goods from the US gave Napoleon what he needed to keep up his struggle with Britain. He and France were the enemy and it was felt that the Americans were aiding the Mother Country's enemy. (b) Britain felt threatened by the increasing strength and success of the US merchant fleet. They were becoming major competitors with the ship owners and merchants in Britain.

The British issued the **Orders in Council,** which was a series of measures prohibiting American ships from entering any French ports, not only in Europe but also in India and the West Indies. At the same time, Napoleon began efforts for a coastal blockade of the British Isles. He issued a series of Orders prohibiting all nations, including the United States, from trading with the British. He threatened seizure of every ship entering French ports after they stopped at any British port or colony, even threatening to seize every ship inspected by British cruisers or that paid any duties to their government. The British were stopping American ships and impressing American seamen to service on British ships and Americans were outraged.

In 1807, Congress passed the **Embargo Act** forbidding American ships from sailing to foreign ports. It couldn't be completely enforced and it really hurt business and trade in America so in 1809 it was repealed. Two additional acts passed by Congress after James Madison became president attempted to regulate trade with other nations and to get Britain and France to remove the restrictions they had put on American shipping. The catch was that whichever nation removed restrictions, the US agreed not to trade with the other one. Clever Napoleon was the first to do this, prompting Madison to issue orders prohibiting trade with Britain, ignoring warnings from the British not to do so. Of course, this didn't work either and although Britain eventually rescinded the Orders in Council, war came in June of 1812 and ended Christmas Eve, 1814, with the signing of the Treaty of Ghent. During the war, Americans were divided over not only whether it was necessary to even fight but also over what territories should be fought for and taken. The nation was still young and just not prepared for war. The primary American objective was to conquer Canada but it failed.

Two naval victories and one military victory stand out for the United States. Oliver Perry gained control of Lake Erie and Thomas MacDonough fought on Lake Champlain. Both of these naval battles successfully prevented the British invasion of the United States from Canada. Nevertheless, the troops landed below Washington on the Potomac, marched into the city, and burned the public buildings, including the White House. Andrew Jackson's victory at New Orleans was a great morale booster to Americans, giving them the impression the US had won the war. The battle actually took place after Britain and the United States had reached an agreement and it had no impact on the war's outcome. The peace treaty did little for the United States other than bringing peace, releasing prisoners of war, restoring all occupied territory, and setting up a commission to settle boundary disputes with Canada. Interestingly, the war proved to be a turning point in American history. European events had profoundly shaped US policies, especially foreign policies.

Skill 10.4   Recognize the origins of the Monroe Doctrine and its significance for the United States and for other nations of the hemisphere

In President Monroe's message to Congress on December 2, 1823, he delivered what we have always called the **Monroe Doctrine**. The United States was informing the powers of the Old World that the American continents were no longer open to European colonization and that any effort to extend European political influence into the New World would be considered by the United States "as dangerous to our peace and safety." The United States would not interfere in European wars or internal affairs and expected Europe to stay out of American affairs.

The ability of America to expand so much so fast was directly related to its having no real enemies or rivals for power on the continent. The native Indian populations were too unorganized and too weak to be able to stop it. In addition, the European powers were similarly forced out of the continent, a process that accelerated with defeat of Great Britain in the American Revolution. With America's growing power, it was able to proclaim the Monroe Doctrine, which prevented Europeans from infringing upon its territory. The only other countries that could possibly compete with the United States for hegemony on this continent, Mexico and Canada, were much less strong than the United States. Canada was then a semi-colony of Great Britain, even after it gained most of its independence. It remained sparsely populated and in any case, it had a similar culture and a similar economy to the United States. It also has a large area of uninhabited land to develop.

The only other power in this hemisphere, Mexico, posed no real problem for the United States. Though there was a conflict with Mexico in the middle of the 1800s over land issues owing to America's expansionist policy, it was no real contest. America was stronger and it remained a stronger nation than Mexico. By the 1880s, Secretary of State James G. Blaine pushed for expanding US trade and influence to Central and South America and in the 1890s, President Grover Cleveland invoked the Monroe Doctrine to intercede in Latin American affairs when it looked like Great Britain was going to exert its influence and power in the Western Hemisphere. In the Pacific, the United States lent its support to American sugar planters who overthrew the Kingdom of **Hawaii** and eventually annexed it as US territory.

Using the Monroe Doctrine of non-involvement of Europe in the affairs of the Western Hemisphere, President Roosevelt forced Italy, Germany, and Great Britain to remove their blockade of Venezuela; gained the rights to construct the **Panama Canal** by threatening force; assumed the finances of the Dominican Republic to stabilize it and prevent any intervention by Europeans; and in 1916 under President Woodrow Wilson US troops were sent to the Dominican Republic to keep order.

Skill 10.5 Demonstrate knowledge of Jacksonian Democracy, suffrage expansion, the rise of popular political culture, and the development of nationalism in the United States

The election of **Andrew Jackson** as President signaled a swing of the political pendulum from government influence of the wealthy, aristocratic Easterners to the interests of the Western farmers and pioneers and the era of the "common man." Jacksonian democracy was a policy of equal political power for all. After the War of 1812, Henry Clay and supporters favored economic measures that came to be known as the American System. This involved tariffs protecting American farmers and manufacturers from having to compete with foreign products, stimulating industrial growth and employment. With more people working, more farm products would be consumed, prosperous farmers would be able to buy more manufactured goods, and the additional monies from tariffs would make it possible for the government to make the needed internal improvements. To get this going, in 1816, Congress not only passed a high tariff, but also chartered a second Bank of the United States. Upon becoming President, Jackson fought to get rid of the bank.

One of the many duties of the bank was to regulate the supply of money for the nation. The President believed that the bank was a monopoly that favored the wealthy. Congress voted in 1832 to renew the bank's charter but Jackson vetoed the bill, withdrew the government's money, and the bank finally collapsed. Jackson also faced the "null and void," or nullification issue from South Carolina. Congress, in 1828, passed a law placing high tariffs on goods imported into the United States. Southerners, led by South Carolina's then Vice-President of the United States, John C. Calhoun, felt that the tariff favored the manufacturing interests of New England.
Calhoun denounced it as an abomination, and claimed that any state could nullify any of the federal laws it considered unconstitutional. The tariff was lowered in 1832, but not enough to satisfy South Carolina, which promptly threatened to secede from the Union. Although Jackson agreed with the rights of states, he also believed in preservation of the Union. A year later, the tariffs were lowered and the crisis was averted.

As the nation extended its borders into the lands west of the Mississippi, thousands of settlers streamed into this part of the country bringing with them ideas and concepts adapting them to the development of the unique characteristics of the region. Equality for everyone, as stated in the Declaration of Independence, did not yet apply to minority groups, black Americans or American Indians. Voting rights and the right to hold public office were restricted in varying degrees in each state. All of these factors decidedly affected the political, economic, and social life of the country and all three were focused in the attitudes of the three sections of the country on slavery.

European events had profoundly shaped US policies, especially foreign policies. After 1815, the US became much more independent from European influence and began to be treated with growing respect by European nations who were impressed by the fact that the young United States showed no hesitancy in going to war with the world's greatest naval power.

The Judiciary Act set up the US Supreme Court by providing for a Chief Justice and five associate justices. It also established federal district and circuit courts. One of the most important acts of Congress was the first 10 amendments to the Constitution, called the Bill of Rights, which emphasized and gave attention to the rights of individuals.

Under President John Adams, a minor diplomatic upset occurred with the government of France. By this time, the two major political parties called Federalists and Democratic-Republicans had fully developed. Hamilton and his mostly northern followers had formed the Federalist Party, which favored a strong central government and was sympathetic to Great Britain and its interests. The Democratic-Republican Party had been formed by Jefferson and his mostly Southern followers and they wanted a weak central government and stronger relations with and support of France. In 1798, the Federalists, in control of Congress, passed the **Alien and Sedition Acts**, written to silence vocal opposition. These acts made it a crime to voice any criticism of the President or Congress and unfairly treated all foreigners.

The legislatures of Kentucky and Virginia protested these laws, claiming they attacked freedoms and challenging their constitutionality. These Resolutions stated mainly the states had created the federal government, which was considered merely as an agent for the states and was limited to certain powers and could be criticized by the states, if warranted. They went further in stating that states' rights included the power to declare any act of Congress null and void if the states felt it unconstitutional. The controversy died down as the Alien and Sedition Acts expired, one by one, but the doctrine of states' rights was not finally settled until the Civil War.

After the US purchased the Louisiana Territory, Jefferson appointed Captains Meriwether Lewis and William Clark to explore it, to find out exactly what had been bought. The expedition went all the way to the Pacific Ocean, returning two years later with maps, journals, and artifacts. This led the way for future explorers to make available more knowledge about the territory and resulted in the Westward Movement and the later belief in the doctrine of Manifest Destiny.

The election of Andrew Jackson as President signaled a swing of the political pendulum from government influence of the wealthy, aristocratic Easterners to the interests of the Western farmers and pioneers and the era of the "common man." Jacksonian democracy was a policy of equal political power for all.

After the War of 1812, Henry Clay and supporters favored economic measures that came to be known as the American System. This involved tariffs protecting American farmers and manufacturers from having to compete with foreign products, stimulating industrial growth and employment. With more people working, more farm products would be consumed, prosperous farmers would be able to buy more manufactured goods, and the additional monies from tariffs would make it possible for the government to make the needed internal improvements. To get it going, in 1816, Congress not only passed a high tariff, but also chartered a second Bank of the United States. Upon becoming President, Jackson fought to get rid of the bank.

One of the many duties of the bank was to regulate the supply of money for the nation. The President believed that the bank was a monopoly that favored the wealthy. Congress voted in 1832 to renew the bank's charter but Jackson vetoed the bill, withdrew the government's money, and the bank finally collapsed.

Jackson also faced the "null and void," or nullification issue from South Carolina. Congress, in 1828, passed a law placing high tariffs on goods imported into the United States. Southerners, led by South Carolina's then Vice-President of the US, John C. Calhoun, felt that the tariff favored the manufacturing interests of New England, denounced it as an abomination, and claimed that any state could nullify any of the federal laws it considered unconstitutional. The tariff was lowered in 1832, but not far enough to satisfy South Carolina, which promptly threatened to secede from the Union. Although Jackson agreed with the rights of states, he also believed in preservation of the Union. A year later, the tariffs were lowered and the crisis was averted.

Skill 10.6 Demonstrate knowledge of the concept of Manifest Destiny and the causes and consequences of the Mexican War

In the United States, territorial expansion occurred in the expansion westward under the banner of **Manifest Destiny,** the belief in the divinely given right of the nation to expand westward and incorporate more of the continent into the nation. This belief had been expressed, at the end of the Revolutionary War, in the demand that Britain cede all lands east of the Mississippi River to America. The goal of expanding westward was further confirmed with the Northwest Ordinance (1787) and the Louisiana Purchase (1803). Manifest Destiny was the justification for the Mexican-American war (1846-48), which resulted in the annexation of Texas and California, as well as much of the southwest. Due to the US involvement in the War with Mexico, the Spanish-American War, and support of the Latin American colonies of Spain in their revolt for independence, the Spanish colonies were successful in their fight for independence and self-government.

After the US purchased the Louisiana Territory, Jefferson appointed **Captains Meriwether Lewis** and **William Clark** to explore it, to find out exactly what had been bought. The Corps of Discovery went all the way to the Pacific Ocean, returning two years later with maps, journals, and artifacts. This led the way for future explorers to make available more knowledge about the territory and resulted in the Westward Movement and the later belief in the doctrine of Manifest Destiny. The US and Britain had shared the Oregon country. By the 1840s, with the increase in the free and slave populations and the demand of the settlers for control and government by the US, the conflict had to be resolved. In a treaty, signed in 1846 by both nations, a peaceful resolution occurred with Britain giving up its claims south of the 49th parallel.

In the American southwest, the results were exactly the opposite. Spain had claimed this area since the 1540s, had spread northward from Mexico City, and in the 1700s had established missions, forts, villages, towns, and very large ranches. After the purchase of the Louisiana Territory in 1803, Americans began moving into Spanish territory. A few hundred American families in what is now Texas were allowed to live there but had to agree to become loyal subjects to Spain. In 1821, Mexico successfully revolted against Spanish rule, won independence, and chose to be more tolerant towards the American settlers and traders.

The Mexican government encouraged and allowed extensive trade and settlement, especially in Texas. Many of the new settlers were southerners and brought with them their slaves. Slavery was outlawed in Mexico and technically illegal in Texas, although the Mexican government pretty much looked the other way.

Friction increased between land-hungry Americans swarming into western lands and the Mexican government, which controlled these lands. The clash was not only political but also cultural and economic. The Spanish influence permeated all parts of southwestern life: law, language, architecture, and customs. By this time, the doctrine of Manifest Destiny was in the hearts and on the lips of those seeking new areas of settlement and a new life. Americans were demanding US control of not only the Mexican Territory but also Oregon. Peaceful negotiations with Great Britain secured Oregon but it took two years of war to gain control of the southwestern US

In addition, the Mexican government owed debts to US citizens whose property was damaged or destroyed during its struggle for independence from Spain. By the time war broke out in 1845, Mexico had not paid its war debts. The government was weak, corrupt, ir'responsible, torn by revolutions, and not in decent financial shape. Mexico was also bitter over American expansion into Texas and the 1836 revolution, which resulted in Texan independence. In the 1844 Presidential election, the Democrats pushed for annexation of Texas and Oregon and after winning, they started the procedure to admit Texas to the Union.

When statehood occurred, diplomatic relations between the US and Mexico was ended. President Polk wanted US control of the entire southwest, from Texas to the Pacific Ocean. He sent a diplomatic mission with an offer to purchase New Mexico and Upper California but the Mexican government refused to even receive the diplomat. Consequently, in 1846, each nation claimed aggression on the part of the other and war was declared. The treaty signed in 1848 and a subsequent one in 1853 completed the southwestern boundary of the United States, reaching to the Pacific Ocean, as President Polk wished.

Skill 10.7 **Demonstrate knowledge of the rise of New York City, the development of the nation's infrastructure and the effects of industrialization on the economy and society of the new nation**

New York City has played a critical role in the development of the State of New York and the nation in many capacities. The huge harbor made the city an important port in colonial times. The construction of the wooden wall that was intended to keep out aggressors became both an actual and a symbolic center of economy and commerce. The tree at the end of the street where traders and dealers gathered informally later became the site of the New York Stock Exchange. This marked the beginning of New York's importance in the state's economy and the national economy. In time, it made the city a central point in international economy.

The construction of the **Erie Canal**, completed in 1825, further enhanced the importance of the port of New York. It was replaced in 1918 by the Barge Canal. This system of waterways was later expanded even more with the construction of the St. Lawrence Seaway. Transportation on land developed very quickly after the construction of a system of turnpikes, beginning in the 1880s. By 1853, railroads crossed the state and connected to those that crossed the nation.

New York City has one of the largest regional economies in the nation. It is a global center for business and commerce. With London, Hong Kong, Paris and Tokyo, New York City is one of the main cities that control world finance. Many consider it the financial capital of the world. In addition to finance and commerce, New York City is critical to the insurance and real estate industries. It is also the single most important center for publishing, mass media and journalism in the country. In addition, it is critical in medical research, technology, fashion and the arts. More Fortune 500 companies are based in New York City than any other city in the nation. Many international companies are also headquartered in the city.

New York City has historically been the **point of entry** into the US for millions of immigrants. This made the city a major haven for oppressed people throughout the world and the point of entry that made the nation the melting pot that it is. The decision to locate the headquarters of the United Nations in New York has also made it a critical center of international politics and democracy.

As one of the first colonized areas in the nation, New York was a major point of entry for immigrants. The melding of the Dutch, French and British settlers into a unified colony was the first step along the way to becoming the melting pot that New York has been to this day. The large harbor and the growing reputation of the state for business, industry, and commerce, made New York a place of special opportunity for immigrants who were seeking freedom and opportunity.

The development of **Ellis Island** as an immigrant processing center made it the point of entry for millions who came to America in search of political or religious freedom, safe haven from political oppression, and the quest for the American dream. The gift of the Statue of Liberty, and its placement in New York harbor, made New York the symbol of American opportunity and freedom.

As African Americans left the rural South and migrated to the North in search of opportunity, many settled in Harlem in New York City. By the 1920s Harlem had become a center of life and activity for persons of color. The music, art, and literature of this community gave birth to a cultural movement known as **the Harlem Renaissance**. The artistic expressions that emerged from this community in the 1920s and 1930s celebrated the black experience, black traditions, and the voices of black America. Major writers and works of this movement included Langston Hughes (*The Weary Blues*), Nella Larsen (*Passing*), Zora Neale Hurston (*Their Eyes Were Watching God*), Claude McKay, Countee Cullen, and Jean Toomer.

Throughout the history of America, New York has welcomed people from all parts of the world and created within the state a truly international and unique cultural mecca. To be sure, some groups of immigrants created their own subcultures within the state. Many of those continue today. Through the port of New York and the city's ability to acclimate and absorb immigrants and provide them a living, the nation has welcomed a population that has been repeatedly enriched by the cultural mix.

Skill 10.8   Demonstrate knowledge of the major reform movements of the first half of the nineteenth century, identify key reform figures, and analyze the effects of the reform movements on US society

Many **social reform movements** began in the United States including education, women's rights, labor, and working conditions, temperance, prisons and insane asylums. But the most intense and controversial was the abolitionists' efforts to end slavery, an effort alienating and splitting the country, hardening Southern defense of slavery, and leading to four years of bloody war. The **abolitionist movement** had political fallout, affecting admittance of states into the Union and the government's continued efforts to keep a balance between total numbers of free and slave states. Congressional legislation after 1820 reflected this.

Religion has always been a factor in American life. Many early settlers came to America in search of religious freedom. Religion, particularly Christianity, was an essential element of the value and belief structure shared by the Founding Fathers. Yet the Constitution prescribes a separation of Church and State.

The **First Great Awakening** was a religious movement within American Protestantism in the 1730s and 1740s. This was primarily a movement among Puritans seeking a return to strict interpretation of morality and values as well as emphasizing the importance and power of personal religious or spiritual experience. Many historians believe the First Great Awakening unified the people of the original colonies and supported the independence of the colonists.

The **Second Great Awakening** (the Great Revival) was a broad movement within American Protestantism that led to several kinds of activities that were distinguished by region and denominational tradition. In general terms, the Second Great Awakening, which began in the 1820s, was a time of recognition that "awakened religion" must weed out sin on both a personal and a social level. It inspired a wave of social activism. In New England, the Congregationalists established missionary societies to evangelize the West. Publication and education societies arose, most notably the American Bible Society.

This social activism gave rise to the temperance movement, prison reform efforts, help for the handicapped and mentally ill. This period was particularly notable for the abolition movement. In the Appalachian region, the camp meeting was used to revive religion. The camp meeting became a primary method of evangelizing new territory.

The **Third Great Awakening** (the Missionary Awakening) gave rise to the Social Gospel Movement. This period (1858 to 1908) resulted in a massive growth in membership of all major Protestant denominations through their missionary activities. This movement was partly a response to claims that the Bible was fallible. Many churches attempted to reconcile or change biblical teaching to fit scientific theories and discoveries. Colleges associated with Protestant churches began to appear rapidly throughout the nation. In terms of social and political movements, the Third Great Awakening was the most expansive and profound. Coinciding with many changes in production and labor, it won battles against child labor and stopped the exploitation of women in factories. Compulsory elementary education for children came from this movement, as did the establishment of a set work day. Much was also done to protect and rescue children from abandonment and abuse, to improve the care of the sick, to prohibit the use of alcohol and tobacco, as well as numerous other "social ills."

Skilled laborers were organized into a labor union called the **American Federation of Labor**, in an effort to gain better working conditions and wages for its members. Farmers joined organizations such as the National Grange and Farmers Alliances. Farmers were producing more food than people could afford to buy. This was the result of (1) new farmlands rapidly opening on the plains and prairies, and (2) development and availability of new farm machinery and newer and better methods of farming.

American **women** began actively campaigning for the right to vote. Elizabeth Cady Stanton and Susan B. Anthony in 1869 founded the organization called National Women Suffrage Association the same year the Wyoming Territory gave women the right to vote. Soon after, a few states followed by giving women the right to vote, limited to local elections only.

Governmental reform began with the passage of the Civil Service Act, also known as the Pendleton Act. It provided for the Civil Service Commission, a federal agency responsible for giving jobs based on merit rather than as political rewards or favors. Another successful reform was the adoption of the secret ballot in voting, as were such measures as the direct primary, referendum, recall, and direct election of US Senators by the people rather than by their state legislatures. Following the success of reforms made at the national level, the progressives were successful in gaining reforms in government at state and local levels.

Following is just a partial list of well-known Americans who contributed their leadership and talents in various fields and reforms:

Lucretia Mott and **Elizabeth Cady Stanton** for women's rights

Emma Hart Willard, Catharine Esther Beecher, and **Mary Lyon** for education for women

Dr. Elizabeth Blackwell, the first woman doctor

Antoinette Louisa Blackwell, the first female minister

Dorothea Lynde Dix for reforms in prisons and insane asylums

Elihu Burritt and **William Ladd** for peace movements

Robert Owen for a Utopian society

Horace Mann, Henry Barmard, Calvin E. Stowe, Caleb Mills, and **John Swett** for public education

Benjamin Lundy, David Walker, William Lloyd Garrison, Isaac Hooper, Arthur and Lewis Tappan, Theodore Weld, Frederick Douglass, Harriet Tubman, James G. Birney, Henry Highland Garnet, James Forten, Robert Purvis, Harriet Beecher Stowe, Wendell Phillips, and John Brown for abolition of slavery and the **Underground Railroad**

Louisa Mae Alcott, James Fenimore Cooper, Washington Irving, Walt Whitman, Henry David Thoreau, Ralph Waldo Emerson, Herman Melville, Richard Henry Dana, Nathaniel Hawthorne, Henry Wadsworth Longfellow, John Greenleaf Whittier, Edgar Allan Poe, Oliver Wendell Holmes, famous writers

John C. Fremont, Zebulon Pike, Kit Carson, explorers

Henry Clay, Daniel Webster, Stephen Douglas, John C. Calhoun, American statesmen

Robert Fulton, Cyrus McCormick, Eli Whitney, inventors

Noah Webster, American dictionary and spellers

COMPETENCY 11.0 UNDERSTAND THE ORIGINS, EVENTS, AND EFFECTS OF THE CIVIL WAR AND RECONSTRUCTION AND THE GROWTH AND DEVELOPMENT OF THE UNITED STATES THROUGH THE BEGINNING OF THE TWENTIETH CENTURY

Skill 11.1 Analyze the emergence of states' rights ideology and the development of sectionalism, the emergence of slavery as a national issue, the economic differences between the North and the South, and efforts to resolve North-South divisions

At the Constitutional Convention, one of the slavery compromises concerned counting slaves for deciding the number of representatives for the House and the amount of taxes to be paid. Southerners pushed for counting the slaves for representation but not for taxes. The Northerners pushed for the opposite. The resulting compromise, sometimes referred to as the "**three-fifths compromise**," was that both groups agreed that three-fifths of the slaves would be counted for both taxes and representation.

The other compromise over slavery was part of the disputes over how much regulation the central government would control over commercial activities such as trade with other nations and the slave trade. It was agreed that Congress would regulate commerce with other nations including taxing imports. Southerners were worried about taxing slaves coming into the country and the possibility of Congress prohibiting the slave trade altogether. The agreement reached allowed the states to continue importation of slaves for the next 20 years until 1808, at which time Congress would make the decision as to the future of the slave trade. During the 20-year period, no more than $10 per person could be levied on slaves coming into the country.

An additional provision of this compromise was that with the admission of Missouri, slavery would not be allowed in the rest of the Louisiana Purchase territory north of latitude 36 degrees 30'. This was acceptable to the Southern Congressmen since it was not profitable to grow cotton on land north of this latitude line anyway. It was thought that the crisis had been resolved but in the next year, it was discovered that in its state constitution, Missouri discriminated against the free blacks. Anti-slavery supporters in Congress went into an uproar, determined to exclude Missouri from the Union. Henry Clay, known as the Great Compromiser, then proposed a second Missouri Compromise, which was acceptable to everyone. His proposal stated that the Constitution of the United States guaranteed protections and privileges to citizens of states and Missouri's proposed constitution could not deny these to any of its citizens. The acceptance in 1820 of this second compromise opened the way for Missouri's statehood--a temporary reprieve only.

These two "slavery' compromises were a necessary concession to have Southern support and approval for the new document and new government. Many Americans felt that the system of slavery would eventually die out in the US, but by 1808, cotton was becoming increasingly important in the primarily agricultural South and the institution of slavery had become firmly entrenched in Southern culture. It is also evident that as early as the Constitutional Convention, active anti-slavery feelings and opinions were very strong, leading to extremely active groups and societies.

By 1815, the Industrial Revolution had fully reached the United States, and the largely urban northern section of the country gained the most advantage. The northern coastal regions were never blessed with large agricultural areas, and industry took hold in the urban centers, primarily in the production of cotton and woolen cloth, shoes, and machinery. With the development of industry came capital and banking, and northern cities like New York became centers of investment and trade. Labor in the growing industrial centers was supplied mainly by European immigrants.

By contrast, the South was still largely rural and relied on agriculture supported by slave labor. Cotton and tobacco were the mainstays of the southern economy, which relied on the North for capital and manufactured goods, as well as a market for its raw materials. The southern system, reliant upon slavery as it was, also required significant political influence to protect the institution from northern anti-slavery interests. The south had enjoyed a prominent presence in the federal government during the decades since independence.

The industrial North was gaining in political activity, however, and in 1856 the Republican Party was founded to represent northern economic interests. The Republican presidential candidate in 1860 was Abraham Lincoln, who would preside over the coming Civil War, in which the agrarian southern economy was devastated by war and the loss of its supply of slave labor. The war would also prove a boon to northern industry during and after the fighting.

The doctrine of **nullification** states that the states have the right to "nullify" – declare invalid – any act of Congress they believed to be unjust or unconstitutional. The nullification crisis of the mid-nineteenth century climaxed over a new tariff on imported manufactured goods that was enacted by the Congress in 1828. While this tariff protected the manufacturing and industrial interests of the North, it placed an additional burden of cost on the South, which was only affected by the tariff as consumers of manufactured goods. The North had become increasingly economically dependent on industry and manufacturing, while the South had become increasingly agricultural. Despite the fact that the tariff was primarily intended to protect northern manufacturing interests in the face of imports from other countries, the effect on the South was to simply raise the prices of needed goods.

This issue of disagreement reached its climax when John C. Calhoun, Jackson's vice president, led South Carolina to adopt the Ordinance of Nullification, which declared the tariff null and void within state borders. Although this issue came to the brink of military action, it was resolved by the enactment of a new tariff in 1832.

When economic issues and the issue of slavery came to a head, the North declared slavery illegal. The South acted on the principles of the doctrine of nullification, declared the new laws null, and acted upon their presumed right as states to **secede** from the union and form their own government. The North saw secession as a violation of the national unity and contract

Skill 11.2   Identify important events leading to the Civil War and examine Abraham Lincoln's efforts to preserve the Union

The slavery issue flared again and was not to be done away with until the end of the Civil War. It was obvious that newly acquired territory would be divided up into territories and later become states. Factions of Northerners advocated prohibition of slavery and Southerners favored slavery. A third faction arose supporting the doctrine of **popular sovereignty** which stated that people living in territories and states should be allowed to decide for themselves whether or not slavery should be permitted. In 1849, California applied for admittance to the Union and the furor began.

The result was the **Compromise of 1850**, a series of laws designed as a final solution to the issue. Concessions made to the North included the admission of California as a free state and the abolition of slave trading in Washington, D.C. The laws also provided for the creation of the New Mexico and Utah territories. As a concession to Southerners, the residents there would decide whether to permit slavery when these two territories became states. In addition, Congress authorized implementation of stricter measures to capture runaway slaves.

A few years later, Congress took up consideration of new territories between Missouri and present-day Idaho. Again, heated debate over permitting slavery in these areas flared up. Those opposed to slavery used the **Missouri Compromise** to prove their point showing that the land being considered for territories was part of the area the Compromise had been designated as banned to slavery. On May 25, 1854, Congress passed the infamous **Kansas-Nebraska Act** which nullified the provision creating the territories of Kansas and Nebraska. This provided for the people of these two territories to decide for themselves whether or not to permit slavery to exist there. Feelings were so deep and divided that any further attempts to compromise would meet with little, if any, success. Political and social turmoil swirled everywhere. Kansas was called "Bleeding Kansas" because of the extreme violence and bloodshed throughout the territory because two governments existed there, one pro-slavery and the other anti-slavery.

The Supreme Court in 1857 handed down a decision guaranteed to galvanize the country. **Dred Scott** was a slave whose owner had taken him from slave state Missouri, then to free state Illinois, into Minnesota Territory, free under the provisions of the Missouri Compromise, then finally back to slave state Missouri. Abolitionists pursued the dilemma by presenting a court case, stating that since Scott had lived in a free state and free territory, he was in actuality a free man. Two lower courts had ruled before the Supreme Court became involved, one ruling in favor and one against. The Supreme Court decided that residing in a free state and free territory did not make Scott a free man because Scott (and all other slaves) was not an US citizen or a state citizen of Missouri. Therefore, he did not have the right to sue in state or federal courts. The Court went a step further and ruled that the old Missouri Compromise was now unconstitutional because Congress did not have the power to prohibit slavery in the Territories.

Anti-slavery supporters were stunned. They had just recently formed the new Republican Party and one of its platforms was keeping slavery out of the Territories. Now, according to the decision in the Dred Scott case, this basic party principle was unconstitutional. The only way to ban slavery in new areas was by a Constitutional amendment, requiring ratification by three-fourths of all states. At this time, this was out of the question because the supporters would be unable to get a majority due to Southern opposition.

In 1858, **Abraham Lincoln** and **Stephen A. Douglas** were running for the office of US Senator from Illinois and participated in a series of debates, which directly affected the outcome of the 1860 Presidential election. Douglas, a Democrat, was up for re-election and knew that if he won this race, he had a good chance of becoming President in 1860. Lincoln, a Republican, was not an abolitionist but he believed that slavery was morally wrong and he firmly believed in and supported the Republican Party principle that slavery must not be allowed to extend any further.

Douglas, on the other hand, originated the doctrine of "popular sovereignty" and was responsible for supporting and getting through Congress the inflammatory Kansas-Nebraska Act. In the course of the debates, Lincoln challenged Douglas to show that popular sovereignty reconciled with the Dred Scott decision. Either way he answered Lincoln, Douglas would lose crucial support from one group or the other. If he supported the Dred Scott decision, Southerners would support him but he would lose Northern support. If he stayed with popular sovereignty, Northern support would be his but Southern support would be lost. His reply to Lincoln, stating that Territorial legislatures could exclude slavery by refusing to pass laws supporting it, gave him enough support and approval to be re-elected to the Senate. But it cost him the Democratic nomination for President in 1860.

In 1859, **abolitionist John Brown** and his followers seized the federal arsenal at Harper's Ferry in what is now West Virginia. His purpose was to take the guns stored in the arsenal, give them to slaves nearby, and lead them in a widespread rebellion. He and his men were captured by Colonel Robert E. Lee of the United States Army and after a trial with a guilty verdict, he was hanged. Most Southerners felt that the majority of Northerners approved of Brown's actions but in actuality, most of them were stunned and shocked. Southern newspapers took great pains to quote a small but well-known minority of abolitionists who applauded and supported Brown's actions.

The final straw came with the election of Lincoln to the Presidency the next year. Due to a split in the Democratic Party, there were four candidates from four political parties. With Lincoln receiving a minority of the popular vote and a majority of electoral votes, the Southern states, one by one, voted to secede from the Union, as they had promised they would do if Lincoln and the Republicans were victorious. The die was cast.

It is ironic that South Carolina was the first state to secede from the Union and the first shots of the war were fired on Fort Sumter in Charleston Harbor. Both sides quickly prepared for war. The North had more in its favor: a larger population; superiority in finances and transportation facilities; manufacturing, agricultural, and natural resources. The North possessed most of the nation's gold, had about 92% of all industries, and almost all known supplies of copper, coal, iron, and various other minerals. Most of the nation's railroads were in the North and mid-West, allowing men and supplies to be moved wherever needed; food could be transported from the farms of the mid-West to workers in the East and to soldiers on the battlefields. Trade with nations overseas could go on as usual due to control of the navy and the merchant fleet. The Northern states numbered 24 and included western (California and Oregon) and border (Maryland, Delaware, Kentucky, Missouri, and West Virginia) states.

The Southern states numbered eleven and included South Carolina, Georgia, Florida, Alabama, Mississippi, Louisiana, Texas, Virginia, North Carolina, Tennessee, and Arkansas, making up the Confederacy. Although outnumbered in population, the South was completely confident of victory. They knew that all they had to do was fight a defensive war and protect their own territory. The North had to invade and defeat an area almost the size of Western Europe. They figured the North would tire of the struggle and give up. Another advantage of the South was that a number of its best officers had graduated from the US Military Academy at West Point and had had long years of army experience. Many had exercised varying degrees of command in the Indian Wars and the war with Mexico. Men from the South were conditioned to living outdoors and were more familiar with horses and firearms than men from northeastern cities. Since cotton was such an important crop, Southerners felt that British and French textile mills were so dependent on raw cotton that they would be forced to help the Confederacy in the war.

Skill 11.3   Recognize major and key figures of the Civil War and analyze the significance of the Emancipation Proclamation

The major military and political turning points of the war.

The war strategies for both sides were relatively clear and simple. The South planned a defensive war, wearing down the North until it agreed to peace on Southern terms. The only exception was to gain control of Washington, D.C., go north through the Shenandoah Valley into Maryland and Pennsylvania in order to drive a wedge between the Northeast and mid-West, interrupt the lines of communication, and end the war quickly.

The North had three basic strategies:

1. Blockade the Confederate coastline in order to cripple the South;
2. Seize control of the Mississippi River and interior railroad lines to split the Confederacy in two;
3. Seize the Confederate capital of Richmond, Virginia, driving southward joining up with Union forces coming east from the Mississippi Valley.

The South won decisively until the Battle of Gettysburg, July 1 - 3, 1863. Until Gettysburg, Lincoln's commanders, McDowell and McClellan, were less than desirable, Burnside and Hooker, not what was needed. Lee, on the other hand, had many able officers, including Jackson and Stuart, who he depended on heavily. Jackson died at Chancellorsville and was replaced by Longstreet. Lee decided to invade the North and depended on J.E.B. Stuart and his cavalry to keep him informed of the location of Union troops and their strengths. Four things worked against Lee at Gettysburg:

1) The Union troops gained the best positions and the best ground first, making it easier to make a stand there.

2) Lee's move into Northern territory put him and his army a long way from food and supply lines. They were more or less on their own.

3) Lee thought that his Army of Northern Virginia was invincible and could fight and win under any conditions or circumstances.

4) Stuart and his men did not arrive at Gettysburg until the end of the second day of fighting and by then, it was too little too late. He and the men had had to detour around Union soldiers and he was delayed getting the information Lee needed.

Consequently, he made the mistake of failing to listen to Longstreet and following the strategy of regrouping back into Southern territory to the supply lines. Lee felt that regrouping was retreating and almost an admission of defeat. He was convinced the army would be victorious. Longstreet was concerned about the Union troops occupying the best positions and felt that regrouping to a better position would be an advantage. He was also very concerned about the distance from supply lines.

The Civil War took more American lives than any other war in history, the South losing one-third of its soldiers in battle compared to about one-sixth for the North. More than half of the total deaths were caused by disease and the horrendous conditions of field hospitals. Both sections paid a tremendous economic price but the South suffered more severely from direct damages. Destruction was pervasive: towns, farms, trade, industry, and the lives and homes of men, women, and children were destroyed and an entire Southern way of life was lost. The deep resentment, bitterness, and hatred that remained for generations gradually lessened as the years went by but legacies of it surface and remain to this day. The South had no voice in the political, social, and cultural affairs of the nation, lessening to a great degree the influence of the more traditional Southern ideals. The Northern Yankee Protestant ideals of hard work, education, and economic freedom became the standard of the United States and helped influence the development of the nation into a modem, industrial power.

The effects of the Civil War were tremendous. It changed the methods of waging war and has been called the first modern war. It introduced weapons and tactics that, when improved later, were used extensively in wars of the late 1800s and 1900s. Civil War soldiers were the first to fight in trenches, first to fight under a unified command, first to wage a defense called "major cordon defense," a strategy of advance on all fronts. They were also the first to use repeating and breech-loading weapons. Observation balloons were first used during the war along with submarines, ironclad ships, and mines.

Telegraphy and railroads were put to use first in the Civil War. It was considered a modern war because of the vast destruction and was "total war", involving the use of all resources of the opposing sides. There was probably no way it could have ended other than total defeat and unconditional surrender of one side or the other.

By executive proclamation and constitutional amendment, slavery was officially and finally ended, although there remained deep prejudice and racism, which still raises its ugly head today. Also, the Union was preserved and the states were finally truly united. Sectionalism, especially in the area of politics, remained strong for another 100 years but not to the degree and with the violence as existed before 1861. It has been noted that the Civil War may have been American democracy's greatest failure in that from 1861 to 1865 reason, which is basic to democracy, fell to human passion. Yet, democracy did survive.

The victory of the North established that no state has the right to end or leave the Union. Because of unity, the US became a major global power. Lincoln never proposed to punish the South. He was most concerned with restoring the South to the Union in a program that was flexible and practical rather than rigid and unbending. In fact, he never really felt that the states had succeeded in leaving the Union but that they had left the 'family circle" for a short time. His plans consisted of two major steps:

All Southerners taking an oath of allegiance to the Union promising to accept all federal laws and proclamations dealing with slavery would receive a full pardon. The only ones excluded from this were men who had resigned from civil and military positions in the federal government to serve in the Confederacy, those who were part of the Confederate government, those in the Confederate army above the rank of lieutenant, and Confederates who were guilty of mistreating prisoners of war and blacks.

A state would be able to write a new constitution, elect new officials, and return to the Union fully equal to all other states on certain conditions: a minimum number of persons (at least 10% of those who were qualified voters in their states before secession from the Union who had voted in the 1860 election) must take an oath of allegiance.

The economic and social chaos in the South after the war was unbelievable with starvation and disease rampant, especially in the cities. The US Army provided some relief of food and clothing for both white and blacks but the major responsibility fell to the Freedmen's Bureau. Though the bureau agents to a certain extent helped southern whites, their main responsibility was to the freed slaves. They were to assist the freedmen to become self-supporting and protect them from being taken advantage of by others. Northerners looked on it as a real, honest effort to help the South out of the chaos it was in. Most white Southerners charged the bureau with causing racial friction, deliberately encouraging the freedmen to consider former owners as enemies.

After the Civil War the **Emancipation Proclamation** in 1863 and the 13th Amendment in 1865 ended slavery in the United States, but these measures did not erase the centuries of racial prejudices among whites that held blacks to be inferior in intelligence and morality. These prejudices, along with fear of economic competition from newly freed slaves, led to a series of state laws that permitted or required businesses, landlords, school boards and others to physically segregate blacks and whites in their everyday lives.

Skill 11.4   Analyze major challenges, events, and outcomes of the Reconstruction period

Following the Civil War, the nation was faced with repairing the torn Union and readmitting the Confederate states. **Reconstruction** refers to this period between 1865 and 1877 when the federal and state governments debated and implemented plans to provide civil rights to freed slaves and to set the terms under which the former Confederate states might once again join the Union.

Planning for Reconstruction began early in the war, in 1861. Abraham Lincoln's Republican Party in Washington favored the extension of voting rights to black men, but was divided as to how far to extend the right. Moderates, such as Lincoln, wanted only literate blacks and those who had fought for the Union to be allowed to vote. Radical Republicans wanted to extend the vote to all black men. Conservative Democrats did not want to give black men the vote at all. In the case of former Confederate soldiers, moderates wanted to allow all but former leaders to vote, while the radicals wanted to require an oath from all eligible voters that they had never borne arms against the US, which would have excluded all former rebels. On the issue of readmission into the Union, moderates favored a much lower standard, with the radicals demanding nearly impossible conditions for rebel states to return.

Lincoln's moderate plan for Reconstruction was actually part of his effort to win the war. Lincoln and the moderates felt that if it remained easy for states to return to the Union, and if moderate proposals on black suffrage were made, that Confederate states involved in the hostilities might be swayed to re-join the Union rather than continue fighting. The radical plan was to ensure that Reconstruction did not actually start until after the war was over.

In 1863 Abraham Lincoln was assassinated, leaving his Vice President Andrew Johnson to oversee the beginning of the actual implementation of Reconstruction. Johnson struck a moderate pose and was willing to allow former confederates to keep control of their state governments. These governments quickly enacted Black Codes that denied the vote to blacks and granted them only limited civil rights.

The radical Republicans in Congress responded to the **Black Codes** by continuing their hard line on allowing former rebel states back into the Union. In addition, they sought to override the Black Codes by granting US citizenship to blacks by passing a civil rights bill. Johnson, supported by Democrats, vetoed the bill, but Congress had the necessary votes to override it, and the bill became law.

In 1866, the radical Republicans won control of Congress and passed the Reconstruction Acts, which placed the governments of the southern states under the control of the federal military. With this backing, the Republicans began to implement their radical policies such as granting all black men the vote and denying the vote to former confederate soldiers. Congress had passed the 13th, 14th and 15th amendments granting citizenship and civil rights to blacks and made ratification of these amendments a condition of readmission into the Union by the rebel states. The Republicans found support in the South among Freedmen, as former slaves were called, white southerners who had not supported the Confederacy, called Scalawags, and northerners who had moved to the south, known as **Carpetbaggers**.

Federal troops were stationed throughout the South and protected Republicans who took control of Southern governments. Bitterly resentful, white Southerners fought the new political system by joining a secret society called the Ku Klux Klan, using violence to keep black Americans from voting and getting equality. However, before being allowed to rejoin the Union, the Confederate states were required to agree to all federal laws. Between 1866 and 1870, all of them had returned to the Union, but Northern interest in Reconstruction was fading. Reconstruction officially ended when the last Federal troops left the South in 1877. It can be said that Reconstruction had a limited success as it set up public school systems and expanded legal rights of black Americans.

Under President Rutherford B. Hayes, the federal troops were removed from the South. Without this support, the Republican governments were replaced by so-called Redeemer governments, who promised the restoration of the vote to those whites who had been denied it and limitations on civil rights for blacks.

The rise of the Redeemer governments marked the beginning of the **Jim Crow** laws and official segregation. Blacks were still allowed to vote, but ways were found to make it difficult for them to do so, such as literacy tests and poll taxes. Reconstruction, which had set as its goal the reunification of the South with the North and the granting of civil rights to freed slaves, was a limited success, at best, and in the eyes of blacks was considered a failure.

Segregation laws were foreshadowed in the **Black Codes** strict laws proposed by some southern states during the Reconstruction Period that sought to essentially recreate the conditions of pre-war servitude. Under these codes, blacks were to remain subservient to their white employers and were subject to fines and beatings if they failed to work. Freedmen, as newly freed slaves were called, were afforded some civil rights protection during the Reconstruction period, but beginning around 1876, so called Redeemer governments began to take office in southern states after the removal of Federal troops that had supported Reconstruction goals. The Redeemer state legislatures began passing segregation laws, which came to be known as Jim Crow laws.

The Jim Crow laws varied from state to state, but the most significant of them required separate school systems and libraries for blacks and whites and separate ticket windows, waiting rooms and seating areas on trains and, later, other public transportation. Restaurant owners were permitted or sometimes required to provide separate entrances and tables and counters for blacks and whites, so that the two races weren't visible to one another while dining. Public parks and playgrounds were constructed for each race. Landlords were not allowed to mix black and white tenants in apartment houses in some states. The Jim Crow laws were given credibility in 1896 when the Supreme Court handed down its decision in the case *Plessy vs. Ferguson*. In 1890, Louisiana had passed a law requiring separate train cars for blacks and whites. To challenge this law, in 1892 Homer Plessy, a man who had a black great grandparent and so was considered legally black in that state, purchased a ticket in the white section and took his seat. Upon informing the conductor that he was black, he was told to move to the black car. He refused and was arrested. His case was eventually elevated to the Supreme Court.

The Court ruled against Plessy, thereby ensuring that the Jim Crow laws would continue to proliferate and be enforced. The Court held that segregating races was not unconstitutional as long as the facilities for each were identical. This became known as the "separate but equal" principle. In practice, facilities were seldom equal. Black schools were not funded at the same level, for instance. Streets and parks in black neighborhoods were not maintained.

Paralleling the development of segregation legislation in the mid-nineteenth century was the appearance of organized groups opposed to any integration of blacks into white society. The most notable of these was the **Ku Klux Klan.** First organized in the Reconstruction south, the KKK was a loose group made up mainly of former Confederate soldiers who opposed the Reconstruction government and espoused a doctrine of white supremacy. KKK members intimidated and sometimes killed their proclaimed enemies. The first KKK was never completely organized, despite having nominal leadership. In 1871, President Grant took action to use federal troops to halt the activities of the KKK and actively prosecuted them in federal court. Klan activity waned and the organization disappeared.

The **13th Amendment** abolished slavery and involuntary servitude, except as punishment for crime. The amendment was proposed on January 31, 1865. It was declared ratified by the necessary number of states on December 18, 1865. The Emancipation Proclamation had freed slaves held in states that were considered to be in rebellion. This amendment freed slaves in states and territories controlled by the Union. The Supreme Court has ruled that this amendment does not bar mandatory military service.

The **14th Amendment** provides for Due Process and Equal Protection under the Law. It was proposed on June 13, 1866 and ratified on July 28, 1868. The drafters of the Amendment took a broad view of national citizenship. The law requires that states provide equal protection under the law to all persons (not just all citizens). This amendment also came to be interpreted as overturning the Dred Scott case (which said that blacks were not and could not become citizens of the US). The full potential of interpretation of this amendment was not realized until the 1950s and 1960s, when it became the basis of ending segregation in the Supreme Court case *Brown v. Board of Education.* This amendment includes the stipulation that all children born on American soil, with very few exceptions, are US citizens. There have been recommendations that this guarantee of citizenship be limited to exclude the children of illegal immigrants and tourists, but this has not yet occurred. There is no provision in this amendment for loss of citizenship.

The **15th Amendment** grants voting rights regardless of race, color or previous condition of servitude. It was ratified on February 3, 1870.

All three of these Constitutional Amendments were part of the Reconstruction effort to create stability and rule of law to provide, protect, and enforce the rights of former slaves throughout the nation.

Skill 11.5   Recognize key issues in the growth of big business, identify important business people and inventors and analyze the effects of major technological innovations on US industry and society

The **Industrial Revolution**, which began in Great Britain and spread elsewhere, was the development of power-driven machinery (fueled by coal and steam) leading to the accelerated growth of industry with large factories replacing homes and small workshops as work centers. The lives of people changed drastically and a largely agricultural society changed to an industrial one. In Western Europe, the period of empire and colonialism began. The industrialized nations seized and claimed parts of Africa and Asia in an effort to control and provide the raw materials needed to feed the industries and machines in the "mother country." Later developments included power based on electricity and internal combustion, replacing coal and steam.

There was a marked degree of industrialization before and during the Civil War, but at war's end, industry in America was small. After the war, dramatic changes took place. Machines replaced hand labor, extensive nationwide railroad service made possible the wider distribution of goods, invention of new products made available in large quantities, and large amounts of money from bankers and investors for expansion of business operations. American life was definitely affected by this phenomenal industrial growth. Cities became the centers of this new business activity resulting in mass population movements there and tremendous growth.

This new boom in business resulted in huge fortunes for some Americans and extreme poverty for many others. The discontent this caused resulted in a number of new reform movements from which came measures controlling the power and size of big business and helping the poor.

The use of machines in industry enabled workers to produce a large quantity of goods much faster than by hand. With the increase in business, hundreds of workers were hired, assigned to perform a certain job in the production process. This was a method of organization called **division of labor** and by its increasing the rate of production, businesses lowered prices for their products, making the products affordable for more people. As a result, sales and businesses were increasingly successful and profitable.

like assembly line

A great variety of new products or inventions became available, such as the typewriter, the telephone, barbed wire, the electric light, the phonograph, and the gasoline automobile. The increase in business and industry was greatly affected by the many rich natural resources that were found throughout the nation. The industrial machines were powered by the abundant water supply. The construction industry as well as products made from wood depended heavily on lumber from the forests. Coal and iron ore in abundance were needed for the steel industry, which profited and increased from the use of steel in such things as skyscrapers, automobiles, bridges, railroad tracks, and machines. Other minerals such as silver, copper, and petroleum played a large role in industrial growth, especially petroleum, from which gasoline was refined as fuel for the increasingly popular automobile.

The industrial boom produced several very wealthy and powerful captains of industry (Andrew Carnegie, John D. Rockefeller, Jay Gould, J.P. Morgan and Philip Armour). While they were envied and respected for their business acumen and success, they were condemned for exploitation of workers and questionable business practices and they were feared because of their power.

While these **captains of industry** were becoming wealthy, the average worker enjoyed some increase in the standard of living. Most workers were required to put in long hours in dangerous conditions doing monotonous work for low wages. Most were not able to afford to participate in the new comforts and forms of entertainment that were becoming available. Farmers believed they were also being exploited by the bankers, suppliers and the railroads. This produced enough instability to fuel several recessions and two severe depressions.

The completion of the transcontinental railroad in 1869 ended the problem of California's isolation from the rest of the country. The four men who provided the vision and much of the initial financial backing for the construction of the railroad were known as the **Big Four** (**Leland Stanford, Collis P. Huntington, Mark Hopkins, and Charles Crocker**). They became the wealthiest and most powerful men of their generation.

The majority of the work in constructing the railroad was done by Chinese workers, who were paid minimal wages and given very dangerous tasks. Construction took more than six years. There was a great celebration when the tracks of the Central Pacific Railroad met the tracks of the Union Pacific Railroad. The track was attached to the final tie with three commemorative spikes, one silver and two gold.

Skill 11.6   Demonstrate knowledge of the causes and effects of immigration during the period 1870–1910, analyze anti-immigrant movements and legislation, recognize major events and individuals associated with the rise of organized labor, and examine the development of the West and its effects on Native American populations

The nation witnessed significant industrial growth during the Civil War, growth that continued after the war. Steam power generation, sophisticated manufacturing equipment, the ability to move about the country quickly by railroad, and the invention of the steam powered tractor resulted in a phenomenal growth in industrial output. The new steel and oil industries provided a significant impetus to industrial growth and added thousands of new jobs.

The post-Reconstruction era represents a period of great transformation and expansion for the United States, both economically and geographically, particularly for the South, which was recovering from the devastation of the Civil War and migration west of the Mississippi River. Great numbers of former slaves moved west, away from their former masters and lured by the promise of land. White migration was also spurred by similar desires for land and resources, leading to boom economies of cotton, cattle and grain starting in Kansas and spreading westward. Although industrial production grew fastest in the South during this period, it was still predominantly agricultural, which featured land tenancy and sharecropping, which did not really advance the remaining freed slaves economically since most of the land was still owned by the large plantation landowners who retained their holdings from before the Civil War. The economic chasm dividing white landowners and black freedmen only widened as the tenants sank further into debt to their landlords.

Westward movement of significant populations from the eastern United States originated with the discovery of gold in the West in the 1840s and picked up greater momentum after the Civil War. Settlers were lured by what they perceived as unpopulated places with land for the taking. However, when they arrived, they found that the lands were populated by earlier settlers of Spanish descent and Native Americans, who did not particularly welcome the newcomers. These original and earlier inhabitants frequently clashed with those who were moving west. Despite having signed treaties with the United States government years earlier, virtually all were ignored and broken as westward settlement accelerated and the government was called upon to protect settlers who were en route and when they had reached their destinations. This led to a series of wars between the United States and the various Native American Nations that were deemed hostile. Although the bloodshed during these encounters was great, it paled compared to the number of Native Americans who died from epidemics of deadly diseases for which they had no resistance. Eventually, the government sought to relocate inconveniently located peoples to Indian reservations, and to Oklahoma, which lacked the necessary resources and was geographically remote from their home range. The justification for this westward expansion at the expense of the previous inhabitants was that it was America's "Manifest Destiny" to tame and settle the continent from coast-to-coast.

Another major factor affecting the opening of the West to migration of Americans and **displacement of native peoples** was the expansion of the railroad. The transcontinental railroad was completed in 1869, joining the West Coast with the existing rail infrastructure terminating at Omaha, Nebraska, its westernmost point. This not only enabled unprecedented movement of people and goods, it also hastened the near extinction of bison, which the Indians of the Great Plains, in particular, depended on for their survival.

One result of industrialization was the growth of the **Labor Movement**. There were numerous boycotts and strikes, which often became violent when the police or the militia were called in. Labor and farmer organizations were created and became a political force. Industrialization also brought an influx of immigrants from Asia (particularly Chinese and Japanese) and from Europe (particularly European Jews, the Irish, and Russians).

High rates of immigration led to the creation of communities, such as "little Russia" or "little Italy" in various cities. Industrialization also led to overwhelming growth of cities as workers moved closer to their places of work. The economy was booming, but that economy was based on basic needs and luxury goods for which there was to be only limited demand, especially during times of economic recession or depression.

Between 1870 and 1916, more than 25 million immigrants came into the United States adding to the phenomenal population growth taking place. This tremendous growth aided business and industry in two ways: (1) The number of consumers increased, creating a greater demand for products and enlarging markets for products, and (2) with increased production and expanding business, more workers were available for newly created jobs. The completion of the nation's transcontinental railroad in 1869 contributed greatly to the nation's economic and industrial growth. Some examples of the benefits of using the railroads included rapid shipment of raw materials by the mining companies and nationwide distribution of finished products. Many wealthy industrialists and railroad owners saw tremendous profits steadily increasing due to this improved method of transportation.

Skilled laborers were organized into a labor union called the **American Federation of Labor** in an effort to gain better working conditions and wages for its members. Farmers joined organizations such as the National Grange and Farmers Alliances. Farmers were producing more food than people could afford to buy. This was the result of (1) new farmlands rapidly sprouting on the plains and prairies, and (2) development and availability of new farm machinery and newer and better methods of farming. They tried selling their surplus abroad but faced stiff competition from other nations selling the same farm products. Other problems contributed significantly to their situation. Items that farmers needed for daily life were priced exorbitantly high. Having to borrow money to carry on farming activities kept them constantly in debt. Higher interest rates, shortage of money, falling farm prices, dealing with the so-called middlemen, and the increasingly high charges by the railroads to haul farm products to large markets all contributed to the desperate need for reform to relieve the plight of American farmers.

The inventive spirit of the time was a major force propelling the industrial revolution forward. This spirit led to improvement in products, development of new production processes and equipment, and even to the creation of entirely new industries. During the last 40 years of the nineteenth century inventors registered almost 700,000 new patents.

Skill 11.7 **Identify the causes and major events of the Spanish-American War, recognize key issues in the debate over American expansionism, and analyze US involvement in Latin America at the turn of the century**

Spain's tyrannical and short-sighted colonial policy led to a revolt on the island of Cuba (1895-98). The US intervened on Cuba's behalf and defeated Spain. The result of the war was that for the sum of $20 million, Spain gave up all claims to Cuba, Puerto Rico, the Philippine Islands and Guam. This acquisition was part of the dramatic growth of the US When Great Britain finally acknowledged American independence in 1783, the country claimed about 900,000 square miles of territory. By 1899, the purchase of the Louisiana Territory from France and Florida from Spain, the addition of Texas, California and the southwest, and the Oregon Country, and the purchase of Alaska from Russia had more than quadrupled the size of the nation. The American "Empire" was now the fifth largest in the world.

Until the middle of the nineteenth century, American foreign policy and expansionism was essentially restricted to the North American Continent. America had shown no interest in establishing colonies in other lands. Specifically, the US had stayed out of the rush to claim African territories. The variety of imperialism that found expression under the administrations of McKinley and **Theodore Roosevelt** was not precisely comparable to the imperialistic goals of European nations. There was a type of idealism in American foreign policy that sought to use military power in territories and other lands only in the interest of human rights and the spread of democratic principles. Much of the concern and involvement in Central and South America, as well as the Caribbean, was to link the two coasts of the nation and to protect the American economy from European encroachment.

When the revolution began in **Cuba**, it aroused the interest and concern of Americans who were aware of what was happening on their doorstep. When the Spanish attempted to put down the revolt, the women and children of Cuba were treated with great cruelty. They were gathered into camps surrounded by armed guards and given little food. Much of the food that kept them alive came from supplies sent by the US Americans were already concerned over years of anarchy and misrule by the Spanish. When reports of gross atrocities reached America, public sentiment clearly favored the Cuban people. President McKinley had refused to recognize the rebellion, but had affirmed the possibility of American intervention. Spain resented this attitude of the Americans. In February 1898, the American battleship *Maine* was blown up in Havana harbor. Although there was no incontrovertible evidence that the Spanish were responsible, popular sentiment accused Spanish agents and war became inevitable. Two months later, Congress declared war on Spain and the US quickly defeated the Spanish. The peace treaty gave the US possession of Puerto Rico, the Philippines, Guam and Hawaii, which was annexed during the war.

The political, economic, and geographic significance of the Panama Canal, the "Open Door" policy with China, Theodore Roosevelt's "Big Stick" Diplomacy, William Howard Taft's "Dollar" Diplomacy, and Woodrow Wilson's Moral Diplomacy.

Although the idea of a canal in Panama goes back to the early sixteenth century, work did not begin until 1880 by the French. The effort collapsed and the US completed the task, opening the **Panama Canal** in 1914. Construction was an enormous task of complex engineering. The significance of the Canal is that it connects the Gulf of Panama in the Pacific Ocean with the Caribbean Sea and the Atlantic Ocean. It eliminated the need for ships to skirt the southern boundary of South America, effectively reducing the sailing distance from New York to San Francisco by 8,000 miles (over half of the distance). The Canal results in a shorter and faster voyage, thus reducing shipping time and cost.

The US helped Panama win independence from Colombia in exchange for control of the Panama Canal Zone. A large investment was made in eliminating disease from the area, particularly yellow fever and malaria. After WWII, control of the canal became an issue of contention between the US and Panama. Negotiations toward a settlement began in 1974, resulting in the Torrijos-Carter Treaties of 1977. Thus began the process of handing the Canal over to Panama. On December 31, 1999, control of the Canal was handed over to the Panama Canal Authority. Tolls for the use of the Canal have ranged from $0.36, when Richard Halliburton swam it, to about $226,000.

The **Open Door Policy** refers to maintaining equal commercial and industrial rights for the people of all countries in a particular territory. The Open Door policy generally refers to China, but it has also been used in application to the Congo basin. The policy was first suggested by the US, but its basis is the typical nation clause of the treaties made with China after the Opium War (1829-1842). The essential purpose of the policy was to permit equal access to trade for all nations with treaties with China while protecting the integrity of the Chinese empire. This policy was in effect from about 1900 until the end of WWII. After the war, China was recognized as a sovereign state. There was no longer opportunity for other nations to attempt to carve out regions of influence or control. When the Communist Party came to power in China, the policy was rejected. This continued until the late 1970s, when China began to adopt a policy of again encouraging foreign trade.

Big Stick Diplomacy was a term adopted from an African proverb, "speak softly and carry a big stick," to describe President Theodore Roosevelt's policy of the US assuming international police power in the Western Hemisphere. The phrase implied the power to retaliate if necessary. The intention was to safeguard American economic interests in Latin America. The policy led to the expansion of the US Navy and to greater involvement in world affairs. Should any nation in the Western Hemisphere become vulnerable to European control because of political or economic instability, the US had both the right and the obligation to intervene. **Dollar Diplomacy** describes US efforts under President Taft to extend its foreign policy goals in Latin America and East Asia via economic power. The designation derives from Taft's claim that US interests in Latin America had changed from "warlike and political" to "peaceful and economic." Taft justified this policy in terms of protecting the Panama Canal. The practice of dollar diplomacy was from time to time anything but peaceful, particularly in Nicaragua. When revolts or revolutions occurred, the US sent troops to resolve the situation. Immediately upon resolution, bankers were sent in to loan money to the new regimes. The policy persisted until the election of Woodrow Wilson to the Presidency in 1913.

Skill 11.8 **Analyze major efforts to reform US society and politics during the Progressive Era and recognize the roles of important figures in the Progressive movement**

The late 1800s and early 1900s were a period of the efforts of many to make significant reforms and changes in the areas of politics, society, and the economy. There was a need to reduce the levels of poverty and to improve the living conditions of those affected by it. Regulation of big business and ridding government of corruption and making it more responsive to the needs of the people were also on the list of reforms to be accomplished. Until 1890, there was very little success, but from 1890 on, the reformers gained increased public support and were able to achieve some influence in government. Since some of these individuals referred to themselves as "**progressives**," the period of 1890 to 1917 is referred to by historians as the Progressive Era.

This fire was fueled by the writings on investigative journalists – the "muckrakers" – who published scathing exposes of political and business wrongdoing and corruption. The result was the rise of a group of politicians and reformers who supported a wide array of populist causes. The period 1900 to 1917 came to be known as the Progressive Era. Although these leaders came from many different backgrounds and were driven by different ideologies, they shared a common fundamental belief that government should be eradicating social ills and promoting the common good and the equality guaranteed by the Constitution.

The reforms initiated by these leaders and the spirit of **Progressivism** were far-reaching. Politically, many states enacted the initiative and the referendum. The adoption of the recall occurred in many states. Several states enacted legislation that would undermine the power of political machines. On a national level the two most significant political changes were (1) the ratification of the 19th Amendment, which required that all US Senators be chosen by popular election, and (2) the ratification of the nineteenth Amendment, which granted women the right to vote.

? 2ᵒᵈ ??

W.E.B. DuBois, an outstanding African-American leader and spokesman, believed that only continuous and vigorous protests against injustices and inequalities, coupled with appeals to black pride, would effect changes. The results of his efforts was the formation of the Urban League and the NAACP (the National Association for the Advancement of Colored People) which today continue to eliminate discrimination and secure equality and equal rights.

Major economic reforms of the period included aggressive enforcement of the Sherman Antitrust Act; passage of the Elkins Act and the Hepburn Act, which gave the Interstate Commerce Commission greater power to regulate the railroads; the Pure Food and Drug Act, which prohibited the use of harmful chemicals in food; The Meat Inspection Act, which regulated the meat industry to protect the public against tainted meat; over two-thirds of the states passed laws prohibiting child labor; workmen's compensation was mandated; and the Department of Commerce and Labor was created.

Responding to concern over the environmental effects of the timber, ranching, and mining industries, Roosevelt set aside 238 million acres of federal lands to protect them from development. Wildlife preserves were established, the national park system was expanded, and the National Conservation Commission was created. The Newlands Reclamation Act also provided federal funding for the construction of irrigation projects and dams in semi-arid areas of the country.

The Wilson Administration carried out additional reforms. The Federal Reserve Act created a national banking system, providing a stable money supply. The Sherman Act and the Clayton Antitrust Act defined unfair competition, made corporate officers liable for the illegal actions of employees, and exempted labor unions from antitrust lawsuits. The Federal Trade Commission was established to enforce these measures. Finally, the 16th Amendment was ratified, establishing an income tax. This measure was designed to relieve the poor of a disproportionate burden in funding the federal government and make the wealthy pay a greater share of the nation's tax burden.

tax changed in the 16th Amendment... Why? What was Why before!

SUBAREA V.   US HISTORY 1914 TO THE PRESENT

COMPETENCY 12.0   UNDERSTAND THE ORIGINS, EVENTS, AND EFFECTS OF US INVOLVEMENT IN WORLD WARS I AND II, AND MAJOR POLITICAL, CULTURAL, AND ECONOMIC DEVELOPMENTS IN THE UNITED STATES BETWEEN 1914 AND 1945

Skill 12.1   Analyze the origins, domestic effects, and diplomatic consequences of US involvement in World War I

Causes attributed to the United States' participation in World War I included the surge of nationalism, the increasing strength of military capabilities, massive colonization for raw materials needed for industrialization and manufacturing, and military and diplomatic alliances. The spark which started the conflagration was the assassination of Austrian Archduke Francis Ferdinand and his wife in Sarajevo.

In Europe, war broke out in 1914, involved nearly 30 nations, and ended in 1918. One of the major causes of the war was the tremendous surge of **nationalism** during the 1800s and early 1900s. People of the same nationality or ethnic group sharing a common history, language or culture began uniting or demanding the right of unification, especially in the empires of Eastern Europe, such as the Russian Ottoman and Austrian-Hungarian Empires. Getting stronger and more intense were the beliefs of these peoples in loyalty to common political, social, and economic goals considered to be before any loyalty to the controlling nation or empire.

Emotions ran high and minor disputes magnified into major ones, sometimes quickly leading to threats of war. Especially sensitive was the area around the Balkan Peninsula. Along with the imperialistic colonization for industrial raw materials, military build-up (especially by Germany), and diplomatic and military alliances, the conditions for one tiny spark to set off the explosion were in place. In July 1914, a Serbian national assassinated the Austrian heir to the throne and his wife and war began a few weeks later. There were a few attempts to keep war from starting, but these efforts were futile.

In 1916, Wilson was reelected to a second term based on the slogan proclaiming his efforts at keeping America out of the war. For a few months after, he put forth most of his efforts to stopping the war but German submarines began unlimited warfare against American merchant shipping. The development of the German *unterseeboot* or **U-boat** allowed them to efficiently attack merchant ships that were supplying their European enemies from Canada and the US. In 1915, a German U-boat sunk the passenger liner RMS **Lusitania**, killing over 1,000 civilians, including over 100 Americans. This attack outraged the American public and turned public opinion against Germany. The attack on the Lusitania became a rallying point for those advocating US involvement in the European conflict.

Great Britain intercepted and decoded a secret message from Germany to Mexico urging Mexico to go to war against the US The publishing of this information along with continued German destruction of American ships resulted in the eventual entry of the US into the conflict, the first time the country prepared to fight in a conflict not on American soil. Though unprepared for war, governmental efforts and activities resulted in massive defense mobilization with America's economy directed to the war effort. Though America made an important contribution with war materials, its greatest contribution to the war was manpower, as soldiers were desperately needed by the Allies.

Some ten months before the war ended, President Wilson had proposed a program called the **Fourteen Points** as a method of bringing the war to an end with an equitable peace settlement. Of the fourteen, five points laid out general ideals; there were eight pertaining to immediately working to resolve territorial and political problems; and the fourteenth point counseled establishing an organization of nations to help keep world peace.

When Germany agreed in 1918 to an armistice, it assumed that the peace settlement would be drawn up on the basis of these Fourteen Points. However, the peace conference in Paris ignored these points and Wilson had to be content with efforts at establishing the **League of Nations**. Italy, France, and Great Britain, having suffered and sacrificed far more in the war than America did, wanted retribution. The treaties punished severely the Central Powers, taking away arms and territories and requiring payment of reparations. Germany was punished more than the others and, according to one clause in the treaty, was forced to assume the responsibility for causing the war.

Pre-war empires lost tremendous amounts of territories as well as the wealth of natural resources in them. New, independent nations were formed and some predominately ethnic areas came under control of nations of different cultural backgrounds. Some national boundary changes overlapped and created tensions and hard feelings as well as political and economic confusion. The wishes and desires of every national or cultural group would never be realized and satisfied, which resulted in disappointments for both those who were victorious and those who were defeated. Germany received harsher terms than expected from the treaty, which weakened its post-war government, and along with the worldwide depression of the 1930s, set the stage for the rise of Adolf Hitler and his Nationalist Socialist Party and World War II.

World War I saw the introduction of such warfare as use of tanks, airplanes, machine guns, submarines, poison gas, and flame-throwers. Fighting on the Western front was characterized by a series of trenches that were used throughout the war until 1918.

President Wilson lost in his efforts to get the US Senate to approve the peace treaty. The Senate at the time was a reflection of American public opinion and its rejection of the treaty was a rejection of Wilson. The approval of the treaty would have made the US a member of the League of Nations but Americans had just come off a bloody war to ensure that democracy would exist throughout the world. Americans just did not want to accept any responsibility that resulted from its new position of power and were afraid that membership in the League of Nations would embroil the US in future disputes in Europe.

The United States war effort for WWI included over four million who served in the military in some capacity, over two million of whom served overseas. The cost of the war up to April 30, 1919 was over $22.5 billion. Nearly 50,000 Americans were killed in battle and an additional 221,000 were wounded. On the home front, people energetically supported the war effort in every way necessary. The menace of German submarines was causing the loss of ships faster than new ships could be built. At the beginning of the war, the US had little overseas shipping. Scores of shipyards were quickly constructed to build both wooden and steel ships. At the end of the war the United States had more than 2,000 ships.

Wilson repudiated the dollar diplomacy approach to foreign policy within weeks of his inauguration. Wilson's "moral diplomacy" became the model for American foreign policy to this day. Wilson envisioned a federation of democratic nations, believing that democracy and representative government were the foundations of world stability. Specifically, he saw Great Britain and the United States as the champions of self-government and the promoters of world peace. Wilson's beliefs and actions set in motion an American foreign policy that was dedicated to the interests of all humanity rather than merely American national interests. Wilson promoted the power of free trade and international commerce as the key to enlarging the national economy into world markets as a means of acquiring a voice in world events. This approach to foreign policy was based on three elements: (1) maintain a combat-ready military to meet the needs of the nation, (2) promote democracy abroad, and (3) improve the US economy through international trade. Wilson believed that democratic states would be less inclined to threaten US interests.

Herbert Hoover had chaired the Belgian Relief Commission previously. He was named "food commissioner," later called the US Food Administration Board. His function was to manage conservation and distribution of the food supply to ensure that there was adequate food to supply every American both at home and overseas, as well as providing additional food to people who were suffering in Europe.

In December of 1917, the government assumed control of all of the railroads in the nation and consolidated them into a single system with regional directors. The goal of this action was to increase efficiency and enable the rail system to meet the needs of both commerce and military transportation. This was done with the understanding that private ownership would be restored after the war. The restoration occurred in 1920. In 1918 telegraph, telephone and cable services were also taken over by the federal government; they were returned to original management and ownership in 1919.

To secure the huge sums of money needed to finance the war, the government sold "Liberty Bonds" to the people. Nearly $25 billion worth of bonds were sold in four issues of bonds. After the war Victory Bonds were sold. The first Liberty loan was issued at 3.5%, the second at 4%, the remaining ones at 4.25%. A strong appeal was made to the people to buy bonds. The total response meant that more than one-fifth of the inhabitants of the US bought bonds. For the first time in their lives, millions of people had begun saving money.

The war effort required massive production of weapons, ammunition, radios, and other equipment of war and the support of war. During wartime, work hours were shortened, wages were increased and working conditions improved. But when the war ended, business and industrial owners and managers attempted a return to pre-war conditions, the workers revolted. These conditions contributed to the Red Scare and the establishment of new labor laws.

Skill 12.2   Demonstrate knowledge of the movements leading to the passing of the Eighteenth Amendment, establishing Prohibition, and the Nineteenth Amendment, establishing women's suffrage.

The Second Great Awakening was an evangelical Protestant revival that preached personal responsibility for one's actions both individually and socially. This movement was led by preachers such as Charles Finney who traveled the country preaching the gospel of social responsibility. This point of view was taken up by the mainline Protestant denominations (Episcopal, Methodist, Presbyterian, Lutheran, and Congregational). Part of the social reform movement that led to an end to child labor, to better working conditions and to other changes in social attitudes, arose from this new recognition that the Christian faith should be expressed for the good of society.

Closely allied to the Second Great Awakening was **the temperance movement**. This movement to end the sale and consumption of alcohol arose from religious beliefs, the violence many women and children experienced from heavy drinkers, and from the effect of alcohol consumption on the work force. The Society for the Promotion of Temperance was organized in Boston in 1826.

The end of World War I and the decade of the 1920s saw tremendous changes in the United States, signifying the beginning of its development into its modern society today. The shift from farm to city life was occurring in tremendous numbers. Social changes and problems were occurring at such a fast pace that it was extremely difficult and perplexing for many Americans to adjust to them. The 18th Amendment to the Constitution, the so-called Prohibition Amendment, which prohibited selling alcoholic beverages throughout the US, resulted in political problems affecting all aspects of society. The passage of the 19th Amendment gave to women the right to vote in all elections. The decade of the 1920s also showed a marked change in roles and opportunities for women with more and more of them seeking and finding careers outside the home. They began to think of themselves as the equal of men and not as much as housewives and mothers.

Other social issues were addressed. It was during this period that efforts were made to transform the prison system and its emphasis on punishment into a penitentiary system that attempted rehabilitation. It was also during this period that Dorothea Dix led a struggle in the North and the South to establish hospitals for the insane. This group of women emerged in the 1840s, which signified the beginning of the first women's rights movement in the nation's history. Among the early leaders of the movement were Elizabeth Cady Stanton, Lucretia Mott, and Ernestine Rose. At this time very few states recognized women's rights to vote, own property, sue for divorce, or execute contracts. In 1869, Susan B. Anthony, Ernestine Rose and Elizabeth Cady Stanton founded the National Woman Suffrage Association.

Skill 12.3   Demonstrate knowledge of major political, technological, and cultural developments of the 1920s

The end of World War I and the decade of the 1920s saw tremendous changes in the United States, signifying the beginning of its development into its modern society today. The shift from farm to city life was occurring at a rapid rate. Social changes and problems were occurring at such a fast pace that it was extremely difficult and perplexing for many Americans to adjust to them. The 18th Amendment to the Constitution, the so-called Prohibition Amendment, which prohibited selling alcoholic beverages throughout the US, resulted in political problems affecting all aspects of society The passage of the 19th Amendment gave women the right to vote in all elections. The decade of the 1920s also showed a marked change in roles and opportunities for women with more and more of them seeking and finding careers outside the home. They began to think of themselves as the equal of men and not as much as housewives and mothers.

The influence of the automobile, the entertainment industry, and the rejection of the morals and values of pre-World War I life, resulted in the fast-paced **Roaring Twenties**. There were significant effects on events leading to the Depression-era 1930s and another world war. Many Americans greatly desired the pre-war life and supported political policies and candidates in favor of the return to what was considered normal. Many desired an end to government's strong role and wanted to adopt a policy of isolating the country from world affairs, a result of the war.

Prohibition of the sale of alcohol resulted in an increase in bootlegging and the rise of underworld gangs and illegal speakeasies, including the jazz music and dances they promoted. The customers of these clubs were considered "modern," reflected by extremes in clothing, hairstyles and attitudes towards authority and life. Movies and other types of entertainment, along with increased interest in sports figures and the accomplishments of national heroes, such as Lindbergh, influenced Americans to admire, emulate, and support individual accomplishments.

As wild and uninhibited as modern behavior became, this decade witnessed an increase in a religious tradition known as "**revivalism**," emotional preaching. Although law and order were demanded by many Americans, the administration of President Warren G. Harding was marked by widespread corruption and scandal, not unlike the administration of Ulysses S. Grant, except Grant was honest and innocent. The decade of the 1920s also saw the resurgence of such racist organizations as the Ku Klux Klan.

Although the British patent for the **radio** was awarded in 1896, it was not until WWI that the equipment and capability of the use of radio was recognized. The first radio program was broadcast on August 31, 1920. The first entertainment broadcasts began in 1922 from England. One of the first developments in the twentieth century was the use of commercial AM radio stations for aircraft navigation. In addition, radio was used to communicate orders and information between army and navy units on both sides of the war during WWI. Broadcasting became practical in the 1920s when radio receivers were introduced on a wide scale.

The relative economic boom of the 1920s made it possible for many households to own a radio. The beginning of broadcasting and the proliferation of receivers revolutionized communication. The news was transmitted into every home with a radio. With the beginning of entertainment broadcasting, people were able to remain in their homes for entertainment. Rather than obtaining filtered information, people were able to hear the actual speeches and information that became news. By the time of the Stock Market Crash in 1929, approximately 40% of households had a radio.

important!

The 1920s were a period of relative prosperity, under the leadership of Warren G. Harding and Calvin Coolidge. Harding had promised a return to "normalcy" in the aftermath of World War I and the radical reactions of labor. During most of the decade, the output of industry boomed and the **automobile** industry put almost 27 million cars on the road. Per capita income rose for almost everyone except farmers.

A huge wave of labor strikes sought a return to wartime working conditions when the workday was shorter, wages were higher, and conditions were better. Many of these labor strikes turned violent. The majority of the population viewed the early strikes as the work of radicals, who were labeled "reds" (communists). As the news spread and other strikes occurred, the **red scare** swept the country.

Americans feared a Bolshevik-type revolution in America. As a result, people were jailed for expressing views that were considered anarchist, communist or socialist. In an attempt to control the potential for revolution, civil liberties were ignored and thousands were deported. The Socialist Party also came to be viewed as a group of anarchist radicals. Several state and local governments passed a variety of laws designed to reduce radical speech and activity. Congress considered more than 70 anti-sedition bills, though none were passed. Within a year, the red scare had essentially run its course.

The **Ku Klux Klan** (KKK) is a name that has been used by several white supremacist organizations throughout history. Their beliefs encompass white supremacy, anti-Semitism, racism, anti-Catholicism and nativism. Their typical methods of intimidation have included terrorism, violence, cross burning and the like. The birth of the organization was in 1866. At that time, members were veterans of the Confederate Army seeking to resist Reconstruction and the carpetbaggers.

The Klan entered a second period beginning in 1915. Using the new film medium, this group tried to spread its message with _The Birth of a Nation_. They also published a number of anti-Semitic newspaper articles. The group became a structured membership organization. Its membership did not begin to decline until the Great Depression. Although the KKK began in the South, its membership at its peak extended into the Midwest, the Northern states, and even into Canada. Membership during the 1920s reached approximately 4 million – 20% of the adult white male population in many regions and as high as 40% in some areas. The political influence of the group was significant. It essentially controlled the governments of Tennessee, Indiana, Oklahoma and Oregon as well as some Southern legislatures.

Another innovation of the 1920s was the introduction of **mass production**. This is the production of large amounts of standardized products on production lines. The method became very popular when Henry Ford used mass production to build the Model T Ford. The process facilitates high production rates per worker. Thus, it created very inexpensive products. The process is, however, capital intensive. It requires expensive machinery in high proportion to the number of workers needed to operate it.

Henry Ford, 1920s

During the period before and after 1900, a large number of people migrated to the cities of America. Throughout the nineteenth century city populations grew faster than rural populations. The new immigrants were not farmers. Polish immigrants became steelworkers in Pittsburgh; Serbian immigrants became meatpackers in Chicago; Russian Jewish immigrants became tailors in New York City; Slovaks assembled cars in Detroit; Italians worked in the factories of Baltimore.

Several factors promoted urbanization during the decade of the 1920s. The decline of agriculture, the drop in prices for grain and produce, and the end of financial support for farming after WWI caused many farmers to go under during the 1920s. Many sold or lost their farms and migrated to cities to find work.

Continuing industrialization drew increasing numbers of workers to the areas near or surrounding industrial or manufacturing centers. Cities were becoming the locus of political, cultural, financial and economic life. Transportation to the place of work or to shop for necessities facilitated the growth of cities.

Urbanization brought certain needs in its wake, including adequate water supply, management of sewage and garbage, the need for public services, such as fire and police, road construction and maintenance, building of bridges to connect parts of cities, and taller buildings. This last led to the invention of steel-framed buildings and of the elevator. In addition, electricity and telephone lines were needed, department stores and supermarkets grew and the need for additional schools was related to urbanization. With the large migration and low wages came overcrowding, often in old buildings. Slums began to appear and public health issues began to arise.

Skill 12.4   Analyze the causes and consequences of the Great Depression

The Great Depression and the New Deal

The 1929 Stock Market Crash was the powerful event that is generally interpreted as the beginning of the Great Depression in America. Although the crash of the Stock Market was unexpected, it was not without identifiable causes. The 1920s had been a decade of social and economic growth and hope. But the attitudes and actions of the 1920s regarding wealth, production, and investment created several trends that quietly set the stage for the 1929 disaster.

The other factor contributing to the Great Depression was the economic condition of Europe. The US was lending money to European nations to rebuild. Many of these countries used this money to purchase US food and manufactured goods. But they were not able to pay off their debts. Although the US was providing money, food, and goods to Europe, it was not willing to buy European goods. Trade barriers were enacted to maintain a favorable trade balance.

Several other factors have been cited by scholars as contributing to the Great Depression. First, in 1929, the Federal Reserve increased interest rates. Second, some believe that as interest rates rose and the stock market began to decline, people began to hoard money. This was certainly the case after the crash and some believe that it was a cause of the crash.

In September 1929, stock prices began to slip somewhat, yet people remained optimistic. On Monday, October 21, prices began to fall quickly. The volume traded was so high that the tickers were unable to keep up. Investors were frightened and they started selling very quickly, which caused further collapse. For the next two days prices stabilized somewhat. On **Black Thursday**, October 24, prices plummeted again. By this time investors had lost confidence. On Friday and Saturday an attempt to stop the crash was made by some leading bankers. But on Monday the 28th, prices began to fall again, declining by 13% in one day. The next day, **Black Tuesday, October 29**, saw 16.4 million shares traded. Stock prices fell so far that at many times no one was willing to buy at any price.

Unemployment quickly reached 25% nationwide. People thrown out of their homes created makeshift domiciles of cardboard, scraps of wood and tents. With unmasked reference to President Hoover, who was quite obviously overwhelmed by the situation and incompetent to deal with it, these communities were called **Hoovervilles**. Families stood in bread lines, rural workers left the dust bowl of the plains to search for work in California and banks failed. More than 100,000 businesses failed between 1929 and 1932. The despair that swept the nation left an indelible scar on all who endured the Depression.

When the stock market crashed, businesses collapsed. Without demand for products, other businesses and industries collapsed. This set in motion a domino effect, bringing down the businesses and industries that provided raw materials or components to these industries. Hundreds of thousands became jobless. Then the jobless often became homeless. Desperation prevailed. Little had been done to assess the toll that hunger, inadequate nutrition, or starvation took on the health of those who were children during this time. Indeed, food was cheap, relatively speaking, but there was little money to buy it.

The gains and losses of organized labor in the 1930s.

There were several major events or actions that are particularly important to the history of organized labor during this decade:

- The Supreme Court upheld the Railway Labor Act, including its prohibition of employer interference or coercion in the choice of bargaining representatives (1930);
- The Davis-Bacon Act provided that employers of contractors and subcontractors on public construction should be paid the prevailing wages (1931);
- The Anti-Injunction Act prohibited Federal injunctions in most labor disputes (1932);
- Wisconsin created the first unemployment insurance act in the country (1932);
- The Wagner-Peyser Act created the United States Employment Service within the Department of Labor (1933);
- Half a million Southern mill workers walked off the job in the Great Uprising of 1934;
- The Secretary of Labor called the first National Labor Legislation Conference to encourage better cooperation between the Federal Government and the States in defining a national labor legislation program (1934);
- The US joined the International Labor Organization (1934);
- The Wagner Act (The National Labor Relations Act) established a legal basis for unions, set collective bargaining as a matter of national policy required by law, provided for secret ballot elections for choosing unions, and protected union members from employer intimidation and coercion. This law was later amended by the Taft-Hartley Act (1947) and by the Landrum Griffin Act (1959);
- The Guffey Act stabilized the coal industry and improved labor conditions (1935). It was later declared unconstitutional (1936);
- The Social Security Act was approved (1935);
- The Committee for Industrial Organization (CIO) was formed within the AFL to carry unionism to the industrial sector (1935);
- The United Rubber Workers staged the first sit-down strike (1936);
- The United Auto Workers used the sit-down strike against General Motors (1936);
- The Anti-Strikebreaker Act (the Byrnes Act) made it illegal to transport or aid strikebreakers in interstate or foreign trade (1936);

- The Public Contracts Act (the Walsh-Healey Act) of 1936 established labor standards, including minimum wages, overtime pay, child and convict labor provisions and safety standards on federal contracts;
- General Motors recognized the United Auto Workers in 1937;
- US Steel recognized the Steel Workers Organizing Committee in 1937;
- The Wagner Act was upheld by the Supreme Court (1937);
- During a strike of the Steel Workers Organizing Committee against Republic Steel, police attacked a crowd gathered in support of the strike, killing ten and injuring eighty. This came to be called **The Memorial Day Massacre** (1937);
- The CIO was expelled from the AFL over charges of dual unionism or competition (1937);
- The National Apprenticeship Act established the Bureau of Apprenticeship within the Department of Labor (1937);
- The Merchant Marine Act created a Federal Maritime Labor Board (1938);
- The Fair Labor Standards Act created a $0.25 minimum wage, stipulated time-and-a-half pay for hours over 40 per week; and,
- The CIO becomes the Congress of Industrial Organizations.

Skill 12.5   Recognize important social, economic, and political developments of the 1930s

See also Skill 12.4

By far the worst natural disaster of the decade came to be known as the **Dust Bowl.** Due to severe and prolonged drought in the Great Plains and previous reliance on inappropriate farming techniques, a series of devastating dust storms occurred in the 1930s that resulted in destruction, economic ruin for many and dramatic ecological change.

Plowing the plains for agriculture removed the grass and exposed the soil. When the drought occurred, the soil dried out and became dust. Wind blew away the dust. Between 1934 and 1939 winds blew the soil to the east, all the way to the Atlantic Ocean. The dust storms, called "black blizzards" created huge clouds of dust that were visible all the way to Chicago. Topsoil was stripped from millions of acres. In Texas, Arkansas, Oklahoma, New Mexico, Kansas and Colorado, over half a million people were homeless. Many of these people journeyed west in the hope of making a new life in California.

Crops were ruined, the land was destroyed, and people either lost or abandoned homes and farms. Fifteen percent of Oklahoma's population left. Because so many of the migrants were from Oklahoma, the migrants came to be called "**Okies**" no matter where they came from. Estimates of the number of people displaced by this disaster range from 300,000 or 400,000 to 2.5 million.

During the first 100 days in office, the Roosevelt Administration responded to this crisis with programs designed to restore the ecological balance. One action was the formation of the **Soil Conservation Service** (now the Natural Resources Conservation Service). The story of this natural disaster and its toll in human suffering is poignantly preserved in the photographs of Dorothea Lange.

Within the context of fear of radicalism and rampant racism and efforts to repress various groups within the population, it is not surprising that several groups were formed to protect the civil rights and liberties guaranteed to all citizens by the US Constitution. The **American Civil Liberties Union** was formed in 1920. It was originally an outgrowth of the American Union Against Militarism, which had opposed American involvement in WWI, and provided legal advice and assistance for conscientious objectors and those who were being prosecuted under the Espionage Act of 1917 and the Sedition Act of 1918. With the name change there was attention to additional concerns and activities. The agency began to try to protect immigrants threatened with deportation and citizens threatened with prosecution for communist activities and agendas. They also opposed efforts to repress the Industrial Workers of the World and other labor unions.

The ACLU is a non-profit organization whose mission is "to defend and preserve the individual rights and liberties guaranteed to every person in this Country by the Constitution and laws of the United States." [American Civil Liberties Union website] The organization accomplishes its goals through community education, litigation and legislation.

The National Association for the Advancement of Colored People (NAACP) was founded in 1909 to assist African Americans. In the early years, the organization focused on working through the courts to overturn Jim Crow statutes that legalized racial discrimination. The group organized voters to oppose Woodrow Wilson's efforts to integrate racial segregation into federal government policy. Between WWI and WWII, much energy was devoted to stopping the lynching of blacks throughout the country.

The Anti-Defamation League was created in 1913 to stop discrimination against the Jewish people. Its charter states that "Its ultimate purpose is to secure justice and fair treatment to all citizens alike and to put an end forever to unjust and unfair discrimination against ridicule of any sect or body of citizens." The organization has historically opposed all groups considered anti-Semitic and/or racist. This has included the Ku Klux Klan, the Nazis, and a variety of others.

Marcus Garvey, an English-educated Jamaican, established an organization call the **Universal Negro Improvement and Conservation Association and African Communities League** (usually called the Universal Negro Improvement Association). In 1919, this "Black Moses" claimed followers numbering about two million. He spoke of a "new Negro" who was proud to be black. He published a newspaper in which he taught about the "heroes" of the race and the strengths of African culture. He told blacks that they would be respected only when they were economically strong. He created a number of businesses by which he hoped to achieve this goal. He then called blacks to work with him to build an all-black nation in Africa. His belief in racial purity and black separatism was not shared by a number of black leaders. In 1922 he and other members of the organization were jailed for mail fraud. His sentence was commuted and he was deported to Jamaica as an undesirable alien.

Skill 12.6   Demonstrate knowledge of the New Deal response to the Great Depression and analyze challenges to Franklin Roosevelt's domestic and international leadership

See also Skill 12.4

Hoover's bid for re-election in 1932 failed. The new president, Franklin D. Roosevelt, won the White House on his promise to the American people of a "new deal." Upon assuming the office, Roosevelt and his advisers immediately launched a massive program of innovation and experimentation to try to bring the Depression to an end and get the nation back on track. Congress gave the President unprecedented power to act to save the nation. During the next eight years, the most extensive and broadly based legislation in the nation's history was enacted. The legislation was intended to accomplish three goals: relief, recovery, and reform.

The first step in the **New Deal** was to relieve suffering. This was accomplished through a number of job creation projects. The second step, the recovery aspect, was to stimulate the economy. The third step was to create social and economic change through innovative legislation.

The National Recovery Administration attempted to accomplish several goals:

- Restore employment;
- Increase general purchasing power;
- Provide character-building activity for unemployed youth;
- Encourage decentralization of industry and thus divert population from crowded cities to rural or semi-rural communities;
- Develop river resources in the interest of navigation and cheap power and light;
- Complete flood control on a permanent basis;
- Enlarge the national program of forest protection and to develop forest resources;
- Control farm production and improve farm prices;
- Assist home builders and home owners;
- Restore public faith in banking and trust operations; and
- Recapture the value of physical assets, whether in real property, securities, or other investments.

These objectives and their accomplishment implied a restoration of public confidence and courage.

Among the "alphabet organizations" set up to work out the details of the recovery plan, the most prominent were:

- **Agricultural Adjustment Administration** (AAA), designed to readjust agricultural production and prices, thereby boosting farm income;
- **Civilian Conservation Corps** (CCC), designed to give wholesome, useful activity in the forestry service to unemployed young men;
- **Civil Works Administration** (CWA) and the **Public Works Administration** (PWA), designed to give employment in the construction and repair of public buildings, parks, and highways; and,
- **Works Progress Administration** (WPA), whose task was to move individuals from relief rolls to work projects or private employment.

The **Tennessee Valley Authority** (TVA) was of a more permanent nature, designed to improve the navigability of the Tennessee River and increase productivity of the timber and farm lands in its valley. This program built 16 dams that provided water control and hydroelectric generation.

The Public Works Administration employed Americans on over 34,000 public works projects at a cost of more than $4 billion. Among these projects was the construction of a highway that linked the Florida Keys and Miami, the Boulder Dam (now the Hoover Dam) and numerous highway projects.

To provide economic stability and prevent another crash, Congress passed the **Glass-Steagall Act**, which separated banking and investing. The Securities and Exchange Commission was created to regulate dangerous speculative practices on Wall Street. The Wagner Act guaranteed a number of rights to workers and unions in an effort to improve worker-employer relations. The **Social Security Act of 1935** established pensions for the aged and infirm as well as a system of unemployment insurance.

Much of the recovery program was of an emergency nature, but certain permanent national policies emerged. The intention of the public through its government was to supervise, and to an extent regulate, business operations, from corporate activities to labor problems. This included protecting bank depositors and the credit system of the country, employing gold resources and currency adjustments to aid permanent restoration of normal living and, if possible, establishing a line of subsistence below which no useful citizen would be permitted to sink.

Many of the steps taken by the Roosevelt administration have had far-reaching effects. They alleviated the economic disaster of the Great Depression, they enacted controls that would mitigate the risk of another stock market crash and they provided greater security for workers. The nation's economy, however, did not fully recover until America entered World War II.

To be sure, there were negative reactions to some of the measures taken to pull the country out of the Depression. There was a major reaction to the deaths of the WWI veterans in the Labor Day Hurricane, ultimately resulting in a Congressional investigation into possible negligence. The Central Valley Project ruffled feathers of farmers who lost tillable land and some water supply to the construction of the aqueduct and the Hoover Dam. Tennesseans were initially unhappy with the changes in river flow and navigation when the Tennessee Valley Authority began constructing dams and directing of water to form reservoirs and to power hydroelectric plants. Some businesses and business leaders were not happy with the introduction of minimum wage laws and restrictions and controls on working conditions and limitations of work hours for laborers. The numerous import/export tariffs of the period were the subject of controversy.

In the long view, however, much that was accomplished under the New Deal had positive long-term effects on economic, ecological, social and political issues for the next several decades. The Tennessee Valley Authority and the Central Valley Project in California provided a reliable source and supply of water to major cities, as well as electrical power to meet the needs of an increasingly electricity dependent society. For the middle class and the poor, the labor regulations, the establishment of the Social Security Administration, and the separation of investment and banking have served the nation admirably for more than six decades.

The Supreme Court of the United States is the highest appellate court in the country and is a court of original jurisdiction according to the Constitution *"in all cases affecting ambassadors, other public ministers and consuls, and those in which a state shall be a party."* By virtue of its power to declare legislation unconstitutional,I the Supreme Court is also the final arbitrator of all Constitutional questions.

Skill 12.7   Analyze the origins of World War II, identify major wartime military and diplomatic events and developments and examine the domestic effects of total war

World War II (1939 to 1945)

Ironically, the Treaty of Paris, the peace treaty ending World War I, ultimately led to the Second World War. Countries that fought in the first war were either dissatisfied over the "spoils" of war, or were punished so harshly that resentment continued building to an eruption twenty years later. In addition, the economic problems of both winners and losers of the first war were never resolved and the worldwide Great Depression of the 1930s dealt the final blow to any immediate rapid recovery. Democratic governments in Europe were severely strained and weakened, which in turn gave strength and encouragement to those political movements that were extreme and made promises to end the economic chaos in their countries.

Nationalism, which was a major cause of World War I, grew even stronger and seemed to feed the feelings of discontent, which became increasingly rampant. Because of **unstable economic** conditions and political unrest, harsh dictatorships arose in several of the countries, especially where there was no history of experience in democratic government. Countries such as Germany, Japan and Italy began to **aggressively expand their borders** acquiring additional territory.

In all, 59 nations became embroiled in World War II, which began September 1, 1939 and ended September 2, 1945. These dates include both the European and Pacific Theaters of war. The tragic results of this second global conflagration were more deaths and more destruction than in any other armed conflict. It completely uprooted and displaced millions of people. The end of the war brought renewed power struggles, especially in Europe and China, with many Eastern European nations as well as China coming under complete control and domination of the Communists, supported and backed by the Soviet Union. With the development and two-time deployment of an atomic bomb against two Japanese cities, the world found itself in the nuclear age. The peace settlement established the United Nations Organization, which is still existing and operating today.

Internment of people of Japanese ancestry

From the turn of the twentieth century, there was tension between Caucasians and Japanese in California. A series of laws had been passed discouraging Japanese immigration and prohibiting land ownership by Japanese. The Alien Registration Act of 1940 (the Smith Act) required the fingerprinting and registration of all aliens over the age of 14. Aliens were also required to report any change of address within 5 days. Almost 5 million aliens registered under the provisions of this act. The Japanese attack on Pearl Harbor (December 7, 1941) raised suspicion that Japan was planning a full-scale attack on the West Coast. Many believed that American citizenship did not necessarily imply loyalty.

Some authorities feared sabotage of both civilian and military facilities within the country. By February 1942, Presidential Executive Orders had authorized the arrest of all aliens suspected of subversive activities and the creation of exclusion zones where people could be isolated from the remainder of the population and kept where they could not damage national infrastructure. These War Relocation Camps were used to isolate about 120,000 Japanese and Japanese Americans (62% of whom were citizens) during World War II.

Allied response to the Holocaust

International organizations received sharp criticism during WWII for their failure to act to save the European Jews. The Allied Powers, in particular, were accused of gross negligence. Many organizations and individuals did not believe reports of the abuse and mass genocide that was occurring in Europe. Many nations did not want to accept Jewish refugees. The International Red Cross was one of the organizations that discounted reports of atrocities. One particular point of criticism was the failure of the Allied Powers to bomb the death camp at Auschwitz-Birkenau or the railroad tracks leading there.

Military leaders argued that their planes did not have the range to reach the camp; they argued that they could not provide sufficiently precise targeting to safeguard the inmates. Critics have claimed that even if Allied bombs killed all inmates at Auschwitz at the time, the destruction of the camp would have saved thousands of other Jews. The usual response was that had the Allies destroyed the camp, the Nazis would have turned to other methods of extermination.

Within the military theater, women and minorities filled a number of new roles. Women served in the military as drivers, nurses, communications operators, clerks, etc. The Flight Nurses corps was created at the beginning of the war. Among the most notable minority groups in the military were the Tuskegee Airmen, the 442nd Regimental Combat Team and the Navajo Code Talkers.

The Tuskegee Airmen were a group of African American aviators who made a major contribution to the war effort. Although they were not considered eligible for the gold wings of a Navy Pilot until 1948, these men completed standard Army flight classroom instruction and the required flying time. This group of fliers was the first blacks permitted to fly for the military. They flew more than 15,000 missions, destroyed over 1,000 German aircraft and earned more than 150 Distinguished Flying Crosses and hundreds of Air Medals.

The 442nd Regimental Combat Team was a unit composed of Japanese Americans who fought in Europe. This unit was the most highly decorated unit of its size and length of service in the history of the US Army. This self-sufficient force served with great distinction in North Africa, Italy, southern France, and Germany. The medals earned by the group include 21 Congressional Medals of Honor (the highest award given). The unit was awarded 9,486 Purple Hearts (for being wounded in battle). The casualty rate, combining those killed in action, missing in action, and wounded and removed from action, was 93%.

The Navajo Code Talkers have been credited with saving countless lives and accelerating the end of the war. There were over 400 Navajo Indians who served in all six Marine divisions from 1942 to 1945. At the time of WWII, less than 30 non-Navajo people understood the Navajo language. Because it was a very complex language and because it was not a code, it was unbreakable by the Germans or the Japanese. The job of these men was to talk and transmit information on tactics, troop movements, orders and other vital military information. A key asset of the Navajo language, besides being unintelligible to the enemy, was its rapid transmission: it was far faster than translating messages into Morse Code. It is generally accepted that without the Navajo Code Talkers, Iwo Jima could not have been taken.

The statistics on minority representation in the military during WWII are interesting:

Negroes	1,056,841
Chinese	13,311
Japanese	20,080
Hawaiians	1,320
American Indians	19,567
Filipinos	11,506
Puerto Ricans	51,438

The role of women and minority groups at home overturned many expectations and assumptions. Most able-bodied men of appropriate age were called up for military service, although minorities were generally not drafted. Yet many critical functions remained to be fulfilled by those who remained at home.

To a greater extent than any previous war, WWII required industrial production. Those who remained at home were needed to build the planes, tanks, ships, bombs, torpedoes, etc. Although the men who remained at home were working, more labor was desperately needed. In particular, a call went out to women to join the effort and enter the industrial work force. A vast campaign that combined emotional appeals and patriotism was launched to recruit women to these tasks. One of the most famous recruiting campaigns featured "Rosie the Riveter."

Yet all of the recruitment efforts emphasized that the need for women in industry was temporary. By the middle of 1944 more than 19 million women had entered the work force. Women worked building planes and tanks, but they also did more. Some operated large cranes to move heavy equipment; some loaded and fired machine guns and other weapons to ensure that they were in working order; some operated hydraulic presses; some were volunteer firefighters; some were welders, riveters, drill press operators and cab drivers. Women worked all manufacturing shifts making everything from clothing to fighter jets. Most women and their families tended "Victory Gardens" to produce food items that were in short supply. Major developments in aviation, weaponry, communications and medicine were achieved during the war. The years between WWI and WWII produced significant advancement in aircraft technology. But the pace of aircraft development and production was dramatically increased during WWII. Major developments included (1) flight-based weapon delivery systems, (2) the long-range bomber, (3) the first jet fighter, (4) the first cruise missile, and (5) the first ballistic missile. Although they were invented, the cruise and ballistic missiles were not widely used during the war. Glider planes were heavily used in WWII because they were silent upon approach. Another significant development was the broad use of paratrooper units. Finally, hospital planes came into use to extract the seriously wounded from the front and transport them to hospitals for treatment.

Weapons and technology in other areas also improved rapidly during the war. These advances were critical in determining the outcome of the war. Used for the first time were radar, electronic computers, nuclear weapons and new tank designs. More new inventions were registered for patents than ever before. Most of these new ideas were aimed to either kill or prevent being killed.

The war began with the same weaponry used in WWI. The aircraft carrier joined the battleship; the Higgins boat, the primary landing craft, was invented; light tanks were developed to meet the needs of a changing battlefield; other armored vehicles were developed. Submarines were also perfected during this period. Numerous other weapons were also developed or invented to meet the needs of battle during WWII: the bazooka, the rocket propelled grenade, anti-tank weapons, assault rifles, the tank destroyer, mine-clearing Flail tanks, Flame tanks, submersible tanks; cruise missiles, rocket artillery and air launched rockets, guided weapons, torpedoes, self-guiding weapons and Napalm. The Atomic Bomb was also developed and used for the first time during WWII.

Skill 12.8   Demonstrate knowledge of the effort to develop the atomic bomb and analyze the scientific, economic, military and human implications of the Manhattan Project

The significance and ramifications of the decision to drop the atomic bomb

The development of the atomic bomb was probably the most profound military development of the war years. This invention made it possible for a single plane to carry a single bomb that was sufficiently powerful to destroy an entire city. It was believed that possession of the bomb would serve as a deterrent to any nation because it would make aggression against a nation with a bomb tantamount to mass suicide. Two nuclear bombs were dropped in 1945 on the cities of Nagasaki and Hiroshima. They caused the immediate deaths of 100,000 to 200,000 people and far more deaths over time.

This was, and still is, a controversial decision. Those who oppose the use of the atom bomb argued that it was an unnecessary act of mass killing, particularly of non-combatants. Proponents argued that it ended the war sooner, thus resulting in fewer casualties on both sides. The development and use of nuclear weapons marked the beginning of a new age in warfare that created greater distance from the act of killing and eliminated the ability to minimize the effect of war on non-combatants. The introduction and possession of nuclear weapons by the United States led not only to the Cold War but also quickly led to the development of similar weapons by other nations, proliferation of the most destructive weapons ever created, and massive fear of the effects of the use of these weapons, including radiation poisoning and acid rain.

COMPETENCY 13.0   UNDERSTAND POLITICAL, ECONOMIC, AND CULTURAL DEVELOPMENTS IN THE UNITED STATES BETWEEN 1945 AND 1968

Skill 13.1   Analyze the causes of the Cold War, demonstrate knowledge of major Cold War political initiatives and conflicts and examine the domestic effects of the Cold War on US politics and society.

The Cold War was, more than anything else, an ideological struggle between proponents of democracy and those of communism. The two major players were the United States and the Soviet Union, but other countries were involved as well. It was a "cold" war because no large scale fighting took place directly between the two main protagonists.

The Soviet Union kept much more of a tight leash on its supporting countries, including all of Eastern Europe, which made up a military organization called the **Warsaw Pact.** The Western nations responded with a military organization of their own, NATO. Another prime battleground was Asia, where the Soviet Union had allies in China, North Korea and North Vietnam, while the US had allies in Japan, South Korea, Taiwan and South Vietnam. The Korean War and Vietnam War were major conflicts in which both main protagonists played major roles but didn't directly fight each other. The main symbol of the Cold War was the arms race, a continual buildup of missiles, tanks and other weapons that became ever more technologically advanced and increasingly more deadly. The ultimate weapon, which both sides had in abundance, was the nuclear bomb. Spending on weapons and defensive systems eventually occupied great percentages of the budgets of the US and the USSR. Some historians argue that this high level of spending played a large part in the demise of the Soviet Union.

The war was a cultural struggle as well. Adults brought up their children to hate "the Americans" or "the Communists." Cold War tensions spilled over into many parts of life in countries around the world. The ways of life in countries on either side of the divide were so different that they seemed entirely foreign to outside observers.

Since the end of the Second World War, the United States has perceived its greatest threat to be the expansion of communism in the world. To that end, it has devoted a larger and larger share of its foreign policy, diplomacy and both economic and military might to combating it.

In the aftermath of the Second World War, with the Soviet Union having emerged as the *second* strongest global power, the United States embarked on a policy known as **Containment** of the Communist menace. This involved what came to be known as the **Marshall Plan** and the **Truman Doctrine**. The Marshall Plan involved economic aid that was sent to Europe in the aftermath of the Second World War aimed at preventing the spread of communism.

The Cold War continued to varying degrees from 1947 to 1991, when the Soviet Union collapsed. Other Eastern European countries had seen their communist governments overthrown by this time as well, marking the shredding of the Iron Curtain.

The Truman Doctrine offered military aid to those countries that were in danger of communist upheaval. This led to the era known as the **Cold War** in which the United States took the lead along with the Western European nations against the Soviet Union and the Eastern Bloc countries. It was also at this time that the United States finally gave up on George Washington's advice against "European entanglements" and joined the **North Atlantic Treaty Organization** or **NATO**, which was formed in 1949 and was comprised of the United States and several Western European nations for the purposes of opposing communist aggression.

The **United Nations** was also formed at this time (1945) to replace the defunct League of Nations for the purposes of ensuring world peace. Even with American involvement, it would prove largely ineffective in maintaining world peace.

The economic boom following the war led to prosperity for many Americans in the 1950s. This prosperity did not extend to the poor blacks of the South, however; economic disparities between the races became more pronounced. Taking inspiration from similar struggles in India at the time led by **Mahatma Ghandi**, a burgeoning civil rights movement began to gain momentum under such leaders as Dr. Martin Luther King, Jr.

McCarthyism is a term that came to be used to describe the anti-communist movement within the federal government in the late 1940s and 1950s. The movement is named after Senator Joseph McCarthy of Wisconsin, who was one of its prime movers. Several congressional committees convened to investigate and interrogate citizens on their possible sympathies for or connections to the Communist Party. Failure to cooperate with these committees often resulted in the loss of one's job and placement on a "blacklist," which prevented one from being hired for many positions.

After targeting the entertainment industry and educational institutions, McCarthy turned his sights on the Army. This proved unpopular with the American public and his influence began to wane. McCarthy was eventually censured by the Senate for his overzealous attacks.

In the 1950s, the United States embarked on what was called the **Eisenhower Doctrine**, after then President Eisenhower. This doctrine aimed at trying to maintain peace in a troubled area of the world, the Middle East. However, unlike the Truman Doctrine in Europe, it would have little success.

The United States also became involved in a number of world conflicts in the ensuing years. Each had at the core the struggle against communist expansion. Among these were the **Korean War** (1950-1953), the **Vietnam War** (1965-1975), and various continuing entanglements in Central and South America and the Middle East. By the early 1970s, under the leadership of then Secretary of State Henry Kissinger, the United States and its allies embarked on the policy that came to be known as **Détente**. It was aimed at the easing of tensions between the United States and its allies and the Soviet Union and its allies.

Harry S. Truman became president near the end of WWII. He is credited with some of the most important decisions in history. When Japan refused to surrender, Truman authorized the dropping of atomic bombs on Japanese cities dedicated to war support: Hiroshima and Nagasaki. He took to the Congress a 21-point plan that came to be known as the **Fair Deal**. It included expansion of Social Security, a full-employment program, public housing and slum clearance, and a permanent Fair Employment Practices Act. The Truman Doctrine provided support for Greece and Turkey when they were threatened by the Soviet Union. The Marshall Plan (Marshall was Truman's Secretary of State) stimulated significant economic recovery for Western Europe. Truman participated in the negotiations that resulted in the formation of the North Atlantic Treaty Organization. He and his administration believed it necessary to support South Korea when it was threatened by the communist government of North Korea. But he contained American involvement in Korea so as not to risk conflict with China or Russia.

Dwight David Eisenhower succeeded Truman. Eisenhower obtained a truce in Korea and worked during his two terms to mitigate the tension of the Cold War. When Stalin died, he was able to negotiate a peace treaty with Russia that neutralized Austria. His domestic policy took a middle road. He continued most of the programs introduced under both the New Deal and the Fair Deal. When desegregation of schools began, he sent troops to Little Rock, Arkansas to enforce desegregation of the schools. He ordered the complete desegregation of the military. During his administration, the Department of Health, Education and Welfare was established and the National Aeronautics and Space Administration was formed.

John F. Kennedy is widely remembered for his Inaugural Address in which he stated, "Ask not what your country can do for you – ask what you can do for your country." His campaign pledge was to get America moving again. During his brief presidency, his economic programs created the longest period of continuous expansion in the country since WWII. He wanted the US to again take up the mission as the first country committed to the revolution of human rights. Through the Alliance for Progress and the Peace Corps, The US tapped the hopes and idealism of its citizens in reaching out to assist developing nations. He was deeply and passionately involved in the cause of equal rights for all Americans and he drafted new civil rights legislation. He also drafted plans for a broad attack on the systemic problems of privation and poverty. He believed the arts were critical to a society and instituted programs to support the arts.

In 1962, during the administration of President John F. Kennedy, Premier Khrushchev and the Soviets decided, as a protective measure for Cuba against an American invasion, to install nuclear missiles on the island. In October, American U-2 spy planes photographed over Cuba what were identified as missile bases under construction. The White House was faced with a decision on how to handle the situation without starting a war. The administration believed that the only recourse was removal of the missile sites and preventing more being set up. Kennedy announced that the US had set up a quarantine of Soviet ships heading to Cuba. It was in reality a blockade but the word itself could not be used publicly as a blockade was actually considered an act of war.

Lyndon B. Johnson assumed the presidency after the assassination of Kennedy. His vision for America was called "A Great Society." He won support in Congress for the largest group of legislative programs in the history of the nation. These included programs Kennedy had been working on at the time of his death, including a new civil rights bill and a tax cut. He defined the "great society" as "a place where the meaning of man's life matches the marvels of man's labor." The legislation enacted during his administration included an attack on disease, urban renewal, Medicare, aid to education, conservation and beautification, development of economically depressed areas, a war on poverty, voting rights for all and control of crime and delinquency. Johnson managed an unpopular military action in Vietnam and encouraged the exploration of space. During his administration the Department of Transportation was formed and the first black, Thurgood Marshall, was nominated and confirmed to the Supreme Court.

Richard Nixon inherited racial unrest and the Vietnam War, from which he extracted the American military. His administration is probably best known for improved relations with both China and the USSR. However, the Watergate scandal divided the country and led to his resignation. His major domestic achievements were the appointment of conservative justices to the Supreme Court, passing new anti-crime legislation, introducing a broad environmental program, and sponsoring revenue-sharing legislation and ended the draft.

Gerald Ford was the first Vice-President selected under the 25th Amendment. The challenges that faced his administration were a depressed economy, inflation, energy shortages and the need to champion world peace. Once inflation slowed and recession was the major economic problem, he instituted measures that would stimulate the economy. He tried to reduce the role of the federal government. He reduced business taxes and lessened the controls on business. His international focus was on preventing a major war in the Middle East. He negotiated with Russia limitations on nuclear weapons.

Skill 13.2   Examine the social, economic, and cultural effects of the postwar economic boom

The end of World War II was not the end of the economic boom that rescued the United States from the Great Depression. Prosperity continued in many ways right through to the 1960s, despite the presence of so many more people (young ones, at that) in the population.

The specter of the unknown created a huge baby boom that lasted from just before the war through its difficult half-decade and on into the late 1940s. A whole sector of society was bolstered in several stages, each time nearly overnight. Demand for all manner of baby-related things flowed and ebbed with the tides of war and recovery. Women who had worked while their husbands were away at war went right back to being homemakers when the war ended, if their husbands came home. The newly widowed who tried to continue doing the welding, airplane-building, and other heavy lifting jobs that they had done successfully while the war was on found themselves suddenly unqualified for those very jobs when the boys came home.

The huge number of newly minted children had to be cared for, of course, and their mothers primarily took responsibility for that childcare, although fathers began to help out in new ways other than providing money for the household. Many went to college, either for the first time or as returning students. The US government helped pay for many veterans' educations, and the result was many more college-educated men in the workforce than otherwise would have been.

More education meant better qualifications and that combination meant better jobs with better pay. More money coming in helped the family afford a better house, clothes and schools for its children. All of these things became affordable for the average family in a way that they had not been before.

Some private enterprises began to support the veterans' cause as well. One such was the construction company Levitt and Sons, which created a new community in New York called **Levittown**. These from-the-ground-up homes were designed especially for veterans and they were a roaring success. From modest plans of 2,000 Levitt and Sons eventually built more than 17,000 homes, including many ranch-style houses for more affluent Americans.

The success of Levittown was mirrored to a lesser degree in communities across the country, as families settled into better lifestyles and hoped for continued good times ahead. This prosperity was chronicled in a best-selling book by the economist John Kenneth Galbraith. *The Affluent Society* aptly described the runaway success of Levittown and how it was a microcosm of the American prosperity as a whole. The book also exposed one of the hidden truths of Levittown—that it was racially exclusive and that it catered, in many cases, to those who could afford the finer things in life. The book coined the term "conventional wisdom" to describe what many people believed to be true. The conventional wisdom about this period in US history was that while a large sector of its population was enjoying the fruits of its labors, a smaller yet eventually more vocal sector was being denied rights of a number of economic, social, and civil rights. This would all come to a head in the 1960s.

Skill 13.3   Recognize and analyze the changes in US society brought about by innovations in technology and transportation

Major technological developments since 1945:

- Discovery of penicillin (1945)
- Detonation of the first atomic bombs (1945)
- Xerography process invented (1946)
- Exploration of the South Pole
- Studies of X-ray radiation
- US airplane first flies at supersonic speed (1947)
- Invention of the transistor (1947)
- Long-playing record invented (1948)
- Studies begin in the science of chemo genetics (1948)
- Mount Palomar reflecting telescope (1948)
- Idlewild Airport opens in NY City
- Cortisone discovered (1949)
- USSR tests first atomic bomb (1949)
- US guided missile launched and traveled 250 miles (1949)
- Plutonium separated (1950)
- Tranquilizer meprobamate comes to wide use (1950)
- Antihistamines become popular in treating colds and allergies (1950)
- Electric power produced from atomic energy (1951)
- First heart-lung machine devised (1951)

- First solo flight over the North Pole (1951)
- Yellow fever vaccine developed (1951)
- Isotopes used in medicine and industry (1952)
- Contraceptive pill produced (1952)
- First hydrogen bomb exploded (1952)
- Nobel Prize in medicine for discovery of streptomycin (1952)
- USSR explodes hydrogen bomb (1953)
- Lung cancer connected to cigarette smoking (1953)
- First US submarine converted to nuclear power (1954)
- Polio vaccine invented (1954)
- Discovery of Vitamin B12 (1955)
- Discovery of the molecular structure of insulin (1955)
- Beginning of development of "visual telephone" (1956)
- Beginning of Transatlantic cable telephone service (1956)
- USSR launches first earth satellites (Sputnik I and II) (1957)
- Mackinac Straits Bridge in Michigan opens as the longest suspension bridge (1957)
- Stereo recordings introduced (1958)
- NASA created (1958)
- USSR launches rocket with two monkeys aboard (1959)
- Nobel Prize for Medicine for synthesis of RNA and DNA (1959)
- Major domestic policies of presidential administrations from Harry S. Truman to the present.

Skill 13.4   Identify important figures and organizations in the civil rights movement, demonstrate knowledge of major events and accomplishments and analyze the consequences of the civil rights movement

Civil Rights Movement

The phrase "the civil rights movement" generally refers to the nationwide effort made by black people and those who supported them to gain equal rights to whites and to eliminate segregation. Discussion of this movement is generally understood in terms of the period of the 1950s and 1960s.

The **key people** in the civil rights movement are:

Rosa Parks -- A black seamstress from Montgomery Alabama who, in 1955, refused to give up her seat on the bus to a white man. This event is generally understood as the spark that lit the fire of the Civil Rights Movement. She has been generally regarded as the "mother of the Civil Rights Movement."

Martin Luther King, Jr.-- the most prominent member of the Civil Rights movement. King promoted nonviolent methods of opposition to segregation. His "Letter from Birmingham Jail" explained the purpose of nonviolent action as a way to make people notice injustice. He led the march on Washington in 1963, at which he delivered the "I Have a Dream" speech. He received the 1968 Nobel Prize for Peace.

James Meredith – the first African American to enroll at the University of Mississippi.

Emmett Till – a teenage boy who was murdered in Mississippi while visiting from Chicago. The crime of which he was accused was "whistling at a white woman in a store." He was beaten and murdered and his body was dumped in a river. His two white abductors were apprehended and tried. They were acquitted by an all-white jury. After the acquittal they admitted their guilt, but remained free because of double jeopardy laws.

Ralph Abernathy – A major figure in the Civil Rights Movement who succeeded Martin Luther King, Jr. as head of the Southern Christian Leadership Conference.

Malcolm X – a political leader and part of the Civil Rights Movement. He was a prominent Black Muslim.

Stokely Carmichael – one of the leaders of the Black Power movement that called for independent development of political and social institutions for blacks. Carmichael called for black pride and maintenance of black culture. He was head of the Student Nonviolent Coordinating Committee.

Jackie Robinson – became the first black Major League Baseball player of the modern era in 1947 and was inducted into the Baseball Hall of Fame in 1962. He was a member of six World Series teams. He actively campaigned for a number of politicians including Hubert Humphrey and Richard Nixon.

Thurgood Marshall – was the grandson of a slave and was the first African American to serve on the Supreme Court of the United States. As a lawyer he was remembered for his high success rate in arguing before the Supreme Court and for his victory in the Brown v. Board of Education case.

Key events of the Civil Rights Movement included:

Brown vs. Board of Education, 1954

The murder of Emmett Till, 1955

Rosa Parks and the Montgomery Bus Boycott, 1955-56 – After refusing to give up her seat on a bus in Montgomery, Alabama, Parks was arrested, tried, and convicted of disorderly conduct and violating a local ordinance. When word reached the black community a bus boycott was organized to protest the segregation of blacks and whites on public buses. The boycott lasted 381 days, until the ordinance was lifted.

Strategy shift to "direct action" – nonviolent resistance and civil disobedience, 1955 – 1965. This action consisted mostly of bus boycotts, sit-ins and freedom rides.

Formation of the Southern Christian Leadership Conference, 1957. This group was formed by Martin Luther King, Jr., John Duffy, Rev. C. D. Steele, Rev. T. J. Jemison, Rev. Fred Shuttlesworth, Ella Baker, A. Philip Randolph, Bayard Rustin and Stanley Levison. The group provided training and assistance to local efforts to fight segregation. Non-violence was its central doctrine and its major method of fighting segregation and racism.

The Desegregation of Little Rock, 1957. Following up on the decision of the Supreme Court in Brown vs. Board of Education, the Arkansas school board voted to integrate the school system. The NAACP chose Arkansas as the place to push integration because it was considered a relatively progressive Southern state. However, the governor called up the National Guard to prevent nine black students from attending Little Rock's Central High School.

Sit-ins – In 1960, students began to stage sit-ins at local lunch counters and stores as a means of protesting the refusal of those businesses to desegregate. The first was in Greensboro, NC. This led to a rash of similar campaigns throughout the South. Demonstrators began to protest in parks, beaches, theaters, museums, and libraries. When arrested, the protesters made "jail-no-bail" pledges. This called attention to their cause and put the financial burden of providing jail space and food on the cities.

Freedom Rides – Activists traveled by bus throughout the deep South to desegregate bus terminals (required by federal law). These protesters undertook extremely dangerous protests. Many buses were firebombed, attacked by the KKK, and protesters were beaten. They were crammed into small, airless jail cells and mistreated in many ways. Key figures in this effort included John Lewis, James Lawson, Diane Nash, Bob Moses, James Bevel, Charles McDew, Bernard Lafayette, Charles Jones, Lonnie King, Julian Bond, Hosea Williams, and Stokely Carmichael.

The Birmingham Campaign, 1963-64. A campaign was planned to use sit-ins, kneel-ins in churches and a march to the county building to launch a voter registration campaign. The City obtained an injunction forbidding all such protests. The protesters, including Martin Luther King, Jr., believed the injunction was unconstitutional and defied it. They were arrested. While in jail, King wrote his famous "Letter from Birmingham Jail." When the campaign began to falter, the "Children's Crusade" called students to leave school and join the protests. The events became news when more than 600 students were jailed. The next day more students joined the protest. The media was present and broadcast to the nation vivid pictures of fire hoses being used to knock down children and dogs attacking some of them. The resulting public outrage led the Kennedy administration to intervene. About a month later, a committee was formed to end hiring discrimination, arrange for the release of jailed protesters, and establish normative communication between blacks and whites. Four months later, the KKK bombed the Sixteenth Street Baptist Church, killing four girls.

The March on Washington, 1963. This was a march on Washington for jobs and freedom. It was a combined effort of all major civil rights organizations. The goals of the march were meaningful civil rights laws, a massive federal works program, full and fair employment, decent housing, the right to vote, and adequate integrated education. It was at this march that Martin Luther King, Jr. made the famous "I Have a Dream" speech.

Mississippi Freedom Summer, 1964. Students were brought from other states to Mississippi to assist local activists in registering voters, teaching in "Freedom schools" and in forming the Mississippi Freedom Democratic Party. Three of the workers disappeared – murdered by the KKK. It took six weeks to find their bodies. The national uproar forced President Johnson to send in the FBI. Johnson was able to use public sentiment to effect passage in Congress of the Civil Rights Act of 1964.

Selma to Montgomery marches, 1965. Attempts to obtain voter registration in Selma, Alabama had been largely unsuccessful due to opposition from the city's sheriff. M.L. King came to the city to lead a series of marches. He and over 200 demonstrators were arrested and jailed. Each successive march was met with violent resistance by police. In March, a group of over 600 intended to walk from Selma to Montgomery (54 miles). News media were on hand when, six blocks into the march, state and local law enforcement officials attacked the marchers with billy clubs, tear gas, rubber tubes wrapped in barbed wire and bull whips. They were driven back to Selma. National broadcast of the footage provoked a nationwide response. President Johnson again used public sentiment to achieve passage of the Voting Rights Act of 1965. This law changed the political landscape of the South irrevocably.

Brown v. Board of Education, 1954 – the Supreme Court declared that Plessy v. Ferguson was unconstitutional. This was the ruling that had established "Separate but Equal" as the basis for segregation. With this decision, the Court ordered immediate desegregation.

Civil Rights Act of 1964 – bars discrimination in public accommodations, employment and education.

Voting Rights Act of 1965 – suspended poll taxes, literacy tests and other voter tests for voter registration.

Skill 13.5   Recognize the effects on US society of major political developments during the 1960s

The 1960 election was a contest between **John F. Kennedy** and Vice President **Richard Nixon**. The country was divided. The 1960 election was a close election, with President Kennedy winning by only 100,000 votes. President Kennedy faced Cold War challenges including Vietnam and the missile crisis in Cuba. Kennedy introduced economic reforms including a minimum wage increase. The civil rights movement led by Martin Luther King, Jr. was gaining steam and led the President to propose civil rights legislation. During a political trip to Dallas, Texas on November 22, 1963, President Kennedy was assassinated by Lee Harvey Oswald, who was subsequently shot by Jack Ruby, a local nightclub owner. Vice-President Lyndon Johnson became President.

A lot of conspiracy theories developed following the President's assassination. The Warren Commission, chaired by the Chief Justice of the Supreme Court, was created to investigate the assassination. The Commission concluded that Oswald was the assassin and that he acted alone.

President Johnson continued President Kennedy's commitment to civil rights reform and poverty. Johnson led the passage of the **Civil Rights Act of 1964** and proposed a series of policies around the Great Society program. Great Society proposed a war on poverty, and also mandated voting rights reforms, Medicare, Medicaid and other civil rights reforms.

President Johnson won reelection over Barry Goldwater, a conservative who is often credited with building the conservative movement in the United States. The Johnson campaign was able to paint Goldwater as an extremist who might lead the country to nuclear war.

The escalation of the **Vietnam War** led to a period of discontent in the United States. Increasing opposition to the war challenged the administration. President Johnson faced opposition during the 1968 Presidential campaign first from Eugene McCarthy and then from Senator Robert F. Kennedy. President Johnson announced that he would not seek a second term.

Increased civil disobedience followed the assassination of Dr. Martin Luther King, the leader of the civil rights movement. James Earl Ray pleaded guilty to the murder. Rioting occurred in several major cities.

In June, 1968, following his victory in the California primary, Senator Kennedy was assassinated by Sirhan Sirhan, who opposed the Senator's position on Israel. The summer of 1968 ended with riots at the Chicago Democratic convention in opposition to the Vietnam War. Hubert Humphrey won the Democratic nomination for President but lost the election to Richard Nixon.

Skill 13.6　Analyze the significance of the Warren court in the areas of racial justice, individual rights and criminal procedure

The **Warren Court**, under Supreme Court Chief Justice Earl Warren, was responsible for a variety of civil rights reforms and criminal procedures changes. Chief Justice Warren was selected by President Eisenhower in 1953 and served the court until 1969. School desegregation was advanced with the decision of the court in the Brown vs. Board of Education of Topeka case, which ruled that the "separate but equal" policies where schools could be separated by race were unconstitutional. This led to efforts to the integration of the public school system. Reynolds vs. Sims decided that reapportionment of legislative districts had to be based on population. In Miranda vs. Arizona the court decided that police must inform suspects of their rights prior to questioning. These rights include remaining silent and having counsel. Mapp vs. Ohio limited the use of evidence secured by illegal searches.

Skill 13.7　Demonstrate knowledge of major social change movements of the 1960s and analyze the causes and consequences of the political and social upheavals of the period

Since 1964 a number of anti-discrimination laws have been passed by the Congress. These acts have protected the civil rights of several groups of Americans. These laws include:

- Civil Rights Act of 1964;
- Immigration and Nationality Services Act of 1965;
- Voting Rights Act of 1965;
- Civil Rights Act of 1968;
- Age Discrimination in Employment Act of 1967;
- Age Discrimination Act of 1975;
- Pregnancy Discrimination Act of 1978;
- Americans with Disabilities Act of 1990;
- Civil Rights Act of 1991; and
- Employment Non-Discrimination Act.

Minority rights encompasses two ideas: the first is the normal individual rights of members of ethnic, racial, class, religious or sexual minorities; the second is collective rights of minority groups. Various civil rights movements have sought to guarantee that the individual rights of persons are not denied on the basis of being part of a minority group. The effects of these movements may be seen in guarantees of minority representation, affirmative action quotas, etc.

The disability rights movement was a successful effort to guarantee access to public buildings and transportation, equal access to education and employment, and equal protection under the law in terms of access to insurance, and other basic rights of American citizens. As a result of these efforts, public buildings and public transportation must be accessible to persons with disabilities; discrimination in hiring or housing on the basis of disability is also illegal.

A prisoners' rights movement has been working for many years to ensure the basic human rights of persons incarcerated for crimes. Immigrant rights movements have provided for employment and housing rights, as well as preventing abuse of immigrants through hate crimes. In some states, immigrant rights movements have led to bilingual education and public information access. Another group movement to obtain equal rights is the lesbian, gay, bisexual and transgender social movement. This movement seeks equal housing, freedom from social and employment discrimination, and equal recognition of relationships under the law.

The women's rights movement is concerned with the freedoms of women as differentiated from broader ideas of human rights. These issues are generally different from those that affect men and boys because of biological conditions or social constructs. The rights the movement has sought to protect throughout history include:

- The right to vote;
- The right to work;
- The right to fair wages;
- The right to bodily integrity and autonomy;
- The right to own property;
- The right to an education;
- The right to hold public office;
- Marital rights;
- Parental rights;
- Religious rights;
- The right to serve in the military; and
- The right to enter into legal contracts.

Some of the most famous leaders in the women's movement throughout American history are:

- Abigail Adams
- Susan B. Anthony
- Gloria E. Anzaldua
- Betty Friedan
- Olympe de Gouges
- Gloria Steinem
- Harriet Tubman
- Mary Wollstonecraft
- Virginia Woolf
- Germaine Greer

COMPETENCY 14.0   UNDERSTAND POLITICAL, ECONOMIC, AND
CULTURAL DEVELOPMENTS IN THE UNITED STATES
SINCE 1968

Skill 14.1   Demonstrate knowledge of the Watergate affair and the effects
of Watergate on U.S politics and culture

The **Watergate** scandal resulted in the first-ever resignation of a sitting American
president and was the most crucial domestic crisis of the 1970s.

The Supreme Court reasserted the power of judicial review in this case, one of the
most dynamic and divisive of the twentieth century in *United States v. Richard
Nixon*. The issue was whether the President had the ability to keep certain items
secret. In this case, the items were secret recordings that Richard Nixon, the
President at the time, had made of conversations he had had with his advisers.
The recordings were thought to implicate Nixon in the cover-up of the Watergate
break-in, an attempt by a team of thieves to gain information on the activities of
George McGovern, Nixon's opponent in the 1972 election. Nixon claimed that the
tapes were the property of the Executive Branch and, more to the point, of Nixon
himself. Nixon claimed an "executive privilege" that would keep him from having to
relinquish the recordings. The real issue was that recordings had been
subpoenaed by the Judicial Branch. Thus, the dispute was really whether the
Judicial Branch could supersede the authority of the Executive Branch. Like John
Marshall before him, Chief Justice Warren Burger declared that the Judicial Branch
could trump both other branches in its pursuit of justice.

Skill 14.2   Recognize major foreign policy issues and developments
affecting the United States since 1968 and analyze the effects of
these developments on the United States and its place in the
global community

Probably the highlight of the foreign policy of President Richard Nixon, after the end
of the Vietnam War and withdrawal of troops, was his 1972 trip to China. When the
Communists gained control of China in 1949, the policy of the US government was
refusal to recognize the Communist government. It regarded the legitimate
government of China to be that of Chiang Kai-shek, exiled to Taiwan.

By the 1980s, the United States embarked on what some saw as a renewal of the
Cold War. This owed to the fact that the United States was becoming more
involved in trying to prevent communist insurgency in Central America. A massive
expansion of its armed forces and the development of space-based weapons
systems were undertaken at this time.   As this occurred, the Soviet Union, with a
failing economic system and a foolhardy adventure in Afghanistan, found itself
unable to compete. By 1989, events had come to a head. This ended with the
breakdown of the Communist Bloc, the virtual end of the monolithic Soviet Union,
and the collapse of the communist system by the early 1990s.

Political boundaries can be the source of contention between adjacent countries. Following the end of World War II, the Allied forces redrew the southern boundaries of Iraq. The former Iraqi leader Saddam Hussein declared in 1991 that Iraq did not recognize the border and intended to reclaim part of Kuwait, which contained rich oil fields. Iraq's invasion led to a military response from the US and others, in the First Gulf War. The modern state of Israel was also partitioned from Palestine and other countries in 1947, creating separate Jewish and Arab regions. These borders have been a constant source of violent conflict between the two groups ever since, as well as between Israel and its neighbors such as Egypt and Lebanon.

The United States remains active in world affairs by trying to promote peace and reconciliation, with a new specter rising to challenge it and the world, the specter of nationalism. Since 1968, the United States has been part of efforts to respond to the humanitarian crisis worldwide. Often the response has been in partnership with allies, the United Nations or other global organizations. United States' assistance was prompted by starvation in countries due to famine or genocide. In countries like Biafra, Bangladesh and Cambodia, the US provided humanitarian assistance. Most recently humanitarian efforts were provided in response to the earthquake in the Indian Ocean area and the tsunami, which destroyed coastal areas in Southern Asia. The United States has also participated in a number of peacekeeping efforts in the Middle East and Bosnia to help control tensions in the country. Often aid is linked to natural or man-made disasters, such as the Chernobyl nuclear disaster in the Soviet Union. Humanitarian aid is also provided to treat or reduce the risk of disease such as in the African AIDs crisis or the threatened bird flu epidemic in Asia.

Skill 14.3   Demonstrate knowledge of the accomplishments and challenges of the presidencies of Jimmy Carter, Ronald Reagan and Bill Clinton

Iran's Ayatollah Khomeini's extreme hatred for the US was the result of the 1953 overthrow of Iran's Mossadegh government, sponsored by the CIA. To make matters worse, the CIA proceeded to train the Shah's ruthless secret police force. So when the terminally ill exiled Shah was allowed into the US for medical treatment, a fanatical mob stormed into the American embassy taking the 53 Americans as prisoners, supported and encouraged by Khomeini.

President Carter froze all Iranian assets in the US, set up trade restrictions and approved a risky rescue attempt, which failed. He had appealed to the UN for aid in gaining release for the hostages and to European allies to join the trade embargo on Iran. Khomeini ignored the UN requests for releasing the Americans, and Europeans refused to support the embargo so as not to risk losing access to Iran's oil. American prestige was damaged and Carter's chances for reelection were doomed. The hostages were released on the day of Ronald Reagan's inauguration as President, when Carter released Iranian assets as ransom.

Jimmy Carter strove to make the government "competent and compassionate" in response to the American people and their expectations. The economic situation of the nation was intensely difficult when he took office. Although significant progress was made by his administration in creating jobs and decreasing the budget deficit, inflation and interest rates were nearly at record highs. There were several notable achievements: establishment of a national energy policy to deal with the energy shortage, decontrolling petroleum prices to stimulate production, civil service reform that improved government efficiency, deregulation of the trucking and airline industries, and the creation of the Department of Education. He also negotiated the framework for peace in the Middle East, led in the establishment of diplomatic relations with China and reached a Strategic Arms Limitation Agreement with the Soviet Union. He expanded the national park system, supported the Social Security system, and appointed a record number of women and minorities to government jobs.

In 1983, in Lebanon, 241 American Marines were killed when an Islamic suicide bomber drove an explosive-laden truck into the United States Marines headquarters located at the airport in Beirut. This tragic event came as part of the unrest and violence between the Israelis and the Palestinian Liberation Organization (PLO) forces in southern Lebanon.

Ronald Reagan introduced an innovative program that came to be known as the Reagan Revolution. The goal of this program was to reduce the reliance of the American people upon government. The Reagan administration restored the hope and enthusiasm of the nation. His legislative accomplishments include economic growth stimulation, curbing inflation, increasing employment, and strengthening the national defense. He won Congressional support for a complete overhaul of the income tax code in 1986. By the time he left office there was prosperity in peacetime with no depression or recession. His foreign policy was "peace through strength." Reagan nominated Sandra Day O'Connor as the first female justice on the Supreme Court.

In the decade preceding the election of Ronald Reagan in 1980, the United States had experienced increased inflation, an upswing in the crime rate, and a fuel shortage crisis. These factors contributed to a general dissatisfaction with the federal government, and a lack of confidence in the ability of the government to prevent or solve the nation's problems.

It was a time of social division, as well. The 1973 Supreme Court decision in *Roe vs. Wade* upheld the legality of abortion, which angered many conservatives and became a rallying point for the right wing of the Republican Party, which had been out of favor for many years.

This conservative branch of the party had enjoyed prominence in 1964, when Barry Goldwater was selected to run for President on the Republican ticket. Goldwater was defeated and the Republicans found more success four years later with the more moderate Richard Nixon. Nixon's presidency ended in disgrace with his resignation and in the meantime, the Democrats retained their stronghold in both houses of Congress. In 1976, Democrat Jimmy Carter was elected President and it was on his watch that public dissatisfaction was to reach its peak. This dissatisfaction was to provide the conservative Republicans an opportunity to offer a new direction, and the American public was receptive.

Bolstering the more conservative Republicans were large numbers of religious activists who gathered behind television evangelists Jerry Falwell and Pat Robertson. This large bloc not only opposed abortion, but pressed for a conservative agenda that invoked religious doctrine in interpreting and proposing social legislation.

In Ronald Reagan, the rising conservative movement found an eloquent and charismatic representative. Reagan was a former movie star who was comfortable in front of a camera. He had entered politics in California, eventually becoming governor. He had supported the conservative Goldwater in 1964 and had delivered a speech on his behalf at the nominating convention. Reagan was confident, and carried a positive message of American strength that resonated with many voters. He won the presidential election of 1980 against Jimmy Carter in a landslide. He was elected to a second term against Walter Mondale in 1984.

Reagan brought with him a cabinet of conservative advisors who believed in a conservative social agenda, limited government involvement in the economy, and American strength abroad. In 1988, Reagan's vice president, George H.W. Bush, was elected president and continued many of the conservative policies implemented by Reagan. The religious groups that had gained a foothold in the years surrounding Reagan's first election continued to grow and still maintain political influence, particularly in the Republican Party. In 2000, conservative George W. Bush, the son of President George H.W. Bush, was elected President. George W. Bush populated his cabinet with many of the same people who had advised President Reagan 20 years earlier, thereby building on the conservative base that Ronald Reagan had laid.

George H. W. Bush was committed to traditional American values and to making America a "kinder and gentler nation." During the Reagan administration, Bush held responsibility for anti-drug programs and Federal deregulation. When the Cold War ended and the Soviet Union broke apart, he supported the rise of democracy, but took a position of restraint toward the new nations. Bush also dealt with defense of the Panama Canal and Iraq's invasion of Kuwait, which led to the first Gulf War, known as Desert Storm. Although his international affairs record was strong, he was not able to turn around increased violence in the inner cities and a struggling economy.

William Clinton led the nation in a time of greater peace and economic prosperity than has been experienced at any other time in history. His domestic accomplishments include: the lowest inflation in 30 years, the lowest unemployment rate in modern days, the highest home ownership rate in history, lower crime rates in many places and smaller welfare rolls. He proposed and achieved a balanced budget and achieved a budget surplus.

Skill 14.4 Analyze the effects of Supreme Court decisions and major legislation on ideas about civil liberties and civil rights.

In recent years, the phrase "race-neutral" has begun to be used. This term seems to be being applied more and more as a response to affirmative action programs, which attempted to grant preferences to African Americans in order to make up for past injustices. One of the most famous of these series of events culminated in *Regents of the University of California* v. *Bakke* (1978), in which the Court invalidated the denial of a white student from law school because the school had to meet its mandated quota of minority applicants. In 1995, in *Adarand Constructors, Inc.* v. *Pena*, the Court mandated that race neutrality be examined in federal agencies under "strict scrutiny". In effect, the Court had validated the idea of race neutrality and ended the raft of affirmative action programs that had dotted the federal government's departments and agencies.

Along with the idea of the government lending a helping hand to those struggling for basic civil rights came the idea of aiding those who were facing a daunting path through the legal system. Prisoners, especially non-white ones, didn't have a whole lot of rights under the law or certainly in practice. The one Court case that resonates throughout the latter half of the twentieth century is **Miranda v. Arizona**, in which the Court set out a series of information that arresting officers had to impart to those they were arresting, including such Bill of Rights-friendly language as the right to an attorney, the right to avoid self-incrimination and the right to a trial by jury. Other law enforcement cases preceded it and followed it, with the idea that a person who is arrested has the presumption of innocence until guilt has been proven.

In the decade preceding the election of Ronald Reagan in 1980, the United States had experienced increased inflation, an upswing in the crime rate and a fuel shortage crisis. These factors contributed to a general dissatisfaction with the federal government, and a lack of confidence in the ability of the government to prevent or solve the nation's problems. It was also a time of social division. The 1973 Supreme Court decision in **Roe vs. Wade** upheld the legality of abortion, which angered many conservatives and became a rallying point for the right wing of the Republican Party, which had been out of favor for many years.

Perhaps the widest ranging yet personal civil rights case to come about in the last decade is **Bush v. Palm Beach County Canvassing Board**. Presidential candidate George W. Bush sued to invalidate the recount that had begun in the wake of Bush's narrow victory over Al Gore in Florida. Bush claimed, among other things, that his Fifth Amendment due process rights were violated by the various decisions made in the wake of the close vote counts. The result was a decision by the Court to stop all recounting and declare Bush the winner. This was not a classical civil rights case per se, but it was one that argued as such and involved the sort of protection that had been argued under previous Fifth and Fourteenth Amendment cases.

Also refer to Skills 13.4 and 16.4.

Skill 14.5   Recognize changing patterns of immigration to the United States and analyze the effects of immigration on US society

Immigration has played a crucial role in the growth and settlement of the United States from the start. With a large interior territory to fill and ample opportunity, the US encouraged immigration throughout most of the nineteenth century, maintaining an almost completely open policy. Famine in Ireland and Germany in the 1840s resulted in over 3.5 million immigrants from these two countries alone between the years of 1830 and 1860.

Following the Civil War, rapid expansion in rail transportation brought the interior states within easy reach of new immigrants who still came primarily from Western Europe and entered the US on the east coast. As immigration increased several states adopted individual immigration laws, and in 1875 the US Supreme Court declared immigration a federal matter. Following a huge surge in European immigration in 1880, the United States began to regulate immigration, first by passing a tax to new immigrants, then by instituting literacy requirements and barring those with mental or physical illness. A large influx of Chinese immigration to the western states had resulted in the complete exclusion of immigrants from that country in 1882. In 1891, the federal Bureau of Immigration was established. Even with these new limits in place, immigration remained relatively open in the US to those from European countries, and increased steadily until World War I.

The **Chinese Exclusion Act**, approved by the US Congress in 1882 was the ultimate expression of anti-Chinese feeling. It prohibited Chinese immigration for ten years. In 1892, it was extended for another ten years. In 1902, it became permanent. It was not repealed until China and the US became allies against the Japanese during World War II. This law also produced further difficulties for the Chinese, including boycotts of Chinese-produced goods.

With much of Europe left in ruins after WWI, immigration to the US exploded in the years following the war. In 1920 and 1921, some 800,000 new immigrants arrived. Unlike previous immigrants who came mainly from western European countries, the new wave of immigrants was from southern and eastern Europe. The US responded to this sudden shift in the makeup of new immigrants with a quota system, first enacted by Congress in 1921. This system limited immigration in proportion to the ethnic groups that were already settled in the US according to previous census records. This national-origins policy was extended and further defined by Congress in 1924.

This policy remained the official policy of the US for the next 40 years. Occasional challenges to the law from non-white immigrants re-affirmed that the intention of the policy was to limit immigration primarily to white, western Europeans, who the government felt were most likely to assimilate into American culture. Strict limitations on Chinese immigration was extended throughout the period, and only relaxed in 1940. In 1965, Congress overhauled immigration policy, removing the quotas and replacing them with a preference based system. Now, immigrants reuniting with family members and those with special skills or education were given preference. As a result, immigration from Asian and African countries began to increase. The 40-year legacy of the 1920s immigration restrictions had a direct and dramatic impact on the makeup of modern American society. Had Congress not imposed what amounted to racial limits on new arrivals to the country, the US would perhaps be a larger more diverse nation today.

Skill 14.6   Evaluate the growing influence of technology in US society and analyze the effects of technology on the US economy

New technologies have changed the way of life for many. This is the computer age and in many places, computers are found in the grade schools. Technology makes the world seem a much smaller place. Even children have cell phones today. The existence of television and modern technology has us watching a war while it is in progress. Outsourcing is now popular because of technological advances. Call centers for European, American and other large countries are now located in India, Pakistan, etc. Multinational corporations located plants in foreign countries to lower costs.

In many places technology has resulted in a mobile population. Popular culture has been shaped by mass production and the mass media. Mass production and technology has made electronic goods affordable to most. This is the day of the **cell phone** and the PDA. The **Internet** and email allow people anywhere in the world to be in touch and allows people to learn about world events. In industrial countries and in many others, popular culture is oriented towards the electronic era.

Skill 14.7   Examine the 2000 presidential election and the role of the Electoral College and the Supreme Court in determining the outcome of the election

The College of Electors, or the Electoral College as it is more commonly known, has a long and distinguished history of mirroring the political will of the American voters. On some occasions, the results have not been entirely in sync with that political will.

Article II of the Constitution lists the specifics of the Electoral College. The Founding Fathers included the Electoral College as one of the famous "checks and balances" for two reasons: 1) to give states with small populations more of an equal weight in the presidential election, and 2) they didn't trust the common man (women couldn't vote then) to be able to make an informed decision on which candidate would make the best president.

First of all, the same theory that created the US Senate practice of giving two Senators to each state created the Electoral College. The large-population states had their populations reflected in the House of Representatives. New York and Pennsylvania, two of the states with the largest populations, had the highest number of members of the House of Representatives. But these two states still had only two senators, the exact same number that small-population states like Rhode Island and Delaware had.

This was true as well in the Electoral College: Each state had just one vote, regardless of how many members of the House represented that state. So, the one vote that the state of New York cast would be decided by an initial vote of New York's Representatives. If the initial vote were a tie, then that deadlock would have to be broken.

Secondly, when the Constitution was being written, not many people knew a whole lot about government, politics, or presidential elections. A large number of people were farmers or lived in rural areas, where they were far more concerned with making a living and providing for their families than they were with who was running for which office. Many of these common people could not read or write, either, and wouldn't be able to read a ballot in any case. Like it or not, the Founding Fathers thought that even if these common people could vote, they wouldn't necessarily make the best decision for who would make the best president. So, the Electoral College was born.

Technically, the electors do not have to vote for anyone. The Constitution does not require them to do so. And throughout the history of presidential elections, some have indeed voted for someone else. But tradition holds that the electors vote for the candidate chosen by their state, and so the vast majority of electors do just that.

The Electoral College meets a few weeks after the presidential election. Mostly, their meeting is a formality. When all the electoral votes are counted, the president with the most votes wins. In most cases, the candidate who wins the popular vote also wins in the Electoral College. However, this has not always been the case.

Most recently, in 2000 in Florida, the Supreme Court decided the election. The Democratic Party's nominee was Vice-President Al Gore. A presidential candidate himself back in 1988, Gore had served as vice-president for both of President Bill Clinton's terms. As such, he was both a champion of Clinton's successes and a reflection of his failures. The Republican Party's nominee was George W. Bush, governor of Texas and son of former President George Bush. He campaigned on a platform of a strong national defense and an end to questionable ethics in the White House. The election was hotly contested, and many states went down to the wire, being decided by only a handful of votes. The one state that seemed to be flip-flopping as Election Day turned into Election Night was Florida. In the end, Gore won the popular vote, by nearly 540,000 votes. But he didn't win the electoral vote. The vote was so close in Florida that a recount was necessary under federal law. Eventually, the Supreme Court weighed in and stopped all the recounts. The last count had Bush winning by less than a thousand votes. That gave him Florida and the White House.

Because of these irregularities, especially the last one, many have taken up the cry to eliminate the Electoral College, which they see as archaic and capable of distorting the will of the people. After all, they argue, elections these days come down to one or two key states, as if the votes of the people in all the other states don't matter. Proponents of the Electoral College point to the tradition of the entity and all of the other elections in which the electoral vote mirrored the popular vote. Eliminating the Electoral College would no doubt take a constitutional amendment, and those are certainly hard to come by. The debate crops up every four years; in the past decade, though, the debate has lasted longer in between elections.

Also refer to Skill 14.4.

Skill 14.8   Analyze the response of the United States to the attacks of September 11, 2001 and demonstrate knowledge of the war against terrorism and US interventions in Afghanistan and Iraq

Modern global terrorism can trace its roots to 1967 when Israel defeated Arab forces in Palestine. Palestinian fighters, realizing they could not win a military battle against Israel, turned to urban terror tactics to attack Israel's population centers. Taking advantage of modern communications and technology, radical Palestinian organizations undertook a series of airline hijackings, bombings and kidnappings to draw attention to their demands and to terrorize and demoralize their enemies, specifically Israel. In 1972, at the Olympic Games in Munich, radical Palestinians kidnapped nine Israeli athletes who were all killed in a subsequent gun battle. Supported by some Arab states and criminal organizations, the radical Palestinians developed a network of connections through which their techniques and training could flow to other parts of the world.

Terrorist activity continued throughout the 1970s. In 1979, the Soviet Union invaded Afghanistan and an Islamic revolution took place in Iran, two events that were to provide opportunities for terrorist tactics to advance as radical organizations gained valuable military experience and state support from the leadership in Iran. During the 1980s, the use of suicide bombers became an effective technique to strike deeply. Anti-Israeli sentiments grew, as well as anti-US feelings over America's support of Israel. Radical terrorists began to choose western targets, as in the bombing of US Marine barracks in Lebanon in 1983 and the 1988 bombing of a Pan Am airliner over Scotland.

With the withdrawal of the Soviet Union from Afghanistan and its subsequent collapse, the region of Afghanistan became a safe haven for radical groups to organize and train followers in terror tactics. The Taliban, a strict religious sect, took control in Afghanistan and harbored these groups, including Al-Qaeda.

Al-Qaeda is led by Saudi millionaire Osama bin-Laden and claims opposition to a US military presence in Saudi Arabia and elsewhere in the Middle East. In 1993, Al-Qaeda operatives struck at the United States by bombing the World Trade Center in New York City. On September 11, 2001, Al-Qaeda followers hijacked four commercial airliners, flying two of them into the World Trade Center towers and one into the Pentagon in Washington, D.C. The fourth airliner crashed in Pennsylvania. It was the largest single terrorist attack the world had seen, killing thousands of people. The United States reacted by launching an attack on Afghanistan, driving bin-Laden and his followers into the hills.

Since that attack the prospect of global terrorism has become a reality in the modern world, driving much of the world's foreign policy toward Middle Eastern states, as well as domestic security policies.

COMPETENCY 15.0   UNDERSTAND MAJOR DEVELOPMENTS IN GEORGIA'S HISTORY AND GEORGIA'S ROLE IN THE HISTORY OF THE UNITED STATES TO 1877

Skill 15.1   Demonstrate knowledge of Native American cultures of the Southeast and analyze the effects of European exploration and settlement on Native American groups in Georgia

The Mississippian Culture was an early Native American culture that thrived throughout much of the eastern part of North America from approximately 800 to 1500 A.D. From this culture, which was centered on mound building and maize cultivation, descended many of the tribes and related cultures that were encountered by the first Europeans to explore the east coast of North America.

In the region that is now Georgia, the Cherokee and the Creek tribes were the primary groups that inhabited the area from the sixteenth century on.

The Cherokee lived partly in the southern Appalachian Mountains in what is now northern Georgia. They were an agricultural people who raised corn, beans and squash. They lived in numerous villages made up of 30 to 60 houses around a large counsel house.

The Creek was a confederacy of related tribes named after a group that lived mainly along the Ocmulgee River, which runs through the center of present day Georgia. The tribes were linked culturally and shared the same language, Muskogean. Like the Cherokee, the Creek were agricultural people who lived in villages.

In 1540, **Hernando De Soto** was the first European to describe the Native Americans living in the Georgia region. As European settlement in the new world advanced, they brought significant changes to the Native American groups in Georgia. New trade opportunities introduced European goods into Native communities, but sometimes also aggravated tensions between different tribes. Horses and firearms changed how warfare was waged. Natives were exposed to European diseases against which they had no natural defenses. Smallpox in particular became epidemic among Native Americans, decimating their populations.

Exposure to Europeans also brought advances to the Native American tribes. **Sequoyah**, a Cherokee man, after being exposed to the Western system of writing, invented an alphabet to represent the spoken Cherokee language, spurring the development of schools and widespread literacy among the tribe. The alphabet is still used today.

Skill 15.2 **Recognize major events of the colonial period of Georgia's history, including the purpose for initial settlement, the Trustee Period and the development of Georgia as a royal colony**

During the seventeenth century, the east coast of North America was rapidly being settled by European colonists in the North and by the Spanish in the South. In 1670, the British colony of South Carolina was founded directly north of Spanish controlled Florida, creating a tense frontier in what is now Georgia. Military conflict followed until the Spanish missions were withdrawn in 1704 and the area occupied by Yamasee Native Americans friendly to the British.

Relations grew sour between the Yamasee and the British in 1715 over the fur trade, however, and the Yamasee began attacking British colonists. The colonists responded with force and the Yamasee were driven out of the area to Florida. This largely depopulated the coast region between Charleston, the capital of British Carolina, and St, Augustine, the capital of Spanish Florida.

In the early 1730s, James Oglethorpe, a British Member of Parliament, was engaged in a campaign of prison reform in England. English citizens who fell into debt could be thrown into debtor's prisons under deplorable conditions, where they were usually mistreated and often died. Oglethorpe presented a plan to colonize the newly available land in North America with some of these debtors to give them an opportunity to escape the horrors of prison and start over in the New World.

King George II approved Oglethorpe's scheme, and on June 9, 1732, granted a royal charter to him and a group of 20 other philanthropists to found a colony in North America. These 21 trustees called the new colony Georgia in honor of the king.

In the end, the first people chosen to go to the new colony were not debtors, but were chosen by the trustees based on their skills and professions and potential usefulness in the new colony. The first group of 114 people, including Oglethorpe, sailed from England on the *Anne* in November 1732, arriving in Charleston two months later. Oglethorpe scouted ahead into the Georgia region and selected a bluff on the Savannah River to build the first settlement, called Savannah.

Oglethorpe and the trustees wished to avoid duplicating England's strict class system in the new colony, which they felt had led to the practice of imprisoning debtors. They implemented a series of rules in the colony that prohibited slavery and required each man to work his own land. Identical houses were built on equal sized lots to emphasize the equality of all.

The peaceful agrarian community that was envisioned by Oglethorpe grew happily for a time, but positioned as it was on the British frontier with the Spanish, the realities of potential warfare occupied the colony's attentions. Oglethorpe successfully petitioned the British government to grant him military authority in the area and to provide him with a regiment of British troops to defend the frontier. Oglethorpe unsuccessfully attempted to capture St. Augustine, spurring a series of battles between the Spanish and British allied troops under Oglethorpe. The British emerged victorious after holding the line at the Battle of Bloody Marsh in 1742, after which the Spanish did not try to invade Georgia again.

Skill 15.3   Analyze Georgia's role in the American Revolution, the strengths and weaknesses of the Georgia Constitution of 1777 and Georgia's role in the framing and adoption of the US Constitution

As dissatisfaction with taxation increased in the northern colonies, similar rumblings began in Georgia, which joined the other colonies in 1765 in renouncing the **Stamp Act.** Georgia had prospered under its royal charter, however, and many Georgians believed that they needed British protection from neighboring Native Americans.

When news of the Battle of Lexington and Concord reached Georgia, patriotic resolve was strengthened and in May 1775, a group of patriots raided the arsenal at Savannah and took a supply of British gunpowder. Georgian colonists set up their own government shortly thereafter and joined the association of colonies in enforcing a ban on trade with the British. While British Governor James Wright was still the official authority in Georgia, the provincial government founded in July 1775 gave executive authority to a Council of Safety, which held the real power.

Wright was eventually expelled in 1776, after being held hostage by the colonists as British warships approached Savannah. Without a governor, provincial congress was convened at Augusta in April 1776 and a set of Rules and Regulations were adopted outlining a simple structure of government. Three delegates were sent to the Second Continental Congress in Philadelphia in time to sign the Declaration of Independence in July.

Three months later, a convention was called in Savannah to provide for a more permanent form of government in Georgia. The result of this convention was Georgia's first constitution, the **Constitution of 1777.** The new constitution created a single elected assembly that in turn chose a governor. The constitution was remarkable for its time in granting voting rights to a wide group of citizens, although only white men were allowed to vote. The Georgia Constitution also provided for future amendments by state convention. This provision, which was not included in all state constitutions at the time, eventually became common practice throughout the United States. The Constitution of 1777 lacked many of the internal balances of political power that would be included in the United States Constitution, however, and serious movements began in 1788 to redraft it.

Following the American victory in the Revolutionary War, Georgia engaged with the rest of the new states in the debate over a federal constitution. Along with its southern neighbors, Georgia opposed a strong central government advocated by the Federalists, fearing the concentration of political power in the northern states. The Bill of Rights, the first ten amendments to the US Constitution that spell out limits on governmental authority, were included in the proposed Constitution to ensure the rights of the states. In this way, Georgia and the other southern states greatly influenced the shape of the Constitution. Georgia ratified the US Constitution in January 1788.

Skill 15.4   Demonstrate knowledge of major social, religious, economic and political developments in Georgia between 1789 and 1840 and analyze their effects on the development of Georgia society.

In 1785, the Georgia General Assembly set aside a tract of land to be used for the establishment of a college or seminary. In 1798, a portion of the land was sold to raise funds to establish a university and in 1799 the **University of Georgia** was officially founded. Classes began in 1801. The University of Georgia was the first state-chartered university in the United States.

Baptists have been present in Georgia since the first colonists arrived in 1733. At about that time, the Methodist denomination was developing in England and the American colonies during what is called the **First Great Awakening**. This protestant religious movement in the colonies emphasized a personal involvement in one's church and personal responsibility for sin and salvation. In Georgia, as elsewhere, protestant denominations gained in membership throughout the eighteenth century. The Second Great Awakening was a similar wave of religious zeal that moved through Georgia and the rest of the country in the early nineteenth century. Methodist and Baptist churches in particular saw huge growth. The Civil War cooled this revival in the North, but in the South, religious involvement was strengthened.

The **Yazoo land fraud** was a corrupt scheme involving several Georgia politicians, including Governor George Mathews, where public land was sold to private companies for extremely low prices. These companies included many state legislators as stockholders. When the details of the scheme became known, a scandal ensued which resulted in the election of reformer Jared Irwin as Governor. In 1796, Irwin nullified the act that had sold the land.

Before the invention of the cotton gin in 1793, cotton in Georgia grew only along the seaboard. The kind of cotton that would grow in these areas could be easily cleaned of seeds because of its long fibers. The **cotton gin** was a device that could clean the short-fiber cotton that grew better inland. Its invention suddenly opened up large areas of potential farmland in Georgia.

The rapid growth of cotton farming required an expansion of the available labor, which came from slavery. As cotton production expanded, so did the Georgia economy's reliance on slave labor. This increased reliance on slavery heightened Georgia's concern with the growing abolitionist movement in the North and would directly contribute to its eventual secession.

The expansion of cotton farming also resulted in the displacement of the **Cherokee** and **Creek** peoples who inhabited desirable potential planting ground. The Cherokee and Creek were eventually forced out of Georgia and relocated to the Indian Territory in present day Oklahoma.

Skill 15.5 Demonstrate knowledge of the decision for secession and Georgia's role in the Civil War and examine the effects of the Civil War and Reconstruction on Georgia

When the anti-slavery candidate Abraham Lincoln was elected President in 1860, many southern states began to seriously consider the issue of seceding from the Union. The issue of whether slavery should be perpetuated in the growing country by allowing it in new territories had been a contentious matter for decade. The southern slave states were concerned that the federal government had been taken over by abolitionists, and that the complete abolition of slavery was not far away.

The white male voters of Georgia were overwhelmingly opposed to abolition, as their livelihoods depended on the labor of slaves. They differed somewhat on the question of **secession**, however, with some in favor of immediate secession after the election of Lincoln and some in favor of using secession as a bargaining chip to gain assurance from the federal government that it would make no attempt to abolish slavery in the states. On January 19, 1861, a state convention called to consider the question voted to secede.

Georgians played a prominent role in the drafting and adoption of the Constitution of the Confederate States in Alabama and Georgian Alexander Stephens served as the first Vice President, under Confederate President **Jefferson Davis.**

Considered safely within the boundaries of the Confederate States, Georgia was the location of considerable Confederate military operations such as munitions factories and the Andersonville prison camp. Georgia was not safe from attack and in 1864, General William Sherman embarked on a campaign that cut a path of destruction through Georgia. Sherman captured Atlanta on September 2, 1864, and burned the entire city. Sherman continued on to the capital, Milledgeville, and finally to Savannah.

Following the surrender of the southern states, the federal government adopted a system of reconstruction in the south. **Reconstruction** required former Confederate states to adopt new constitutions in order to be readmitted into the Union. Georgia was one of the last states to surrender, and the last state to be readmitted. This was partly because the terms of readmission had changed after the death of Lincoln, requiring Georgia to hold two conventions on a new constitution.

The post-reconstruction government abolished slavery and granted voting rights to all men, black and white. At first, many whites boycotted elections, allowing many blacks to participate in the government for a time.

COMPETENCY 16.0   UNDERSTAND MAJOR DEVELOPMENTS IN GEORGIA'S HISTORY AND GEORGIA'S ROLE IN THE HISTORY OF THE UNITED STATES FROM 1877 TO THE PRESENT

Skill 16.1   Demonstrate knowledge of important political, economic and social changes that occurred in Georgia between 1877 and 1918.

The "New South" is a term sometimes used to describe the South after the Civil War and refers to the South that is based on industry and no longer dependent on slave labor. In Georgia, **Henry Grady** is closely associated with the New South movement in the 1880s, which sought to bring northern investment and industry to the state, particularly in the Atlanta region.

The New South was an ideal more than a reality for Georgia farmers, who found themselves stressed by falling cotton prices after the Civil War. The growing Populist movement in the 1890s blamed the entrenched Democratic Party for many of the farmer's woes and mounted a challenge to the party. Georgia populists sought to include blacks in the movement and called for prison reform. By the turn of the century, **Populism** as a movement had largely faded from Georgia politics, but had lasting effects.

Jim Crow laws were laws enacted after the Civil War, which resulted in the segregation of whites and blacks, with blacks being forced to use inferior facilities. During Reconstruction, southern states were forced to adopt protections for free black citizens. Once the Reconstruction governments were replaced with "Redeemer" governments, laws were enacted that required separate schools and public facilities for blacks and whites, thereby replacing the Black Codes that had been in effect prior to the Civil War.

Jim Crow laws had the effect of denying voting rights to many black citizens by requiring the payment of a **poll tax**. The all white Democratic Party also discouraged black participation in politics and elections.

Despite these prejudices, many blacks prospered following the war, especially in the growing industrial center of Atlanta. As the white elite witnessed the emergence of a black economic elite in Atlanta, some argued that allowing blacks to vote had caused them to think of themselves as equal to whites and that the vote should be taken away from blacks.

Tension grew between the races, eventually erupting in violence in Atlanta in 1906. Unsubstantiated reports circulated that black men had attacked four white women. A mob of white men and boys gathered and raided black neighborhoods, destroying black businesses and killing several people. The state militia was called in to control the mob, which eventually subsided. As a result of the riot, even further restrictions were placed on black voting rights.

Skill 16.2 **Demonstrate knowledge of the effects of World Wars I and II in Georgia and recognize major economic and political developments of the interwar period.**

World War I greatly impacted Georgia, which became the location of several military training camps. Thousands of troops from all over the country passed through Georgia on their way to war. In 1918, the troop ship *Otranto* sunk tragically, killing almost 400 men of which 130 were from Georgia.

When President Wilson instituted the draft, many white Georgians tried to prevent black men from being called into service, especially landowners who employed black sharecroppers. Not wanting to lose their labor force, they would sometimes not deliver draft notices, or prevent blacks from registering. Many blacks were arrested and jailed for evading the draft as a result.

Agriculture was not only threatened by the potential loss of farm labor. The boll weevil is an insect that affects cotton. It began its spread northward from Mexico in the late nineteenth century and reached Georgia around 1915. Within 10 years, the number of acres planted in cotton in Georgia halved because of the pest. The boll weevil forced farmers to diversify their crops, leading to the rise of peanut farming, which became an important agricultural product.

Eugene Talmadge began his career in state politics as the Commissioner of Agriculture in 1926. Outspoken and opinionated, Talmadge won popular support of the rural community and rapidly became a polarizing influence in the Democratic Party. He was elected governor in 1932 and re-elected in 1934. After unsuccessful bids for the US Senate, Talmadge was again elected governor in 1940.

Talmadge was a forceful leader who would bypass legislative action and remove appointees who disagreed with his views. Talmadge undertook to remove faculty members from the state University system who he thought wanted to integrate the schools or held the belief of racial equality. As a result of his raid on the system, the University lost its accreditation. The more moderate Ellis Arnall challenged Talmadge in the gubernatorial race of 1942, promising to restore accreditation and won. Talmadge was re-elected governor in 1946, but died before taking office.

Talmadge was a major opponent of President Franklin Roosevelt's New Deal, a series of public programs beginning in 1933 designed to assist Depression wracked Americans and promote economic recovery. Talmadge and others saw the New Deal as the federal government interference with local affairs, but the program, which provided farm subsidies, built new infrastructure and provided direct assistance to poor Georgians was popular among the people. President Roosevelt himself was popular in Georgia, having adopted Warm Springs as a second home during his time in office.

The New Deal did help many poor southerners, but failed to bring the dramatic turnaround which the South had sought. It was World War II and the related boom in war industry that transformed Georgia's economy. Defense contractors found a large and willing labor force in Georgia, and shipbuilding and aircraft manufacturing became important industries, employing hundreds of thousands of people. With many men away in the military, women entered the workforce in large numbers for the first time. Black workers also benefited from the labor shortage, entering positions that had formerly been reserved for white men. Segregation was still enforced, however.

Skill 16.3   Analyze major political and economic developments in Georgia since World War II.

New methods of agriculture kept farming a viable endeavor once again, but Georgia was no longer entirely dependent on agriculture. The City of Atlanta made an early commitment to developing air travel in 1925 with the establishment of an airfield. The airfield grew throughout the twentieth century, and under the administration of Mayor Maynard Jackson was transformed into the **Hartsfield International Airport,** a huge building project that opened in 1980. Later named the Hartsfield-Jackson International airport, the facility is currently the busiest airport in the world.

Ellis Arnall was elected Governor of Georgia in 1942 at the age of 35. Arnall made several significant reforms, including the elimination of poll taxes and the lowering of the voting age. He also proposed checks to the power of the governor, feeling that Eugene Talmadge had abused his power previously. Arnall left office in 1947, and ran again in 1966 against the segregationist Lester Maddox. Maddox emerged the victor in that race and served as governor until 1971.

Herman Talmadge was the only son of former Governor Eugene Talmadge. He ran his father's successful campaign for Governor in 1946, and was briefly appointed Governor by the legislature when his father died before taking office. Herman Talmadge was himself elected Governor in 1948. Talmadge worked to bring industry to Georgia and supported segregation. He served as Governor until 1954, when he ran for the US Senate and was elected. Talmadge served in the Senate until 1981.

Between Reconstruction and the 1960s, the Democratic Party dominated Georgia politics. Republicans had been installed by the federal government during reconstruction and were quickly replaced by Democrats after the federal troops that supported the Republican state governments were withdrawn. The civil rights era began drawing sharp lines between old line Democrats and Democrats that were more moderate. This division sometimes split the vote and allowed Republicans to gain footholds.

Another change in Georgia politics in the 1960s was the end of the county unit system of conducting state primaries. Under this system, all of a county's unit votes were awarded to the candidate that received the most individual votes within that county. This system favored rural counties, and allowed for the election of candidates who had actually lost the popular vote, as was the case in the 1946 primary where Eugene Talmadge won the primary for Governor. Primary politics were important in Georgia. Because of the dominance of the Democratic Party, winning the primary virtually ensured winning the general election. The US Supreme Court declared the county unit system illegal in 1963.

In 1962, **Jimmy Carter** was elected to the Georgia legislature after challenging fraudulent returns in his election. He went on to serve as Governor of Georgia and was elected President of the United States in 1976, defeating President Gerald Ford.

Skill 16.4   Examine the role of Georgia and prominent Georgians in the civil rights movement.

Dr. Martin Luther King, Jr., was born in Atlanta in 1929. He studied sociology and theology in college and became a Baptist pastor in Montgomery, Alabama in 1953. In 1955, in Montgomery, **Rosa Parks**, a black woman, was arrested for refusing to give her bus seat to a white man, as was required under the segregation laws of the time. King organized a boycott of Montgomery buses, which lasted over a year. During this time, King was himself arrested and his home was bombed. The matter eventually reached the United States Supreme Court, which ruled that segregation of public transportation was illegal.

King became a national spokesman for civil rights for African Americans and non-violent protest of segregation. Through organized protests and powerful public speeches, King brought national attention to the issue of civil rights culminating in 1963 with the **March on Washington**. The March was an organized demonstration by several African American organizations calling for an end to segregation and legal discrimination. The demonstration was successful in influencing the passage of the **Civil Rights Act of 1964.** Dr. King continued to speak out against violence and in opposition to the US involvement in Viet Nam. Dr. King was assassinated in 1968.

Maynard Jackson was the first African American mayor of Atlanta. The grandson of prominent civil rights leader John Wesley Dobbs, Jackson brought a commitment to civil rights to his office. He implemented an affirmative action program that increased the number of city contracts with African American businesses and introduced public involvement in neighborhood planning. Jackson also undertook to reform the Atlanta Police Department to provide more opportunity for black advancement.

Andrew Young was a key aide to Dr. King during the growth of the civil rights movement. Young organized voter registration drives and encouraged political participation among African Americans. Following Dr. King's assassination, Young ran for Congress and became one of the first black congressmen in the twentieth century, where he continued to advocate for improvement in civil rights legislation. Young succeeded Maynard Jackson as Mayor of Atlanta.

Skill 16.5   Recognize the effects of new immigrant communities on Georgia's society.

Georgia is one of several states that has seen an increase in immigration over the past decade. Mexico is the origin of most immigrants to Georgia. Asian immigrants are another significant group.

Georgia mirrors the rest of the country in the effects these new immigrant communities have on its society. Exposure to new cultures enriches a society by introducing new ideas and traditions, but also creates tension when cultural differences arise. In Georgia, as in other states with a historic tradition of racial segregation, these issues are particularly sensitive. As in other parts of the country where immigration is increasing, organizations have appeared which aim to control immigration.

Bibliography

Adams, James Truslow. (2006). "The March of Democracy," Vol 1. "The Rise of the Union". New York: Charles Scribner's Sons, Publisher.

Barbini, John & Warshaw, Steven. (2006). "The World Past and Present." New York: Harcourt, Brace, Jovanovich, Publishers.

Berthon, Simon & Robinson, Andrew. (2006. "The Shape of the World." Chicago: Rand McNally, Publisher.

Bice, David A. (2006). "A Panorama of Florida II". (Second Edition). Marceline, Missouri: Walsworth Publishing Co., Inc.

Bram, Leon (Vice-President and Editorial Director). (2006). "Funk and Wagnalls New Encyclopedia." United States of America.

Burns, Edward McNall & Ralph, Philip Lee. (2006. "World Civilizations Their History and Culture" (5th ed.). New York: W.W. Norton & Company, Inc., Publishers.

Dauben, Joseph W. (2006). "The World Book Encyclopedia." Chicago: World Book Inc. A Scott Fetzer Company, Publisher.

De Blij, H.J. & Muller, Peter O. (2006). "Geography Regions and Concepts" (Sixth Edition). New York: John Wiley & Sons, Inc., Publisher.

Encyclopedia Americana. (2006). Danbury, Connecticut: Grolier Inc, Publisher.

Heigh, Christopher (Editor). (2006). "The Cambridge Historical Encyclopedia of Great Britain and Ireland." Cambridge: Cambridge University Press, Publisher.

Hunkins, Francis P. & Armstrong, David G. (2006). "World Geography People and Places." Columbus, Ohio: Charles E. Merrill Publishing Co. A Bell & Howell Company, Publishers.

Jarolimek, John; Anderson, J. Hubert & Durand, Loyal, Jr. (2006). "World Neighbors." New York: Macmillan Publishing Company. London: Collier Macmillan Publishers.

McConnell, Campbell R. (2006). "Economics-Principles, Problems, and Policies" (Tenth Edition). New York: McGraw-Hill Book Company, Publisher.

Millard, Dr. Anne & Vanags, Patricia. (2006). "The Usborne Book of World History." London: Usborne Publishing Ltd., Publisher.

Novosad, Charles (Executive Editor). (2006). "The Nystrom Desk Atlas." Chicago: Nystrom Division of Herff Jones, Inc., Publisher.

Patton, Clyde P.; Rengert, Arlene C.; Saveland, Robert N.; Cooper, Kenneth S. & Cam, Patricia T. (2006). "A World View." Morristown, N.J.: Silver Burdette Companion, Publisher.

Schwartz, Melvin & O'Connor, John R. (2006). "Exploring A Changing World." New York: Globe Book Company, Publisher.

"The Annals of America: Selected Readings on Great Issues in American History 1620-1968." (2006). United States of America: William Benton, Publisher.

Tindall, George Brown & Shi, David E. (2006). "America-A Narrative History" (Fourth Edition). New York: W.W. Norton & Company, Publisher.

Todd, Lewis Paul & Curti, Merle. (2006). "Rise of the American Nation" (Third Edition). New York: Harcourt, Brace, Jovanovich, Inc., Publishers.

Tyler, Jenny; Watts, Lisa; Bowyer, Carol; Trundle, Roma & Warrender, Annabelle (2006) 'The Usbome Book of World Geography." London: Usbome Publishing Ltd., Publisher.

Willson, David H. (2006). "A History of England." Hinsdale, Illinois: The Dryder

Sample Essay Question

Discuss the emergence, expansion, and evolution of Islam.

Islam is a monotheistic faith that traces its traditions to Abraham and considers the Jewish patriarchs and prophets, especially Moses, King Solomon and Jesus Christ, as earlier "Prophets of God."

Mohammed was born in 570 CE in a small Arabian town. Around 610, **Mohammed** came to some prominence through a new religion called **Islam** or submission to the will of God. His followers were called **Moslems.** His first converts were members of his family and his friends. As the new faith began to grow, it remained a secret society. But when Moslems began to make their faith public, they met with opposition and persecution from the pagan Arabians who feared the loss of profitable trade with the pilgrims who came to the Kaaba every year. In 622, Mohammed and his close followers fled persecution in Mecca and found refuge in **Medina.** His flight is called the **Hegira.** Mohammed took advantage of feuds between Jews and Arabs and became the ruler, making it the capital of a rapidly growing state.

Islam changed significantly. It became a fighting religion and Mohammed became a political leader. The group survived by raiding caravans on the road to Mecca and by plundering nearby Jewish tribes. It attracted many converts from Bedouin tribes. By 630, Mohammed conquered Mecca and made it the religious center of Islam, toward which all Moslems turned to pray. By taking over the sacred city, Mohammed made it easier for converts to join the religion. By the time of his death in 632, most of the people of Arabia had become adherents of Islam.

Mohammed left behind a collection of revelations (**surahs**) he believed were delivered by the angel Gabriel. The **Quran** was reputedly dictated to Muhammad as the Word of God, published in a book called the **Koran.** The revelations were never dated or kept in any kind of order. After Mohammed's death they were organized by length in diminishing order. The Koran contains Mohammed's teachings on moral and theological questions, his legislation on political matters, and his comments on current events. Five basic principles of Islam are Allah, Praying five times a day facing Mecca, Charity, Fasting during Ramadan and the Pilgrimage to Mecca.

The Islamic armies spread their faith by conquering the Arabian Peninsula, Mesopotamia, Egypt, Syria and Persia by 650 CE and expanding to North Africa and most of the Iberian Peninsula by 750 CE. During this period of expansion, the Muslim conquerors established great centers of learning in the Middle East.

Sample Test

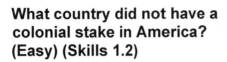

1. What country did not have a colonial stake in America? (Easy) (Skills 1.2)

   A. France

   B. Spain

   C. Mexico

   D. China

2. The end to hunting, gathering, and fishing of prehistoric people was due to: (Rigorous)(Skill 1.2)

   A. Domestication of animals.

   B. Building crude huts and houses ·

   C. Development of agriculture

   D. Organized government in villages

3. The early ancient civilizations developed systems of government: (Average) (Skill 1.2)

   A. To provide for defense against attack

   B. To regulate trade

   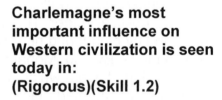

   C. To regulate and direct the economic activities of the people as they worked together in groups

   D. To decide on the boundaries of the different fields during planting seasons

4. Charlemagne's most important influence on Western civilization is seen today in: (Rigorous)(Skill 1.2)

   A. Relationship of church and state

   B. Strong military for defense

   C. The criminal justice system

   D. Education of women

5. Jim Crow refers to: (Average) (Skill 1.3)

   A. Equality

   B. Labor Movement

   C. Racism

   D. Free trade

6. The chemical process of radiocarbon dating would be most useful and beneficial in the field of:
(Average) (Skill 1.4)

    A. Archaeology

    B. Geography

    C. Sociology

    D. Anthropology

7. The study of the exercise of power and political behavior in human society today would be conducted by experts in:
(Average) (Skill 1.4)

    A. History

    B. Sociology

    C. Political Science

    D. Anthropology

8. The study of a people's language and writing would be part of all of the following except:
(Average)(Skill 1.4, 2.1)

    A. Sociology

    B. Archaeology

    C. History

    D. Geography

9. Which of the following is not a social science reference resource:
(Easy)(Skill 2.1)

    A. Encyclopedias

    B. Almanacs

    C. Atlas

    D. Moody's

10. A primary source is written:
(Average)(Skill 2.4)

    A. Five years after the period being studies

    B. Ten years after the period being studied

    C. During the period being studied

    D. Anytime

11. Distortions in maps occur because:
(Average)(Skill 2.5)

    A. Of carelessness

    B. Of imprecise instruments

    C. Maps are flat and the earth is a sphere

    D. Cost of precision is prohibitive

12. The Fertile Crescent was bounded by:
(Average)(Skill 3.1)

A. Mediterranean Sea

B. Arabian Desert

C. Taurus Mountains

D. Ural Mountains

13. Which ancient civilization is credited with being the first to develop irrigation techniques through the use of canals, dikes, and devices for raising water?
(Rigorous)(Skill 3.1)

A. The Sumerians

B. The Egyptians

C. The Babylonians

D. The Akkadians

 14. All of the following applies to the Kushites except:
(Rigorous)(Skill 3.2)

A. Female rulers

B. Male rulers

C. Polytheism

D. Lion warrior god

15. Development of a solar calendar, invention of the decimal system, and contributions to the development of geometry and astronomy are all the legacy of:
(Average) (Skill 3.2)

A. The Babylonians

B. The Persians

C. The Sumerians

D. The Egyptians

16. The world religion which includes a caste system is:
(Easy) (Skill 3.4)

A. Buddhism

B. Hinduism

C. Sikhism

D. Jainism

17. Which of the following is not a religion of China:
(Easy) (Skill 3.5)

A. Confucianism

B. Taoism

C. Buddhism

D. Shintoism

18. The Cradle of Western Civilization is considered to be:
(Easy) (Skill 3.6)

A. The Ottoman Empire

B. Egypt

C. Rome

D. Ancient Greece

19. Direct democracy was:
(Easy)(Skill 3.6)

A. Practiced in Egypt

B. Based on direct, personal, active participation

C. A basis of Roman law

D. Practiced in Sumaria

20. The "father of political science" is considered to be:
(Average)(Skill 3.7)

A. Aristotle

B. John Locke

C. Plato

D. Thomas Hobbes

21. The first ancient civilization to introduce and practice monotheism was the:
(Average)(Skill 3.8)

A. Sumerians

B. Minoans

C. Phoenicians

D. Hebrews

22. China's last imperial ruling dynasty was one of its most stable and successful and, under its rule, Chinese culture made an outstanding impression on Western nations. This dynasty was:
(Rigorous)(Skill 4.1)

A. Min

B. Manchu

C. Han

D. Chou

23. The achievements of the Mongol Empire include all but the following:
(Rigorous)(Skill 4.1)

A. Reunification of China

B. Unification of the Central Asian Republic

C. Expansion of Europe's knowledge of the world

D. Exploration of the Americas

24. The network of roads connecting Asia and the Mediterranean was known as the:
(Average)(Skill 4.2)

A. Asian Road

B. Silk Road

C. European Road

D. Mediterranean Road

25. The Bantu were from:
(Easy)(Skill 4.3)

A. Asia

B. Europe

C. Africa

D. Russia

26. Which does not apply to the ancient kingdom of Mali:
(Rigorous)(Skill 4.4)

A. Christianity

B. Traditional African beliefs

C. Islam

D. Ruled by a king

27. Which was not a part of the Triangular Trade System:
(Rigorous) (Skill 4.5)

A. England

B. Africa

C. New World

D. Japan

28. Which native American group was known for their calendars?
(Average) (Skill 4.6)

A. The Incas

B. The Atacamas

C. The Mayans

D. The Tarapacas

29. Native South American tribes included all of the following except:
(Easy)(Skill 4.6)

A. Aztec

B. Inca

C. Minoans

D. Maya

30. **An ancient Indian civilization known for its worshipping of the dead was the: (Rigorous) (Skill 4.6)**

A. The Mayans

B. The Atacamas

C. The Incas

D. The Tarapacas

31. **The principle of zero in mathematics is the discovery of the ancient civilization found in: (Average)(Skill 4.6)**

A. Egypt

B. Persia

C. Mayas

D. Babylon

32. **India's greatest ruler is considered to be: (Average) (Skill 4.7)**

A. Akbar

B. Asoka

C. Babur

D. Jahan

33. **Which one of the following is not an important legacy of the Byzantine Empire? (Rigorous) (Skill 5.1)**

A. It protected Western Europe from various attacks from the East by such groups as the Persians, Ottoman Turks, and Barbarians.

B. It played a part in preserving the literature, philosophy, and language of ancient Greece.

C. Its military organization was the foundation for modern armies.

D. It kept the legal traditions of Roman government, collecting and organizing many ancient Roman laws.

34. **The Roman Empire gave so much to the world, especially the Western world. Of the legacies below, the most influential, effective and lasting is: (Rigorous) (Skill 5.1)**

A. The language of Latin

B. Roman law, justice, and political system

C. Engineering and building

D. The writings of its poets an historians

35. Which of the following was not characteristic of the Bedouin:
(Average) (Skill 5.3)

A. Nomadic wanderers

B. City dwellers

C. Infanticide — What?.

D. Suppression of women

36. The holy book of Islam is the:
(Easy) (Skill 5.3)

A. Kaaba

B. Torah

C. Koran

D. Bible

37. The Crusades were fought between the:
(Easy)(Skill 5.4)

A. Arabs and Israelies

B. Muslims and Christian Byzantines

C. Romans and Greeks

D. British and Romans

38. Which one of the following did not contribute to the early medieval European civilization?
(Rigorous) (Skill 5.5)

A. The heritage from the classical cultures

B. The Christian religion

C. The influence of the German Barbarians

D. The spread of ideas through trade and commerce

39. In Western Europe, the achievements of the Renaissance were unsurpassed and made these countries outstanding cultural centers on the continent. All of the following were accomplishments except:
(Rigorous)(Skill 5.6)

A. Investment of the printing press

B. A rekindling of interest in the learning of classical Greece and Rome

C. Growth in literature, philosophy and art

D. Better military tactics

40. **Which French Renaissance writer contributed to literature and philosophy? (Average)(Skill 5.6)**

A. Francois Rabelais,

B. Desiderius Erasmus

C. Michel de Montaigne

D. Sir Francis Bacon

41. **The changing focus during the Renaissance when artists and scholars were less concerned with religion but centered their efforts on a better understanding of people and the world was called: (Average)(Skill 5.6)**

A. Realism

B. Humanism

C. Individualism

D. Intellectualism

42. **The "father of anatomy" is considered to be: (Easy) (Skill 5.6)**

A. Vesalius

B. Servetus

C. Galen

D. Harvey

43. **Studies in astronomy, skills in mapping, and other contributions to geographic knowledge came from: (Easy) (Skill 5.6)**

A. Galileo

B. Columbus

C. Eratosthenes

D. Ptolemy

44. **The ideas and innovations of the period of the Renaissance were spread throughout Europe mainly because of: (Average) (Skill 5.6)**

A. Extensive exploration

B. Craft workers and their guilds

C. The invention of the Printing press

D. Increased travel and trade

45. **Who is considered to be the most important figure in the spread of Protestantism across Switzerland? (Easy) (Skill 5.7)**

A. Calvin

B. Zwingli

C. Munzer

D. Leyden

46. The English explorer who gave England its claim to North American was:
(Easy) (Skill 6.1)

A. Raleigh

B. Hawkins

C. Drake

D. Cabot

47. The Age of Exploration begun in the 1400s was led by:
(Average)(Skill 6.1)

A. The Portuguese

B. The Spanish

C. The English

D. The Dutch

48. The foundation of modern democracy is embodied in the ideas of:
(Rigorous) (Skill 6.4)

A. St. Thomas Aquinas

B. Rousseau

C. John Locke

D. Montesquieu

49. Who applied Locke's principles to the American situation?
(Rigorous) (Skill 6.4)

A. Thomas Paine

B. Samuel Adams

C. Benjamin Franklin

D. Thomas Jefferson ?

50. The idea that morality lay not in the natural of God but in the human soul itself was a philosophy of:
(Average)(Skill 6.4)

A. Rousseau

B. Immanuel Kant

C. Montesquieu

D. John Locke 2nd

51. The "divine right" of kings was the key political characteristic of:
(Easy) (Skill 6.6)

A. The Age of Absolutism

B. The Age of Reason

C. The Age of Feudalism

D. The Age of Despotism

52. Studies in astronomy, skills in mapping, and other contributions to geographic knowledge came from:
(Rigorous) (Skill 6.6)

A. Galileo

B. Columbus

C. Eratosthenes

D. Ptolemy

53. The major force in eighteenth and nineteenth century politics was:
(Average) (Skill 6.7)

A. Nationalism

B. Revolution

C. War

D. Diplomacy

54. Which one of the following was not a reason why the United States went to war with Great Britain in 1812?
(Rigorous)(Skill 6.8)

A. Resentment by Spain over the sale exploration, and settlement of the Louisiana Territory

B. The westward movement of farmers because of the need for more land

C. Canadian fur traders were agitating the northwestern Indians to fight American expansion'

D. Britain continued to seize American ships on the high seas and force American seamen to serve aboard British ships

55. Colonial expansion by Western European powers in the eighteenth and nineteenth centuries was due primarily to:
(Average) (Skill 7.1)

A. Building and opening the Suez Canal ·

B. The Industrial Revolution ·

C. Marked improvements in transportation

D. Complete independence of all the Americas and loss of European domination and influence

56. Marxism believes which two
groups are in continual
conflict?
(Easy)(Skill 7.1)

A. Farmers and landowners

B. Kings and the nobility

C. Workers and owners

D. Structure and
superstructure

57. Laissez-faire economics is
based on:
(Easy)(Skill 7.1)

A. Free markets without
government interference

B. Free markets with
government intervention

C. Government control of the
marketplace

D. Government ownership of
the means of production

58. Competition leads to:
(Rigorous) (Skill 7.1)

A. Fights

B. Waste

C. Overproduction

D. Efficient use of resources

59. The concept of the invisible
hand was created by:
(Easy)(Skill 7.1)

A. Thomas Robert Malthus

B. John Stuart Mill

C. Adam Smith

D. John Maynard Keynes

60. Nineteenth century German
unification was the result of
the hard work of:
(Average) (Skill 7.2)

A. Otto von Bismarck

B. Kaiser William II

C. Von Moltke

D. Hindenburg

61. Nineteenth century imperialism by Western European nations had important and far-reaching effects on the colonial peoples they ruled. All four of the following are the result of this. Which one was most important and had lasting effects on key 20th century events?
(Rigorous)(Skill 7.3)

A. Local wars were ended

B. Living standards were raised

C. Demands for self government and feelings of nationalism surfaced

D. Economic developments occurred

62. The results of the Renaissance, Enlightenment, Commercial and Industrial Revolutions were more unfortunate for the people of:
(Rigorous)(Skill 7.3)

A. Asia

B. Latin America

C. Africa

D. Middle East

63. What event sparked the onset of World War I:
(Average)(Skill 7.4)

A. Assassination of Archduke Francis Ferdinand

B. Hitler's invasion of Poland

C. The collapse of the Weimar Republic

D. The assassination of Czar Nicholas Romanov

64. Who was not one of the World War II Allies?:
(Easy)(Skill 7.7)

A. Japan

B. Russia

C. United States

D. Great Britain

65. A well-known World War II figure who ruled fascist Italy was?
(Average) (Skill 7.7)

A. Hitler

B. Stalin

C. Tojo

D. Mussolini

66. **A political system in which there is a one party state, centralized control, and a repressive police system with private ownership is called:**
(Average) (Skill 7.7)

A. Communism

B. Fascism

C. Socialism

D. Constitutional Monarchy

67. **Which country was not a part of the Axis in World War II?**
(Easy) (Skill 7.7)

A. Germany

B. Italy

C. Japan

D. United States

68. **The international organization established to work for world peace at the end of the Second World War is the:**
(Average)(Skill 7.8)

A. League of Nations

B. United Federation of Nations

C. United Nations

D. United World League

69. **Which one of the following would not be considered a result of World War II?**
(Rigorous)(Skill 7.8)

A. Economic depressions and slow resumption of trade and financial aid

B. Western Europe was no longer the center of world power

C. The beginnings of new power struggles not only in Europe but in Asia as well

D. Territorial and boundary changes for many nations, especially in Europe

70. **The doctrine of comparative advantage explains:**
(Average) (Skill 8.9)

A. Why nations trade

B. How to fight a war

C. Time zones

D. Political divisions

71. **The Common Market is a form of:**
(Average) (Skill 8.9)

A. Industrialization

B. Military defense

C. Control

D. Trade liberalization

72. **The only colony not founded and settled for religious, political or business reasons was:**
(Easy)(Skill 9.2)

A. Delaware

B. Virginia

C. Georgia

D. New York

73. **The year 1619 was a memorable for the colony of Virginia. Three important events occurred resulting in lasting effects on US history. Which of the following is not one of the events?**
(Average) (Skill 9.2)

A. Twenty African slaves arrived.

B. The London Company granted the colony a charter making it independent.

C. The colonists were given the right by the London Company to govern themselves through representative government in the Virginia House of Burgesses.

D. The London Company sent to the colony 60 women who were quickly married, establishing families and stability in the colony.

74. **Which one of the following is not a reason why Europeans came to the New World?**
(Easy) (Skill 9.3)

A. To find resources in order to increase wealth

B. To establish trade

C. To increase a ruler's power and importance

D. To spread Christianity

75. **The source of authority for national, state, and local governments in the US is:**
(Average) (Skill 9.6)

A. The will of the people

B. The US Constitution

C. Written laws

D. The Bill of Rights

76. **France decided in 1777 to help the American colonies in their war against Britain. This decision was based on: (Rigorous)(Skill 9.8)**

   A. The naval victory of John Paul Jones over the British ship Serapis"

   B. The survival of the terrible winter at Valley Forge

   C. The success of colonial guerilla fighters in the South

   D. The defeat of the British at Saratoga

77. **"These are the times that try men's souls" were words penned by: (Rigorous)(Skill 9.8)**

   A. Thomas Jefferson

   B. Samuel Adams

   C. Benjamin Franklin

   D. Thomas Paine

78. **Under the brand new Constitution, the most urgent of the many problems facing the new federal government was that of: (Average) (Skill 9.9)**

   A. Maintaining a strong army and navy

   B. Establishing a strong Foreign policy

   C. Raising money to pay salaries and war debts

   D. Setting up courts, passing federal laws, and providing for law enforcement officers

79. **The Federalists: (Rigorous) (Skill 10.5)**

   A. Favored state's rights

   B. Favored a weak central government

   C. Favored a strong federal government

   D. Supported the British

80. **After the War of 1812, Henry Clay and others proposed economic measures, including raising tariffs to protect American farmers and manufacturers from foreign competition. These measures were proposed in the period known as: (Rigorous)(Skill 10.5)**

   A. Era of Nationalism

   B. American Expansion

   C. Era of Good Feeling

   D. American System

81. **The belief that the United States should control all of North America was called: (Easy)(Skill 10.6)**

   A. Westward Expansion

   B. Pan Americanism

   C. Manifest Destiny

   D. Nationalism

82. **Leaders in the movement for woman's rights have included all but: (Rigorous) (Skill 10.8)**

   A. Elizabeth Cady Stanton

   B. Lucretia Borgia

   C. Susan B. Anthony

   D. Lucretia Mott

83. **The Pilgrims came to America to: (Average) (Skill 10.8)**

   A. To drill for oil

   B. To be the official representatives of the king

   C. To take over the East India Company

   D. To flee religious persecution

84. **A famous canal is the: (Easy) (Skill 10.9)**

   A. Pacific Canal

   B. Arctic Canal

   C. Panama Canal

   D. Atlantic Canal

85. There is no doubt of the vast improvement of the US Constitution over the weak Articles of Confederation. Which one of the four accurate statements below is a unique yet eloquent description of the document?
(Rigorous)(Skill 11.1)

A. The establishment of a strong central government in no way lessened or weakened the individual states.

B. Individual rights were protected and secured.

C. The Constitution is the best representation of the results of the American genius for compromise.

D. Its flexibility and adaptation to change gives it a sense of timelessness.

86. What Supreme Court ruling dealt with the issue of civil rights?
(Rigorous) (Skill 11.2)

A. Jefferson vs Madison

B. Lincoln vs Douglas

C. Dred Scott v. Sanford

D. Marbury vs Madison

87. As a result of the Missouri Compromise:
(Rigorous) (Skill 11.2)

A. Slavery was not allowed in the Louisiana Purchase

B. The Louisiana Purchase was nullified

C. Louisiana separated from the Union

D. The Embargo Act was repealed

88. The principle of "popular sovereignty" allowing people in any territory to make their own decision concerning slavery was stated by;
(Rigorous)(Skill 11.2)

A. Henry Clay

B. Daniel Webster

C. John C. Calhoun

D. Stephen A. Douglas

89. The Union had many strengths over the Confederacy. Which was not a strength?
(Average) (Skill 11.2)

A. Railroads

B. Industry

C. Slaves

D. Manpower

90. **After the Civil War, the US adapted an attitude of isolation from foreign affairs. But the turning point marking the beginning of the US becoming a world power was:**
(Rigorous) (Skill 11.3)

  A. World War I

  B. Expansion of business and trade overseas

  C. The Spanish-American War

  D. The building and financial of the Panama Canal

91. **The three-day Battle of Gettysburg was the turning point of the Civil War for the North leading to ultimate victory. The battle in the West reinforcing the North's victory and sealing the South's defeat was the day after Gettysburg at:**
(Rigorous) (Skill 11.3)

  A. Perryville

  B. Was after Gettysburg

  C. Stones River

  D. Shiloh

92. **The Radical Republicans who pushed the harsh Reconstruction measures through Congress after Lincoln's death lost public and moderate Republican support when they went too far:**
(Rigorous) (Skill 11.4)

  A. In their efforts to challenge the President

  B. By dividing ten southern states into military-controlled districts

  C. By making the ten southern states give freed African Americans the right to vote

  D. Sending carpetbaggers into the South to build up support for Congressional legislation

93. **Historians state that the West helped to speed up the Industrial Revolution. Which one of the following statements was not a reason for this?**
(Rigorous) (Skill 11.6)

A. Food supplies for the ever increasing urban populations came from farms in the West

B. A tremendous supply of gold and silver from western mines provided the capital needed to built industries

C. Descendants of western settlers, educated as engineers, geologists, and metallurgists in the East, returned to the West to mine the mineral resources needed for industry

D. Iron, copper, and other minerals from western mines were important resources in manufacturing products

94. **The post-Civil War years were a time of low public morality, a time of greed, graft, and dishonesty. Which one of the reasons listed would not be accurate?**
(Rigorous) (Skill 11.6)

A. The war itself because of the money and materials needed to carry on the War

B. The very rapid growth of industry and big business after the War

C. The personal example set by President Grant

D. Unscrupulous heads of large impersonal corporations

95. **The American labor union movement started gaining new momentum:**
(Average) (Skill 11.6)

A. During the building of the railroads

B. After 1865 with the growth of cities

C. With the rise of industrial giants such as Carnegie and Vanderbilt

D. During the war years of 1861-1865

96. **It can be reasonably stated that the change in the United States from primarily an agricultural country into an industrial power was due to all of the following except: (Rigorous)(Skill 11.6)**

    A. Tariffs on foreign imports

    B. Millions of hardworking immigrants

    C. An increase in technological developments

    D. The change from steam to electricity for powering industrial machinery

97. **After 1783, the largest "land owner" in the Americas was: (Average) (Skill 11.7)**

    A. Britain

    B. Spain

    C. France

    D. United States

98. **In the United States, federal investigations into business activities are handled by the: (Rigorous)(Skill 11.8)**

    A. Department of Treasury

    B. Security & Exchange Commission

    C. Government Accounting Office

    D. Federal Trade Commission

99. **Drought is a problem in Africa and other places because: (Average) (Skill 12.5)**

    A. There is flooding

    B. The rivers change course

    C. People flock to see the drought

    D. The dried out soil turns to dust and cannot grow food

100. **Which of the following contributed to the severity of the Great Depression in California? (Rigorous)(Skill 12.5)**

    A. An influx of Chinese immigrants.

    B. The dust bowl drove People out of the cities.

    C. An influx of Mexican immigrants.

    D. An influx of Oakies.

101. **The term Red Scare refers to: (Average) (Skill 12.3)**

    A. The Halloween holiday

    B. The fear of communists

    C. Sun Spots

    D. Labor strikes

102. Of all the major causes of both World Wars I and II, the most significant one is considered to be:
(Average)(Skill 12.7)

A. Extreme nationalism

B. Military buildup and aggression

C. Political unrest

D. Agreements and alliances

103. Which of the following is an organization or alliance for defense purposes?
(Average) (Skill 13.1)

A. North Atlantic Treaty Organization

B. The Common Market

C. The European Union

D. North American Free Trade Association

104. Which country was a Cold War foe?
(Average) (Skill 13.1)

A. Russia

B. Brazil

C. Canada

D. Argentina

105. Which one of the following was not a post World War II organization?
(Average) (Skill 13.1)

A. Monroe Doctrine

B. Marshall Plan

C. Warsaw Pact

D. North Atlantic Treaty Organization

106. After World War II, the United States:
(Rigorous) (Skill 13.2)

A. Limited its involvement in European affairs

B. Shifted foreign policy emphasis from Europe to Asia

C. Passed significant legislation pertaining to aid to farmers and tariffs on imports

D. Entered the greatest period of economic growth in its history

107. **Which of the following is not a name associated with the Civil Rights movement? (Rigorous) (Skill 13.4)**

A. Rosa Parks

B. Emmett Till

C. Tom Dewey

D. Martin Luther King, Jr.

108. **During the 1920s, the United States almost completely stopped all immigration. One of the reasons was: (Rigorous)(Skill 14.5)**

A. Plentiful cheap unskilled labor was no longer needed by industrialists

B. War debts from World War I made it difficult to render financial assistance

C. European nations were reluctant to allow people to leave since there was a need to rebuild populations and economic stability

D. The United States did not become a member of the League of Nations

109. **A significant change in immigration policy occurred after World War II when the United States: (Average) (Skill 14.5)**

A. Eliminated restrictions

B. Prevented Japanese immigration

C. Imposed policies based on ethnicity and country of origin

D. Banned immigration

110. **From about 1870 to 1900 the settlement of America's "last frontier", the West, was completed. One attraction for settlers was free land but it would have been to no avail without: (Rigorous) (Skill 14.7)**

A. Better farming methods and technology

B. Surveying to set boundaries

C. Immigrants and others to seek new land

D. The railroad to get them there

111. **The Electoral College:**
(Average) (Skill 14.7)

   A. Elects the Senate but not the House

   B. Elects the House but not the Senate

   C. Elects both the House and Senate

   D. Elects the President

112. **The Native American tribes of the Georgia area are: (Average)(Skill 15.1)**

   A. Cherokee and Creek

   B. Cherokee and Hopi

   C. Creek and Seminole

   D. Seminole and Hopi

113. **Which Native American tribe in Georgia was friendly to the British? (Rigorous)(Skill 15.2)**

   A. Creek

   B. Yamasee

   C. Navajo

   D. Cherokee

114. **The first settlement in Georgia was: (Average) (Skill 15.2)**

   A. Macon

   B. Atlanta

   C. Valdosta

   D. Savannah

115. **The first Constitution for Georgia was adopted in: (Rigorous)(Skill 15.3)**

   A. 1776

   B. 1777

   C. 1778

   D. 1779

116. **When did Georgia ratify the U.S. Constitution: (Rigorous)(Skill 15.3)**

   A. 1779

   B. 1785

   C. 1788

   D. 1790

117. **The University of Georgia was:**
(Average)(Skill 15.4)

   A. founded as a private school

   B. founded as a military school

   C. the first state chartered university in the U.S.

   D. established in 1779

118. **The First and Second Great Awakenings refer to:**
(Rigorous) (Skill 15.4)

   A. religious movements

   B. political movements

   C. military movements

   D. industrialization

119. **The major crop of Georgia was:**
(Average) (Skill 15.4)

   A. Cotton

   B. Corn

   C. Soybeans

   D. Wheat

120. **During the Civil War, Georgia:**
(Rigorous)(Skill 15.5)

   A. opposed slavery

   B. Opposed secession

   C. Abstained from the war

   D. Seceded from the Union

121. **Jim Crow laws did all but the following:**
(Rigorous) (Skill 16.1)

   A. Promoted segregation of blacks and whites

   B. Promoted integration of blacks and whites

   C. Provided for a poll tax

   D. Forced blacks to use inferior facilities

122. **Why did white Georgians try to prevent blacks from serving in World War I?**
(Rigorous)(Skill 16.2)

   A. Blacks were needed as sharecroppers for the agricultural crops

   B. They did not want to serve with blacks

   C. They felt that blacks were not qualified for military service

   D. They felt that the blacks would not return to Georgia after the war

123. **Why did Georgia's Gov. Talmadge oppose the New Deal?**
(Rigorous) (Skill 16.2)

A. He felt it wasn't needed

B. He felt the New Deal programs were federal interference in local affairs

C. He did not agree with the purpose of the spending policies

D. He didn't like President Roosevelt personally

124. **The Atlanta born man who became prominent in the Civil Rights movement was:**
(Rigorous) (Skill 16.4)

A. Eugene Talmadge

B. Ellis Arnall

C. Herman Talmadge

D. Dr. Martin Luther King, Jr.

125. **All of the following are prominent Georgians except?**
(Rigorous)(Skill 16.4)

A. Jimmy Carter

B. Rosa Parks

C. Maynard Jackson

D. Andrew Young

Answer Key

1. D	41. B	81. C	121. B
2. C	42. A	82. B	122. A
3. C	43. D	83. D	123. B
4. A	44. C	84. C	124. D
5. C	45. A	85. C	125. B
6. A	46. D	86. C	
7. C	47. A	87. A	
8. A	48. C	88. D	
9. D	49. D	89. C	
10. C	50. B	90. C	
11. C	51. A	91. B	
12. D	52. D	92. A	
13. A	53. A	93. C	
14. B	54. A	94. C	
15. D	55. B	95. B	
16. B	56. C	96. A	
17. D	57. A	97. B	
18. D	58. D	98. D	
19. B	59. C	99. D	
20. A	60. A	100. D	
21. D	61. C	101. B	
22. B	62. C	102. A	
23. D	63. A	103. A	
24. B	64. A	104. A	
25. C	65. D	105. A	
26. A	66. B	106. D	
27. D	67. D	107. C	
28. C	68. C	108. A	
29. C	69. A	109. C	
30. C	70. A	110. D	
31. C	71. D	111. D	
32. A	72. C	112. A	
33. C	73. B	113. B	
34. B	74. B	114. D	
35. B	75. A	115. B	
36. C	76. D	116. C	
37. B	77. D	117. C	
38. D	78. C	118. A	
39. D	79. C	119. A	
40. C	80. D	120. D	

RIGOR TABLE

Easy	Average	Rigorous
1, 9, 16, 17, 18, 19, 25, 29, 36, 37, 42, 43, 45, 46, 51, 56, 57, 59, 64, 67, 72, 74, 79, 81, 84	3, 5, 6, 7, 8, 10, 11, 12, 15, 20, 21, 24, 28, 31, 32, 35, 40, 41, 44, 47, 50, 53, 55, 58, 60, 63, 65, 66, 68, 70, 71, 73, 75, 78, 83, 89, 95, 97, 99, 101, 102, 103, 104, 105, 109, 111, 112, 114, 117, 119	2, 4, 13, 14, 22, 23, 26, 27, 30, 33, 34, 38, 39, 48, 49, 52, 54, 61, 62, 69, 76, 77, 80, 82, 85, 86, 87, 88, 90, 91, 92, 93, 94, 96, 98, 100, 106, 107, 108, 110, 113, 115, 116, 118, 120, 121, 122, 123, 124, 125

Rationales for Sample Questions

1.　**What country did not have a colonial stake in America?**
　　(Easy) (Skills 1.2)

　　A. France

　　B. Spain

　　C. Portugal

　　D. China

D. China
European countries and Portugal were aggressively involved in the rapid colonization of the New World to gain knowledge and power. China, however, was not as interested as it was well established under the Qing dynasty which endured until 1911.

2.　**The end to hunting, gathering, and fishing of prehistoric people was due to:**
　　(Rigorous) (Skill 1.2)

　　A. Domestication of animals

　　B. Building crude huts and houses

　　C. Development of agriculture

　　D. Organized government in Villages

C. Development of agriculture
Although the domestication of animals, the building of huts and houses and the first organized governments were all very important steps made by early civilizations, it was the development of agriculture that ended the once dominant practices of hunting, gathering, and fishing among prehistoric people. The development of agriculture provided a more efficient use of time and for the first time a surplus of food. This greatly improved the quality of life and contributed to early population growth.

3. **The early ancient civilizations developed systems of government: (Average)(Skill 1.2)**

    A. To provide for defense against attack

    B. To regulate trade

    C. To regulate and direct the economic activities of the people as they worked together in groups

    D. To decide on the boundaries of the different fields during planting seasons

C. To regulate and direct the economic activities of the people as they worked together in groups
Although ancient civilizations were concerned with defense, trade regulation and the maintenance of boundaries in their fields, they could not have done any of them without first regulating and directing the economic activities of the people as they worked in groups. This provided for a stable economic base from which they could trade and actually had something worth providing defense for.

4. **Charlemagne's most important influence on Western civilization is seen today in: (Rigorous)(Skill 1.2)**

    A. Relationship of church and state

    B. Strong military for defense

    C. The criminal justice system

    D. Education of women

A. Relationship of church and state
Charlemagne was the leader of the Germanic Franks responsible for the promotion of the Holy Roman Empire across Europe. Although he unified governments and aided the Pope, he re-crowned himself in 802 A.D. to demonstrate that his power and right to rule was not a grant from the Pope, but rather a secular achievement. Therefore, although he used much of the Church's power in his rise to power, the Pope in turn used Charlemagne to ascend the Church to new heights. Thus, Charlemagne had an influence on the issues between Church and state and was well-known for his respect of learning.

5.   **Jim Crow refers to:**
     (Average) (Skill 1.3)

     A. Equality

     B. Labor Movement

     C. Racism

     D. Free trade

C. Racism
Jim Crow is a term used to describe the policies of racism and discrimination. It has nothing to do with the (B) labor movement or (D) free trade and is the opposite of (A) the concept of equality.

6.   **The chemical process of radiocarbon dating would be most useful and**
     beneficial in the field of:
     (Average) (Skill 1.4)

     A. Archaeology

     B. Geography

     C. Sociology

     D. Anthropology

A. Archaeology
Radiocarbon dating is a chemical process that helps generate a more absolute method for dating artifacts and remains by measuring the radioactive materials present in them today and calculating how long it takes for certain materials to decay. Since geographers mainly study locations and special properties of earth's living things and physical features, sociologists mostly study human society and social conditions and anthropologists generally study human culture and humanity, the answer is archaeology because archeologists study past human cultures by studying their remains.

7. **The study of the exercise of power and political behavior in human society today would be conducted by experts in:**
    (Average)(Skill 1.4)

    A. History

    B. Sociology

    C. Political Science

    D. Anthropology

C. Political Science
Experts in the field of political science today would likely conduct the study of exercise of power and political behavior in human society. However, it is also reasonable to suggest that such studies would be important to historians (study of the past, often in an effort to understand the present), sociologists (often concerned with power structure in the social and political worlds) and even some anthropologists (study of culture and their behaviors).

8. **The study of a people's language and writing would be part of all of the following except:**
    (Average) (Skill 1.4, 2.1)

    A. Sociology

    B. Archaeology

    C. History

    D. Geography

A. Sociology
The study of a people's language and writing would be a part of studies in the disciplines of sociology (study of social interaction and organization), archaeology, (study of ancient artifacts including written works), and history (the study of the past). Language and writing would be less important to geography that tends to focus more on locations and spatial relations than on the people in those regions and their languages or writings.

9. **Which of the following is not a social science reference resource:
(Easy) (Skill 2.1)**

   A. Encyclopedias

   B. Almanacs

   C. Atlas

   D. Moody's

D. Moody's
Moody's is a business reference resource. Encyclopedias, almanacs and atlases are social science reference resources.

10. **A primary source is written:
(Average) (Skill 2.4)**

   A. Five years after the period being studies

   B. Ten years after the period being studied

   C. During the period being studied

   D. Anytime

C. During the period being studied
Primary and secondary sources can be different kinds of material, but primary sources are written during the period in which the event occurs or immediately following the event.

11.   **Distortions in maps occur because:**
      (Average) (Skill 2.5)

      A. Of carelessness

      B. Of imprecise instruments

      C. Maps are flat and the earth is a sphere

      D. Cost of precision is prohibitive

C. Maps are flat and the earth is a sphere

Although maps have advantages over globes and photographs, they do have one major disadvantage. The major problem of all maps comes about because most maps are flat and the Earth is a sphere. It is impossible to reproduce exactly on a flat surface an object shaped like a sphere. In order to put the earth's features onto a map they must be stretched in some way. This stretching is called **distortion.** Distortion does not mean that maps are wrong it simply means that they are not perfect representations of the Earth or its parts.

12.   **The Fertile Crescent was bounded by:**
      (Average) (Skill 3.1)

      A. Mediterranean Sea

      B. Arabian Desert

      C. Taurus Mountains

      D. Ural Mountains

D. Ural Mountains

(A) Mediterranean Sea forms the Western border of the Fertile Crescent (B) the Arabian Desert is the Southern boundary and (C) the Taurus Mountains form the Northern boundary. (D) The Ural Mountains are further North in Russia and form the border between Russia and Europe.

13.   Which ancient civilization is credited with being the first to develop irrigation techniques through the use of canals, dikes, and devices for raising water?
(Rigorous)(Skill 3.1)

   A. The Sumerians

   B. The Egyptians

   C. The Babylonians

   D. The Akkadians

A. The Sumerians
The ancient civilization of the Sumerians invented the wheel; developed irrigation through use of canals, dikes, and devices for raising water; devised the system of cuneiform writing; learned to divide time; and built large boats for trade

14.   All of the following applies to the Kushites except:
(Rigorous)(Skill 3.2)

   A. Female rulers

   B. Male rulers

   C. Polytheism

   D. Lion warrior god

B. Male rulers
The Kushites differed from other tribes in that they had (A) female rulers. They practiced (C) polytheism and worshipped a (D) lion warrior god. They did not have (b) male rulers.

15. **Development of a solar calendar, invention of the decimal system, and contributions to the development of geometry and astronomy are all the legacy of:**
(Average)(Skill 3.2)

   A. The Babylonians

   B. The Persians

   C. The Sumerians

   D. The Egyptians

D. The Egyptians
The (A) Babylonians of ancient Mesopotamia flourished for a time under their great contribution of organized law and code, called Hammurabi's Code (1750 BC), after the ruler Hammurabi. The fall of the Babylonians to the Persians in 539 BC made way for the warrior-driver Persian Empire that expanded from Pakistan to the Mediterranean Sea until the conquest of Alexander the Great in 331 BC. The Sumerians of ancient Mesopotamia were most noted for their early advancements as one of the first civilizations and their contributions towards written language known as cuneiform. It was the (D) Egyptians who were the first true developers of a solar calendar, the decimal system, and made significant contributions to the development of geometry and astronomy

16.   The world religion which includes a caste system is:
       (Easy) (Skill 3.4)

       A. Buddhism

       B. Hinduism

       C. Sikhism

       D. Jainism

B. Hinduism
Buddhism, Sikhism, and Jainism all rose out of protest against Hinduism and its practices of sacrifice and the caste system. The caste system, in which people were born into castes, would determine their class for life including who they could marry, what jobs they could perform, and their overall quality of life.

17.   Which of the following is not a religion of China:
       (Easy)(Skill 3.5)

       A. Confucianism

       B. Taoism

       C. Buddhism

       D. Shintoism

D. Shintoism
(A) Confucianism, (B) Taoism and (C) Buddhism are all religions of China. (D) Shintoism is a religion of Japan.

18. The Cradle of Western Civilization is considered to be:
(Easy) (Skill 3.6)

A. The Ottoman Empire

B. Egypt

C. Rome

D. Ancient Greece

D. Ancient Greece
Ancient Greece is often called the **Cradle of Western Civilization** because of the enormous influence it had not only on the time in which it flourished, but on western culture ever since.

19. Direct democracy was:
(Easy)(Skill 3.6)

A. Practiced in Egypt

B. Based on direct, personal, active participation

C. A basis of Roman law

D. Practiced in Sumaria

B. Based on direct, personal, active participation
Direct democracy was (A) not practiced in Egypt, (B) Rome or (D) Sumaria. It was an Athenian concept. The **Athenian** form of democracy, with each citizen having an equal vote in his own government, is a philosophy upon which all modern democracies are based.

20.   The "father of political science" is considered to be:
       (Average) (Skill 3.7)

       A. Aristotle

       B. John Locke

       C. Plato

       D. Thomas Hobbes

A. Aristotle
(D) Thomas Hobbes (1588-1679) wrote the important work *Leviathan* in which he pointed out that people are by all means selfish, individualistic animals that will always look out for themselves and therefore, the state must combat this nature desire. (B) John Locke (1632-1704) whose book *Two Treatises of Government* has long been considered a founding document on the rights of people to rebel against an unjust government was an important figure in the founding of the US Constitution and on general politics of the American Colonies. (C) Plato (427-347 BC) and Aristotle (384-322 BC) both contributed to the field of political science.

Both believed that political order would result in the greatest stability. In fact, Aristotle studied under Plato. Both Plato and Aristotle studied the ideas of causality and the Prime Mover, but their conclusions were different. Aristotle, however, is considered to be "the father of political science" because of his development of a scientific system to study justice and political order.

21.   The first ancient civilization to introduce and practice monotheism was the:
       (Average)(Skill 3.8)

       A. Sumerians

       B. Minoans

       C. Phoenicians

       D. Hebrews

D. Hebrews
The (A) Sumerians and (C) Phoenicians both practiced religions in which many gods and goddesses were worshipped. Often these Gods/Goddesses were based on a feature of nature such as a sun, moon, weather, rocks, water, etc. The (B) Minoan culture shared many religious practices with the Ancient Egyptians. It seems that the king was somewhat of a god figure and the queen, a goddess. Much of the Minoan art point to the worship of multiple gods. Therefore, only the (D) Hebrews introduced and fully practiced monotheism, or the belief in one god.

22.   China's last imperial ruling dynasty was one of its most stable and
      successful and, under its rule, Chinese culture made an outstanding
      impression on Western nations. This dynasty was:
      (Rigorous) (Skill 4.1)

      A. Min

      B. Manchu

      C. Han

      D. Chou

B. Manchu
The (A) Ming Dynasty lasted from 1368-1644 and was among the more successful
dynasties but focused attention towards foreign trade and encouraged growth in the
arts. Therefore, it was the (B) Manchu Dynasty, the last imperial ruling dynasty,
which came to power in the 1600s and expanded China's power in Asia greatly that
was and still is considered to be among the most important, most stable, and most
successful of the Chinese dynasties. The (C) Han and (D) Chou Dynasties were
part of the "ancient" dynasties of China and while important in Chinese History, their
influence did not hold impression on Western nations as the Manchu.

23.   The achievements of the Mongol Empire include all but the following:
      (Rigorous)(Skill 4.1)

      A. Reunification of China

      B. Unification of the Central Asian Republic

      C. Expansion of Europe's knowledge of the world

      D. Exploration of the Americas

D. Exploration of the Americas
The Mongol Empire was founded by Genghis Khan. They had a strict code that had
to be obeyed or there were strict consequences. They had many achievements
among which were the (A) reunification of China, (B) the unification of the Central
Asian Republic and (C) expansion of Europe's knowledge of the world. They did not
(D) explore the Americas.

24. **The network of roads connecting Asia and the Mediterranean was known as the:**
     (Average)(Skill 4.2)

     A. Asian Road

     B. Silk Road

     C. European Road

     D. Mediterranean Road

B. Silk Road
(B) The **Silk Road** was a network of routes connecting Asia and the Mediterranean, and passing through India and the Middle East. It is named after the silk trade but was also the route for trade in other materials such as livestock, wine and minerals. The network included overland routes as well as naval routes, extending over 8,000 miles.

25. **The Bantu were from:**
     (Easy)(Skill 4.3)

     A. Asia

     B. Europe

     C. Africa

     D. Russia

C. Africa
(C) Bantu-speaking people currently populate most of sub-Equatorial Africa, not (A) Asia, (B) Europe or (D) Russia.

26.   **Which does not apply to the ancient kingdom of Mali:**
       (Rigorous)(Skill 4.4)

       A. Christianity

       B. Traditional African beliefs

       C. Islam

       D. Ruled by a king

A. Christianity
(A) Christianity was not a part of the ancient kingdom of Mali. They practiced a blend of (B) traditional African beliefs and (C) Islam and were (D) ruled by their own king.

27.   **Which was not a part of the Triangular Trade System:**
       (Rigorous)   (Skill 4.5)

       A. England

       B. Africa

       C. New World

       D. Japan

D. Japan
The slave trade was part of the triangular trade system, which linked (A) England, (B) Africa and the (C) New World. Trade goods such as beads, cloth and weapons were shipped to the west coast of Africa where they were exchanged for slaves. Slaves were then transported to the West Indies and sold, with the profits used to purchase rum, sugar or molasses. This was then shipped back to England, and the process started again. (D) Japan was not a part of the triangular trade system.

28.   **Which native American group was known for their calendars? (Average)(Skill 4.6)**

A. The Incas

B. The Atacamas

C. The Mayans

D. The Tarapacas

C. The Mayans
The most advanced Native American civilization was the Maya, who lived primarily in Central America. They were the only Native American civilization to develop writing, which consisted of a series of symbols that have yet to be deciphered. The Mayas also built huge pyramids and other stone figures and sculptures, mostly of the gods they worshiped. The Mayas are most famous, however, for their calendars and for their mathematics. The Mayan calendars were the most accurate on the planet until the 16th Century.

29.   **Native South American tribes included all of the following except: (Easy) (Skill 4.6)**

A. Aztec

B. Inca

C. Minoans

D. Maya

C. Minoans
The (A) Aztec were a tribe in Mexico and Central America. (B) The Inca and (D) the Maya were South American tribes. The Minoans were an early civilization but not from the Americas.

30. **An ancient Indian civilization known for its worshipping of the dead was the:**
(Rigorous) (Skill 4.6)

A. The Mayans

B. The Atacamas

C. The Incas

D. The Tarapacas

C. The Incas
The Incas of Peru were an ancient civilization that practiced the worship of the dead.

31. **The principle of zero in mathematics is the discovery of the ancient civilization found in:**
(Average)(Skill 4.6)

A. Egypt

B. Persia

C. Mayas

D. Babylon

C. Mayas
Although the Egyptians practiced algebra and geometry, the Persians developed an alphabet, and the Babylonians developed Hammurabi's Code, which would come to be considered among the most important contributions of the Mesopotamian civilization, it was the created that created the idea of zero in mathematics changing drastically our ideas about numbers.

32. **India's greatest ruler is considered to be:**
    (Average)(Skill 4.7)

    A. Akbar

    B. Asoka

    C. Babur

    D. Jahan

A. Akbar
Akbar (1556-1605) is considered to be India's greatest ruler. He combined a drive for conquest with a magnetic personality and went so far as to invent his own religion, Dinillahi, a combination of Islam, Christianity, Zoroastrianism, and Hinduism. Asoka (273 B.C.-232 B.C.) was also an important ruler as he was the first to bring together a fully united India. Babur (1483-1540) was both considered to be a failure as he struggled to maintain any power early in his reign, but later to be somewhat successful in his quest to reunite Northern India. Jahan's (1592-1666) rule of India is considered to be the golden age of art and literature in the region.

33. **Which one of the following is not an important legacy of the Byzantine Empire?**
    (Rigorous) (Skill 5.1)

    A. It protected Western Europe from various attacks from the East by such groups as the Persians, Ottoman Turks, and Barbarians.

    B. It played a part in preserving the literature, philosophy, and language of ancient Greece.

    C. Its military organization was the foundation for modern armies.

    D. It kept the legal traditions of Roman government, collecting and organizing many ancient Roman laws.

C. Its military organization was the foundation for modern armies
The Byzantine Empire (1353-1453) was the successor to the Roman Empire in the East and protected Western Europe from invaders such as the Persians and Ottomans. The Byzantine Empire was a Christian incorporation of Greek philosophy, language, and literature along with Roman government and law. Therefore, although regarded as having a strong infantry, cavalry, and Engineering corps along with excellent morale amongst its soldiers, the Byzantine Empire is not particularly considered a foundation for modern armies.

34.　　The Roman Empire gave so much to the world, especially the Western world. Of the legacies below, the most influential, effective and lasting is:
(Rigorous) (Skill 5.1)

A. The language of Latin

B. Roman law, justice, and political system

C. Engineering and building

D. The writings of its poets an historians

B. Roman law, justice, and political system
Of the lasting legacies of the Roman Empire, it is their law, justice, and political system that has been the most effective and influential on our Western world today. The idea of a Senate and different houses is still maintained by our United States government and their legal justice system is also the foundation of our own. We still use many Latin words in our justice system, terms such as *habeas corpus* and *voir dire*. English, Spanish, Italian, French, and others are all based on Latin.

The Roman language, Latin itself has died out. The Roman engineering and building and their writings and poetry have also been influential but not nearly to the degree that their governmental and justice systems have been.

35.　　Which of the following was not characteristic of the Bedouin:
(Average) (Skill 5.3)

A. Nomadic wanderers

B. City dwellers

C. Infanticide

D. Suppression of women

B. City dwellers
The Bedouins were basically (A) Nomadic wanderers, not (B) city dwellers. They were cruel and practiced (C) infanticide and (D) suppression of women.

36.   **The holy book of Islam is the:**
       (Easy)(Skill 5.3)

       A. Kaaba

       B. Torah

       C. Koran

       D. Bible

C. Koran
The (A) Kaaba is a small temple. The (B) is the holy book of Judaism and the Bible is the holy book of Christianity. (C) the Koran is the holy book of Islam.

37.   **The Crusades were fought between the:**
       (Easy) (Skill 5.4)

       A. Arabs and Israelies

       B. Muslims and Christian Byzantines

       C. Romans and Greeks

       D. British and Romans

B. Muslims and Christian Byzantines
The Christian Byzantines fought the Crusades to stop the spread of Islam.

38. **Which one of the following did not contribute to the early medieval European civilization?**
(Rigorous)(Skill 5.5)

    A. The heritage from the classical cultures

    B. The Christian religion

    C. The influence of the German Barbarians

    D. The spread of ideas through trade and commerce

D. The spread of ideas through trade and commerce
The heritage of the classical cultures such as Greece, the Christian religion which became dominant, and the influence of the Germanic Barbarians (Visigoths, Saxons, Ostrogoths, Vandals and Franks) were all contributions to early medieval Europe and its plunge into feudalism. During this period, lives were often difficult and lived out on one single manor, with very little travel or spread of ideas through trade or commerce. Civilization seems to have halted progress during these years.

39. **In Western Europe, the achievements of the Renaissance were unsurpassed and made these countries outstanding cultural centers on the continent. All of the following were accomplishments except:**
(Rigorous)(Skill 5.6)

    A. Investment of the printing press

    B. A rekindling of interest in the learning of classical Greece and Rome

    C. Growth in literature, philosophy and art

    D. Better military tactics

D. Better military tactics
The Renaissance in Western Europe produced many important achievements that helped push immense progress among European civilization. Some of the most important developments during the Renaissance were Gutenberg's invention of the printing press in Germany and a reexamination of the ideas and philosophies of classical Greece and Rome that eventually helped Renaissance thinkers to approach more modern ideas. Also important during the Renaissance was the growth in literature (Petrarch, Boccaccio, Erasmus), philosophy (Machiavelli, More, Bacon) and art (Van Eyck, Giotto, da Vinci). Therefore, improved military tactics is the only possible answer as it was clearly not a characteristic of the Renaissance in Western Europe.

40. **Which French Renaissance writer contributed to literature and philosophy?**
(Average) (Skill 5.6)

A. Francois Rabelais

B. Desiderius Erasmus

C. Michel de Montaigne

D. Sir Francis Bacon

C. Michel de Montaigne
(A) Francois Rabelais (1490-1553) was a French writer and physician who was both a practicing monk (first Franciscan then later Benedictine) and a respected humanist thinker of the Renaissance. (B) Desiderius Erasmus (1466-1536) was a Dutch humanist who was very critical of the Catholic Church but was equally conflicted with Luther's Protestant Reformation. Although Luther had once considered him an ally, Erasmus opposed Luther's break from the church and favored a more internal reform to corruption, he never left the Catholic Church. (D) Sir Francis Bacon (1561-1626) was an English philosopher and writer who pushed the idea that knowledge must come from thorough scientific knowledge and experiment, and insufficient data must not be used in reaching conclusions. (C) Michel de Montaigne (1533-1592), a French essayist from a mixed background, half Catholic and half Jewish, did write some about the dangers of absolute powers, primarily monarchs but also of the Church. His attitude changed as his examination of his own life developed into a study of mankind and nature.

41. The changing focus during the Renaissance when artists and scholars were less concerned with religion but centered their efforts on a better understanding of people and the world was called:
(Average)(Skill 5.6)

    A. Realism

    B. Humanism

    C. Individualism

    D. Intellectualism

B. Humanism
Realism is a medieval philosophy that contemplated independence of existence of the body, the mind, and God. The idea of individualism is usually either a reference to an economic or political theory. Intellectualism is the placing of great importance and devotion to the exploring of the intellect. Therefore, the changing focus during the Renaissance when artists and scholars were less concerned with religion but centered their efforts on a better understanding of people and the world was called humanism.

42. The "father of anatomy" is considered to be:
(Easy) (Skill 5.6)

    A. Vesalius

    B. Servetus

    C. Galen

    D. Harvey

A. Vesalius
Andreas Vesalius (1514-1564) is considered to be the "father of anatomy" as a result of his revolutionary work on the human anatomy based on dissections of human cadavers. Prior to Vesalius, men such as Galen, (130-200) had done work in the field of anatomy, but they had based the majority of their work on animal studies.

43. **Studies in astronomy, skills in mapping, and other contributions to geographic knowledge came from:**
    (Easy) (Skill 5.6)

    A. Galileo

    B. Columbus

    C. Eratosthenes

    D. Ptolemy

D. Ptolemy

Ptolemy (2nd century AD) was important in the fields of astronomy and geography. His theory stated that the earth was the center of the universe and all the other planets rotated around it, a theory that was proven false, while Ptolemy was important for his contributions to the fields of mapping, mathematics, and geography. Galileo (1564-1642) was also important in the field of astronomy but did not make the mapping and geographic contributions of Ptolemy. He invented and used the world's first telescope and advanced Copernicus' theory that the earth revolved around the sun, much to the dismay of the Church.

44. **The ideas and innovations of the period of the Renaissance were spread throughout Europe mainly because of:**
    (Average)(Skill 5.6)

    A. Extensive exploration

    B. Craft workers and their guilds

    C. The invention of the printing press

    D. Increased travel and trade

C. The invention of the printing press

The ideas and innovations of the Renaissance were spread throughout Europe for a number of reasons. While exploration, increased travel, and spread of craft may have aided the spread of the Renaissance to small degrees, nothing was as important to the spread of ideas as Gutenberg's invention of the printing press in Germany.

45.   Who is considered to be the most important figure in the spread of
       Protestantism across Switzerland?
       (Easy)(Skill 5.7)

       A. Calvin

       B. Zwingli

       C. Munzer

       D. Leyden

A. Calvin
While Huldreich Zwingli (1484-1531) was the first to spread the Protestant
Reformation in Switzerland around 1519, it was John Calvin (1509-1564), whose
less radical approach to Protestantism who really made the most impact in
Switzerland. Calvin's ideas separated from the Lutherans over the "Lord's Supper"
debate over the sacrament, and his branch of Protestants became known as
Calvinism. Calvin certainly built on Zwingli's early influence but really made the
religion widespread throughout Switzerland. Thomas Munzer (1489-1525) was a
German Protestant reformer whose radical and revolutionary ideas about God's will
to overthrow the ruling classes and his siding with the peasantry got him beheaded.
Munzer has since been studied and admired by Marxists for his views on class.
Leyden (or Leiden) was a founder of the University of Leyden, a Protestant place for
study in the Netherlands.

46.   The English explorer who gave England its claim to North American
       was:
       (Easy) (Skill 6.1)
       A. Raleigh

       B. Hawkins

       C. Drake

       D. Cabot

D. Cabot
Sir Walter Raleigh (1554-1618) was an English explorer and navigator, who was
sent to the New World in search of riches. He founded the lost colony at Roanoke,
Virginia, and was later imprisoned for a supposed plot to kill the King for which he
was later released. Sir John Hawkins (1532-1595) and Sir Francis Drake (1540-
1596) were both navigators who worked in the slave trade, made some voyages to
the New World, and commanded ships against and defeated the Spanish Armada in
1588. John Cabot (1450-1498) was the English explorer who gave England claim to
North America.

47. **The Age of Exploration begun in the 1400s was led by:**
    (Average)(Skill 6.1)

    A. The Portuguese

    B. The Spanish

    C. The English

    D. The Dutch

A. The Portuguese
Although the Age of Exploration had many important players among them, the Dutch, Spanish and English, it was the Portuguese who sent the first explorers to the New World.

48. **The foundation of modern democracy is embodied in the ideas of:**
    (Rigorous) (Skill 6.4)

    A. St. Thomas Aquinas

    B. Rousseau

    C. John Locke

    D. Montesquieu

C. John Locke
(A) It was St. Thomas Aquinas (1225-1274) who merged Aristotelian ideas with Christianity, who helped lay the ideas of modern constitutionalism and the limiting of government by law. (B) Rousseau (1712-1778) and (D) Montesquieu (1689-1755) were political philosophers who explored the idea of what has come to be known as liberalism. They pushed the idea that through understanding the interconnectedness of economics, geography, climate and psychology, that changes could be made to improve life. (C) John Locke (1632-1704), whose book *Two Treatises of Government* has long been considered a founding document on the rights of people to rebel against an unjust government, was an important figure in the founding of the US Constitution and on general politics of the American Colonies. Locke is the one who laid the basis for modern democracy.

49.   Who applied Locke's principles to the American situation?
      (Rigorous) (Skill 6.4)

      A. Thomas Paine

      B. Samuel Adams

      C. Benjamin Franklin

      D. Thomas Jefferson

D. Thomas Jefferson
Thomas Paine (1737-1809), the great American political theorist, wrote "these are the times that try men's souls" in his 16 part pamphlet *The Crisis*. Paine's authoring of *Common Sense* was an important step in spreading information to the American colonists about their need for independence from Great Britain. It was Thomas Jefferson who took the ideals and principles of John Locke and applied them to the situation in America.

50.   The idea that morality lay not in the natural of God but in the human
      soul itself was a philosophy of:
      (Average) (Skill 6.4)

      A. Rousseau

      B. Immanuel Kant

      C. Montesquieu

      D. John Locke

B. Immanuel Kant
Immanuel Kant (1724-1804) was the German metaphysician and philosopher, who was a founding proponent of the idea that world organization was the means for achieving universal peace. Kant's ideas helped to found such world peace organizations as the League of Nations in the wake of World War I.

51.   **The "divine right" of kings was the key political characteristic of:**
       (Easy) (Skill 6.6)

       A. The Age of Absolutism

       B. The Age of Reason

       C. The Age of Feudalism

       D. The Age of Despotism

A. The Age of Absolutism
The "divine right" of kings was the key political characteristic of The Age of Absolutism and was most visible in the reign of King Louis XIV of France, as well as during the times of King James I and his son, Charles I. The divine right doctrine claims that kings and absolute leaders derive their right to rule by virtue of their birth alone. They see this both as a law of God and nature.

52.   **Studies in astronomy, skills in mapping, and other contributions to**
       geographic knowledge came from:
       (Rigorous) (Skill 6.6)

       A. Galileo

       B. Columbus

       C. Eratosthenes

       D. Ptolemy

D. Ptolemy
Ptolemy (2nd century AD) was important in the fields of astronomy and geography. His theory stated that the earth was the center of the universe and all the other planets rotated around it, a theory that was proven false, while Ptolemy was important for his contributions to the fields of mapping, mathematics, and geography. Galileo (1564-1642) was also important in the field of astronomy but did not make the mapping and geographic contributions of Ptolemy. He invented and used the world's first telescope and advanced Copernicus' theory that the earth revolved around the sun, much to the dismay of the Church.

53. **The major force in eighteenth and nineteenth century politics was:**
(Average) (Skill 6.7)

   A. Nationalism

   B. Revolution

   C. War

   D. Diplomacy

A. Nationalism
Nationalism was the driving force in politics in the eighteenth and nineteenth century. Groups of people that shared common traits and characteristics wanted their own government and countries. This led to some revolution, war and the failure of diplomacy.

54. **Which one of the following was not a reason why the United States went to war with Great Britain in 1812?**
(Rigorous) (Skill 6.8)

   A. Resentment by Spain over the sale exploration, and settlement of the Louisiana Territory

   B. The westward movement of farmers because of the need for more land

   C. Canadian fur traders were agitating the northwestern Indians to fight American expansion'

   D. Britain continued to seize American ships on the high seas and force American seamen to serve aboard British ships

A. Resentment by Spain over the sale, exploration, and settlement of the Louisiana Territory
The United States went to war with Great Britain in 1812 for a number of reasons including the expansion of settlers westward and the need for more land, the agitation of Indians by Canadian fur traders in eastern Canada, and the continued seizures of American ships by the British on the high seas. Therefore, the only statement given that was not a reason for the War of 1812 was the resentment by Spain over the sale, exploration and settlement of the Louisiana Territory. In fact, the Spanish continually held more hostility towards the British than towards the United States. The War of 1812 is often considered to be the second American war for independence.

55.   **Colonial expansion by Western European powers in the eighteenth and nineteenth centuries was due primarily to:**
      (Average) (Skill 7.1)

      A. Building and opening the Suez Canal

      B. The Industrial Revolution

      C. Marked improvements in transportation

      D. Complete independence of all the Americas and loss of   European domination and influence

B. The Industrial Revolution

Colonial expansion by Western European powers in the late eighteenth and nineteenth centuries was due primarily to the Industrial Revolution in Great Britain that spread across Europe and needed new natural resources and therefore, new locations from which to extract the raw materials needed to feed the new industries

56.   **Marxism believes which two groups are in continual conflict?**
      (Easy) (Skill 7.1)

      A. Farmers and landowners

      B. Kings and the nobility

      C. Workers and owners

      D. Structure and superstructure

C. Workers and owners

Marxism believes that the workers and owners are in continual conflict. Marxists refer to these two groups as the proletariat and the bourgeoisie. The proletariat is exploited by the bourgeoisie and will, according to Marxism, rise up over the bourgeoisie in class warfare in an effort to end private control over the means of production.

57.   **Laissez-faire economics is based on:**
       (Easy)(Skill 7.1)

      A. Free markets without government interference

      B. Free markets with government intervention

      C. Government control of the marketplace

      D. Government ownership of the means of production

A. Free markets without government interference
Laissez-faire literally means leave it alone. Laissez-faire economics is based on (a) no government intervention in the market place.

58.   **Competition leads to:**
       (Rigorous) (Skill 7.1)

      A. Fights

      B. Waste

      C. Overproduction

      D. Efficient use of resources

D. Efficient use of resources
Competition is the basis for the functioning of markets. It may cause a few a disagreements between market participants but it does not lead to (B) waste or (C) overproduction since competition results in (D) the efficient use of resources.

59.   **The concept of the invisible hand was created by:**
       (Easy)(Skill 7.1)

    A. Thomas Robert Malthus

    B. John Stuart Mill

    C. Adam Smith

    D. John Maynard Keynes

C. Adam Smith
Adam Smith was a believer in laissez-faire economic which meant no government interference in the economy. He believed that the economy would function as if it were guided by an invisible hand to achieve the most efficient outcomes.

60.   **Nineteenth century German unification was the result of the hard work of:**
       (Average)(Skill 7.2)

    A. Otto von Bismarck

    B. Kaiser William II

    C. Von Moltke

    D. Hindenburg

A. Otto von Bismarck
(A) Otto von Bismarck is the man most often credited with the unification of Germany. Bismarck became the first Chancellor of a unified Germany. He ultimately lost power to his successor Kaiser William II, who ultimately led Germany into World War I, when nationalist sentiment proved too strong for the united Germany. Ultimately, Germany's concessions in the Treaty of Versailles to end World War I, and Adolf Hitler's Nazi regime's defeat at the hands of Allied forces in World War II had destroyed the unified Germany that Bismarck had achieved in the mid to late 1800s.

61.   Nineteenth century imperialism by Western European nations had important and far-reaching effects on the colonial peoples they ruled. All four of the following are the result of this. Which one was most important and had lasting effects on key 20th century events? (Rigorous) (Skill 7.3)

      A. Local wars were ended

      B. Living standards were raised

      C. Demands for self government and feelings of nationalism surfaced

      D. Economic developments occurred

C. Demands for self-government and feelings of nationalism surfaced
The 19th century imperialism by Western European nations had some very serious and far-reaching effects. The most important and lasting effect on events of the 20th century is the demands for self-government and the rise of nationalism. Both World War I and World War II were caused to a large degree by the rise of nationalist sentiment across Europe and Asia. Nationalism has also fueled numerous liberation movements and revolutionary movements across the globe from Central and South America to the South Pacific to Africa and Asia.

62.   The results of the Renaissance, Enlightenment, Commercial and Industrial Revolutions were more unfortunate for the people of: (Rigorous) (Skill 7.3)

      A. Asia

      B. Latin America

      C. Africa

      D. Middle East

C. Africa
The results of the Renaissance, Enlightenment, Commercial and Industrial Revolutions were quite beneficial for many people in much of the world. New ideas of humanism, religious tolerance, and secularism were spreading. Increased trade and manufacturing were surging economies in much of the world. The people of Africa, however, suffered during these times as they became largely left out of the developments. Also, the people of Africa were stolen, traded, and sold into slavery to provide a cheap labor force for the growing industries of Europe and the New World.

**63.   What event sparked the onset of World War I?
(Average)(Skill 7.4)**

    A. Assassination of Archduke Francis Ferdinand

    B. Hitler's invasion of Poland

    C. The collapse of the Weimar Republic

    D. The assassination of Czar Nicholas Romanov

A. Assassination of Archduke Francis Ferdinand
Nationalist pressures were surging in the pre World War I and tensions were high. (A) Archduke Ferdinand and his wife were visiting Sarajevo when they were assassinated. This led to the onset of the war. (B) Hitler's invasion of Poland occurred before World War II. (C) The Weimar Republic collapsed during World War I and the (D) Russian Czar was assassinated after Russia withdrew from the war.

**64.   Who was not one of the World War II Allies?
(Easy) (Skill 7.7)**

    A. Japan

    B. Russia

    C. United States

    D. Great Britain

A. Japan
(B) Russia, (C) the United States and (D) Great Britain were the Allies. (D) Japan was one of the Axis powers.

65.   A well-known World War II figure who ruled fascist Italy was?
       (Average) (Skill 7.7)

       A. Hitler

       B. Stalin

       C. Tojo

       D. Mussolini

D. Mussolini
(A) Adolf Hitler (1889-1945), the Nazi leader of Germany, and (C) Hideki Tojo (1884-1948), the Japanese General and Prime Minister, were well known World War II figures who led Axis forces into war on a quest of spreading fascism. (B) Joseph Stalin (1879-1953) was the Communist Russian head of state during World War II. Although all three were repressive in their actions, it was (D) Benito Mussolini (1883-1945), the Fascist and widely-considered incompetent.

66.   A political system in which there is a one party state, centralized control,
       and a repressive police system with private ownership is called
       (Average) (Skill 7.7)

       A. Communism

       B. Fascism

       C. Socialism

       D. Constitutional Monarchy

B. Fascism
(A) Communism and (C) Socialism both are based on the public ownership of the means of production. (D) A constitutional monarchy would have private ownership. (B) Fascism is the only form of government that has all of the characteristics mentioned in the statement.

67. **Which country was not a part of the Axis in World War II?
(Easy) (Skill 7.7)**

    A. Germany

    B. Italy

    C. Japan

    D. United States

D. United States
(A) Germany, (B) Italy and (C) Japan were the member of the Axis in World War II.
(D) The United States was a member of the Allies which opposed the Axis.

68. **The international organization established to work for world peace at
the end of the Second World War is the:
(Average)(Skill 7.8)**

    A. League of Nations

    B. United Federation of Nations

    C. United Nations

    D. United World League

C. United Nations
The international organization established to work for world peace at the end of the
Second World War was the United Nations. From the ashes of the failed League of
Nations, established following World War I, the United Nations continues to be a
major player in world affairs today.

69. **Which one of the following would not be considered a result of World War II?**
    (Rigorous) (Skill 7.8)

    A. Economic depressions and slow resumption of trade and financial aid

    B. Western Europe was no longer the center of world power

    C. The beginnings of new power struggles not only in Europe but in Asia as well

    D. Territorial and boundary changes for many nations, especially in Europe

A. Economic depressions and slow resumption of trade and financial aid
Following World War II, the economy was vibrant and flourished from the stimulant of war and an increased dependence of the world on United States industries. Therefore, World War II didn't result in economic depressions and slow resumption of trade and financial aid. Western Europe was no longer the center of world power. New power struggles arose in Europe and Asia and many European nations underwent changing territories and boundaries.

70. **The doctrine of comparative advantage explains:**
    (Average) (Skill 8.9)

    A. Why nations trade

    B. How to fight a war

    C. Time zones

    D. Political divisions

A. Why nations trade
The principle of comparative advantage is the basis for the theory of international trade and says that nations engage in trade with other nations when they can produce the good at a comparatively lower price than the other nation can.

71. **The Common Market is a form of:**
    (Average)(Skill 8.9)

    A. Industrialization

    B. Military defense

    C. Control

    D. Trade liberalization

D. Trade liberalization
The Common Market is a form of (D) trade liberalization. This is a way of lowering trade barriers between nations. Free unrestricted trade results in the most efficient use of resources, and higher levels of output, income and employment in the trading countries.

72. **The only colony not founded and settled for religious, political or business reasons was:**
    (Easy) (Skill 9.2)

    A. Delaware

    B. Virginia

    C. Georgia

    D. New York

C. Georgia
The Swedish and the Dutch established Delaware and New York as Middle Colonies. They were established with the intention of growth by economic prosperity from farming across the countryside. The English, with the intention of generating a strong farming economy settled Virginia, a Southern Colony. Georgia was the only one of these colonies not settled for religious, political or business reasons as it was started as a place for debtors from English prisons.

73. The year 1619 was a memorable for the colony of Virginia. Three important events occurred resulting in lasting effects on US history. Which of the following is not one of the events?
     (Average)(Skill 9.2)

     A. Twenty African slaves arrived.

     B. The London Company granted the colony a charter making it independent.

     C. The colonists were given the right by the London Company to govern themselves through representative government in the Virginia House of Burgesses.

     D. The London Company sent to the colony 60 women who were quickly married, establishing families and stability in the colony.

B. The London Company granted the colony a charter making it independent.
In the year 1619, the Southern colony of Virginia had an eventful year including the first arrival of twenty African slaves, the right to self-governance through representative government in the Virginia House of Burgesses (their own legislative body), and the arrival of sixty women sent to marry and establish families in the colony. The London Company did not, however, grant the colony a charter in 1619.

74. Which one of the following is not a reason why Europeans came to the New World?
     (Easy) (Skill 9.3)

A. To find resources in order to increase wealth

B. To establish trade

C. To increase a ruler's power and importance

D. To spread Christianity

B. To establish trade
The Europeans came to the New World for a number of reasons; often they came to find new natural resources to extract for manufacturing. The Portuguese, Spanish and English were sent over to increase the monarch's power and spread influences such as religion (Christianity) and culture. Therefore, the only reason given that Europeans didn't come to the New World was to establish trade.

TEACHER CERTFICATION STUDY GUIDE

75. **The source of authority for national, state, and local governments in the US is:**
(Average) (Skill 9.6)

A. The will of the people

B. The US Constitution

C. Written laws

D. The Bill of Rights

A. The will of the people
The source of authority for national, state, and local governments in the United States is the will of the people. Although the United States Constitution, the Bill of Rights, and the other written laws of the land are important guidelines for authority, they may ultimately be altered or changed by the will of the people.

76. **France decided in 1777 to help the American colonies in their war against Britain. This decision was based on:**
(Rigorous) (Skill 9.8)

A. The naval victory of John Paul Jones over the British ship Serapis"

B. The survival of the terrible winter at Valley Forge

C. The success of colonial guerilla fighters in the South

D. The defeat of the British at Saratoga

D. The defeat of the British at Saratoga
The defeat of the British at Saratoga was the overwhelming factor in the Franco-American alliance of 1777 that helped the American colonies defeat the British. Some historians believe that without the Franco-American alliance, the American Colonies would not have been able to defeat the British and American would have remained a British colony.

GACE HISTORY   293

77.   "These are the times that try men's souls" were words penned by:
      (Rigorous)(Skill 9.8)

      A. Thomas Jefferson

      B. Samuel Adams

      C. Benjamin Franklin

      D. Thomas Paine

D. Thomas Paine
Thomas Paine (1737-1809), the great American political theorist, wrote "these are the times that try men's souls" in his 16 part pamphlet *The Crisis*. Paine's authoring of *Common Sense* was an important step in spreading information to the American colonists about their need for independence from Great Britain.

78.   Under the brand new Constitution, the most urgent of the many
      problems facing the new federal government was that of:
      (Average) (Skill 9.9)

      A. Maintaining a strong army and navy

      B. Establishing a strong foreign policy

      C. Raising money to pay salaries and war debts

      D. Setting up courts, passing federal laws, and providing for law enforcement
          officers

C. Raising money to pay salaries and war debts
Maintaining strong military forces, establishment of a strong foreign policy, and setting up a justice system were important problems facing the United States under the newly ratified Constitution. However, the most important and pressing issue was how to raise money to pay salaries and war debts from the Revolutionary War. Alexander Hamilton (1755-1804) then Secretary of the Treasury proposed increased tariffs and taxes on products such as liquor. This money would be used to pay off war debts and to pay for internal programs. Hamilton also proposed the idea of a National Bank.

79.   **The Federalists:**
        (Rigorous) (Skill 10.5)

        A. Favored state's rights

        B. Favored a weak central government

        C. Favored a strong federal government

        D. Supported the British

C. Favored a strong federal government
The Federalists were opposed to (A) state's rights and a (B) weak federal government. (D) Most of them opposed the British. (C) The Federalists favored a strong federal government.

80.   **After the War of 1812, Henry Clay and others proposed economic measures, including raising tariffs to protect American farmers and manufacturers from foreign competition. These measures were proposed in the period known as:**
        (Rigorous) (Skill 10.5)

        A. Era of Nationalism

        B. American Expansion

        C. Era of Good Feeling

        D. American System

D. American System
Although there is no official (A) "Era of Nationalism", it could be used to describe the time leading up to and including the First and Second World Wars, as nationalism was on the rise. (B) American Expansion describes the movement of American settlers across the frontier towards the West. The so-called (C) "Era of Good Feeling" is the period after the War of 1812 but doesn't describe the policies proposed by Clay. The economic measures, including raising tariffs to protect American farmers and manufacturers from foreign competition, was known as the (D) American System

81. **The belief that the United States should control all of North America was called:**
(Easy) (Skill 10.6)

A. Westward Expansion

B. Pan Americanism

C. Manifest Destiny

D. Nationalism

C. Manifest Destiny
The belief that the United States should control all of North America was called (B) Manifest Destiny. This idea fueled much of the violence and aggression towards those already occupying the lands such as the Native Americans. Manifest Destiny was certainly driven by sentiments of (D) nationalism and gave rise to (A) westward expansion.

82. **Leaders in the movement for woman's rights have included all but:**
(Rigorous) (Skill 11.2)

A. Elizabeth Cady Stanton

B. Lucretia Borgia

C. Susan B. Anthony

D. Lucretia Mott

B. Lucretia Borgia
The only name not associated with the woman's rights movement is Lucretia Borgia. The others were all pioneers in the movement with Susan B. Anthony and Elizabeth Cady Stanton being the founders of the National Woman Suffrage Association in 1869.

83. **The Pilgrims came to America to:**
(Average) (Skill 10.8)

A. To drill for oil

B. To be the official representatives of the king

C. To take over the East India Company

D. To flee religious persecution

D. To flee religious persecution
The Pilgrims and others suffered religious persecution and because of this came to America.

84. **A famous canal is the:**
(Easy) (Skill 10.9)

A. Pacific Canal

B. Arctic Canal

C. Panama Canal

D. Atlantic Canal

C. Panama Canal
(C) The only canal is the selection of answers is the Panama Canal. The Pacific, Artic and Atlantic are oceans, not canals.

85. **There is no doubt of the vast improvement of the US Constitution over the weak Articles of Confederation. Which one of the four accurate statements below is a unique yet eloquent description of the document? (Rigorous) (Skill 11.1)**

   A. The establishment of a strong central government in no way lessened or weakened the individual states.

   B. Individual rights were protected and secured.

   C. The Constitution is the best representation of the results of the American genius for compromise.

   D. Its flexibility and adaptation to change gives it a sense of timelessness.

C. The Constitution is the best representation of the results of the American genius for compromise
The U.S. Constitution was indeed a vast improvement over the Articles of Confederation and the authors of the document took great care to assure longevity. It clearly stated that the establishment of a strong central government in no way lessened or weakened the individual states. In the Bill of Rights, citizens were assured that individual rights were protected and secured. Possibly the most important feature of the new Constitution was its flexibility and adaptation to change which assured longevity.

Therefore, the only statement made that doesn't describe some facet of the Constitution is "The Constitution is the best representation of the results of the American genius for compromise". On the contrary, the Constitution made sure that citizens could critique and make changes to their government and encourages such critiques and changes as necessary for the preservation of democracy.

86. **What Supreme Court ruling dealt with the issue of civil rights?**
(Rigorous) (Skill 11.2)

   A. Jefferson vs Madison

   B. Lincoln vs Douglas

   C. Dred Scott v. Sanford

   D. Marbury vs Madison

C. Dred Scott v. Sanford
Marbury vs Madison established the principal of judicial review. The Supreme Court ruled that it held no authority in making the decision (regarding Marbury's commission as Justice of the Peace in District of Columbia) as the Supreme Court's jurisdiction (or lack thereof) in the case, was conflicted with Article III of the Constitution. (D) The Dred Scot case is the well-know civil rights case that had to do with the rights of the slave.

87. **As a result of the Missouri Compromise:**
(Rigorous) (Skill 11.2)

   A. Slavery was not allowed in the Louisiana Purchase

   B. The Louisiana Purchase was nullified

   C. Louisiana separated from the Union

   D. The Embargo Act was repealed

A. Slavery was not allowed in the Louisiana Purchase
The Missouri Compromise was the agreement that eventually allowed Missouri to enter the Union. It did not nullify (B) the Louisiana Purchase and (D) the Embargo Act and did not (C) separate Louisiana from the Union. (A) As a result of the Missouri Compromise slavery was specifically banned north of the boundary 36° 30'.

88. The principle of "popular sovereignty" allowing people in any territory to make their own decision concerning slavery was stated by; (Rigorous)(Skill 11.2)

    A. Henry Clay

    B. Daniel Webster

    C. John C. Calhoun

    D. Stephen A. Douglas

D. Stephen A. Douglas
(A) Henry Clay (1777-1852) and (B) Daniel Webster (1782-1852) were prominent Whigs whose main concern was keeping the United States one nation. They opposed Andrew Jackson and his Democratic party around the 1830s in favor of promoting what Clay called "the American System". (C) John C. Calhoun (1782-1850) served as Vice-President under John Quincy Adams and Andrew Jackson, and then as a state senator from South Carolina. He was very pro-slavery and a champion of states' rights. The principle of "popular sovereignty", in which people in each territory could make their own decisions concerning slavery, was the doctrine of (D) Stephen A. Douglas (1813-1861). Douglas was looking for a middle ground between the abolitionists of the North and the pro-slavery Democrats of the South. However, as the polarization of pro- and anti-slavery sentiments grew, he lost the presidential election to Republican Abraham Lincoln, who later abolished slavery.

89. The Union had many strengths over the Confederacy. Which was Not a strength?
    (Average) (Skill 11.2)

    A. Railroads

    B. Industry

    C. Slaves

    D. Manpower

C. Slaves
At the time of the Civil War, the South was mostly a plantation economy based on using slaves. The industry, railroads and manpower was located in the North, which made transportation and weapons easy for the North to obtain and use than the South.

90.	After the Civil War, the US adapted an attitude of isolation from foreign affairs. But the turning point marking the beginning of the US becoming a world power was:
(Rigorous)(Skill 11.3)

A. World War I

B. Expansion of business and trade overseas

C. The Spanish-American War

D. The building and financial of the Panama Canal

C. The Spanish-American War
The turning point marking the beginning of the United States becoming a super power was the Spanish-American War. This was seen as an extension of the Monroe doctrine, calling for United States dominance in the Western Hemisphere and removal of European powers in the region. The United States' relatively easy defeat of Spain in the Spanish-American War marked the beginning of a continuing era of dominance for the United States. In addition, in the post-Civil War era, Spain was the largest landowner in the Americas. Their easy defeat at the hands of the United States in Cuba, the Philippines and elsewhere showed the strength of the United States across the globe.

91.	The three-day Battle of Gettysburg was the turning point of the Civil War for the North leading to ultimate victory. The battle in the West reinforcing the North's victory and sealing the South's defeat was the day after Gettysburg at:
(Rigorous) (Skill 11.3)

A. Perryville

B. Was after Gettysburg

C. Stones River

D. Shiloh

B. Was after Gettysburg
The Battle of Vicksburg was crucial in reinforcing the North's victory and sealing the south's defeat for a couple of reasons. First, the Battle of Vicksburg potentially gave the Union full control of the Mississippi River. More importantly, the battle split the Confederate Army and allowed General Grant to reach his goal of restoring commerce to the important northwest area.

92. The Radical Republicans who pushed the harsh Reconstruction measures through Congress after Lincoln's death lost public and moderate Republican support when they went too far: (Rigorous) (Skill 11.4)

   A. In their efforts to challenge the President

   B. By dividing ten southern states into military-controlled districts

   C. By making the ten southern states give freed African Americans the right to vote

   D. Sending carpetbaggers into the South to build up support for Congressional legislation

A. In their efforts to impeach the President
The public support and the moderate Republicans were actually being drawn towards the more radical end of the Republican spectrum following Lincoln's death during Reconstruction. Because many felt as though Andrew Johnson's policies towards the South were too soft and were running the risk of rebuilding the old system of white power and slavery. Even moderate Republicans in the North felt as though it was essential to rebuild the South but with the understanding that they must be abide by the Fourteenth and Fifteenth Amendment assuring Blacks freedom and the right to vote. The radical Republicans were so frustrated that the President would make concessions to the old Southerners that they attempted to impeach him. This turned back the support that they had received from the public and from moderates.

93. **Historians state that the West helped to speed up the Industrial Revolution. Which one of the following statements was not a reason for this?**
(Rigorous) (Skill 11.6)

    A. Food supplies for the ever increasing urban populations came from farms in the West

    B. A tremendous supply of gold and silver from western mines provided the capital needed to built industries

    C. Descendants of western settlers, educated as engineers, geologists, and metallurgists in the East, returned to the West to mine the mineral resources needed for industry

    D. Iron, copper, and other minerals from western mines were important resources in manufacturing products

C. Descendants of western settlers, educated as engineers, geologists, and metallurgists in the East, returned to the West to mine the mineral resources needed for industry.
The West helped to speed up the Industrial Revolution in a number of important and significant ways. First, the land yielded crops for the growing urban populations. Second, the gold and silver supplies coming out of the Western mines provided the capital needed to build industries. Also, resources such as iron and copper were extracted from the mines in the West and provided natural resources for manufacturing. The descendants of western settlers typically didn't become educated and then returned to the West as miners. The miners were typically working class with little or no education.

94. **The post-Civil War years were a time of low public morality, a time of greed, graft, and dishonesty. Which one of the reasons listed would not be accurate?**
(Rigorous) (Skill 11.6)

   A. The war itself because of the money and materials needed to carry on the War

   B. The very rapid growth of industry and big business after the War

   C. The personal example set by President Grant

   D. Unscrupulous heads of large impersonal corporations

C. The personal example set by President Grant
The post-Civil War years were a particularly difficult time for the nation and public morale was especially low. The war had plunged the country into debt and ultimately into a recession by the 1890s. Racism was rampant throughout the South and the North where freed Blacks were taking jobs for low wages. The rapid growth of industry and big business caused a polarization of rich and poor, workers and owners. Many people moved into the urban centers to find work in the new industrial sector, jobs were typically low-wage, long hours and poor working conditions. The heads of large impersonal corporations were arrogant in treating their workers inhumanely and letting morale drop to a record low. The heads of corporations showed their greed and malice towards the workingman by trying to prevent and disband labor unions.

95.   **The American labor union movement started gaining new momentum:
(Average) (Skill 11.6)**

   A. During the building of the railroads

   B. After 1865 with the growth of cities

   C. With the rise of industrial giants such as Carnegie and Vanderbilt

   D. During the war years of 1861-1865

B. After 1865 with the growth of cities

The American Labor Union movement had been around since the late 18th and early 19th centuries. The Labor movement began to first experience persecution by employers in the early 1800s. The American Labor Movement remained relatively ineffective until after the Civil War. In 1866, the National Labor Union was formed, pushing such issues as the eight-hour workday and new policies of immigration. This gave rise to the Knights of Labor and eventually the American Federation of Labor (AFL) in the 1890s and the Industrial Workers of the World (1905). Therefore, it was the period following the Civil War that empowered the labor movement in terms of numbers, militancy, and effectiveness.

96.   **It can be reasonably stated that the change in the United States from
primarily an agricultural country into an industrial power was due to
all of the following except:
(Rigorous) (Skill 11.6)**

   A. Tariffs on foreign imports

   B. Millions of hardworking immigrants

   C. An increase in technological developments

   D. The change from steam to electricity for powering industrial machinery

A. Tariffs on foreign imports

It can be reasonably stated that the change in the United States from primarily an agricultural country into an industrial power was due to a great degree of three of the reasons listed above. It was a combination of millions of hard-working immigrants, an increase in technological developments, and the change from steam to electricity for powering industrial machinery. The only reason given that really had little effect was the tariffs on foreign imports.

97.   After 1783, the largest "land owner" in the Americas was:
        (Average)   (Skill 11.7)

        A. Britain

        B. Spain

        C. France

        D. United States

B. Spain
Despite the emergence of the United States as an independent nation in control of the colonies over the British, and the French control of Canada, Spain remained the largest "land owner" in the Americas controlling much of the southwest as well as much of Central and South America.

98.   In the United States, federal investigations into business activities are
        handled by the:
        (Rigorous)(Skill 11.8)

        A. Department of Treasury

        B. Security & Exchange Commission

        C. Government Accounting Office

        D. Federal Trade Commission

D. Federal Trade Commission
The Department of Treasury (A), established in 1789, is an executive government agency that is responsible for advising the president on fiscal policy. There is no such thing as a Government Accounting Office. In the United States, Federal Trade Commission or FTC handles federal investigations into business activities. The establishment of the FTC in 1915 as an independent government agency was done so as to assure fair and free competition among businesses.

99.   **Drought is a problem in Africa and other places because:
       (Average) (Skill 12.5)**

       A. There is flooding

       B. The rivers change course

       C. People flock to see the drought

       D. The dried out soil turns to dust and cannot grow food

D. The dried out soil turns to dust and cannot grow food
Since a drought is a period of dryness and a lack of rain, there (A) is no flooding and (B) the rivers do not change course especially since most of them are dry.

People may go to see the area but for the most part, (D) drought is accompanied by famine since the soil cannot grow food.

100.   **Which of the following contributed to the severity of the Great
       Depression in California?
       (Rigorous)(Skill 12.5)**

       A. An influx of Chinese immigrants.

       B. The dust bowl drove People out of the cities.

       C. An influx of Mexican immigrants.

       D. An influx of Oakies.

D. An influx of Oakies
The answer is "An influx of Oakies" (D). The Dust Bowl of the Great Plains destroyed agriculture in the area. People living in the plains areas lost their livelihood and many lost their homes and possessions in the great dust storms that resulted from a period of extended drought. People from all of the states affected by the Dust Bowl made their way to California in search of a better life. Because the majority of the people were from Oklahoma, they were all referred to as "Oakies." These migrants brought with them their distinctive plains culture. The great influx of people seeking jobs exacerbated the effects of the Great Depression in California.

101.　The term Red Scare refers to:
　　　(Average) (Skill 12.3)

　　　A. The Halloween holiday

　　　B. The fear of communists

　　　C. Sun Spots

　　　D. Labor strikes

B. The fear of communists
(C) Communists were known as Reds so the term Red Scare referred to a fear of Communists in the government.

102.　Of all the major causes of both World Wars I and II, the most significant one is considered to be:
　　　(Average) (Skill 12.7)

　　　A. Extreme nationalism

　　　B. Military buildup and aggression

　　　C. Political unrest

　　　D. Agreements and alliances

A. Extreme nationalism
Although military buildup and aggression, political unrest, and agreements and alliances were all characteristic of the world climate before and during World War I and World War II, the most significant cause of both wars was extreme nationalism. Nationalism is the idea that the interests and needs of a particular nation are of the utmost and primary importance above all else. Some nationalist movements could be liberation movements while others were oppressive regimes; much depends on their degree of nationalism. The nationalism that sparked WWI included a rejection of German, Austro-Hungarian, and Ottoman imperialism by Serbs, Slavs and others culminating in the assassination of Archduke Ferdinand by a Serb nationalist in 1914. Following WWI and the Treaty of Versailles, many Germans and others in the Central Alliance Nations, malcontent at the concessions and reparations of the treaty started a new form of nationalism. Adolf Hitler and the Nazi regime led this extreme nationalism. Hitler's ideas were an example of extreme, oppressive nationalism combined with political, social and economic scapegoating and was the primary cause of WWII.

103. **Which of the following is an organization or alliance for defense purposes?**
(Average) (Skill 13.1)

   A. North Atlantic Treaty Organization

   B. The Common Market

   C. The European Union

   D. North American Free Trade Association

A. North Atlantic Treaty Organization
(B) The Common Market, (C) The European Union and (D) the North American Free Trade Organization are all forms of economic integration and are in place to promote free trade and factor mobility. (D) The North Atlantic Treaty Organization, NATO, is the organization that provides for the defense of Europe.

104. **Which country was a Cold War foe?**
(Average) (Skill 13.1)

   A. Russia

   B. Brazil

   C. Canada

   D. Argentina

A. Russia
(B) Brazil and (D) Argentina are in South America and (C) Canada is in North America. (A) Russia is the country that was a Cold War superpower and foe of the United States.

105. **Which one of the following was not a post World War II organization? (Average) (Skill 13.1)**

    A. Monroe Doctrine

    B. Marshall Plan

    C. Warsaw Pact

    D. North Atlantic Treaty Organization

A. Monroe Doctrine
(B) The Marshall Plan provided funds for the reconstruction of Europe after World War II. (C) The Warsaw Pact and (D) NATO were both organizations that came into being for defense purpose. The Warsaw Pact was for the defense of Eastern Europe and NATO was for the defense of Western Europe. (A) The Monroe Doctrine was a nineteenth century agreement in which the United States was committed to defend all countries in the hemisphere.

106. **After World War II, the United States: (Rigorous) (Skill 13.2)**

    A. Limited its involvement in European affairs

    B. Shifted foreign policy emphasis from Europe to Asia

    C. Passed significant legislation pertaining to aid to farmers and tariffs on imports

    D. Entered the greatest period of economic growth in its history

D. Entered the greatest period of economic growth in its history
After World War II, the United States did not limit or shift its involvement in European affairs. In fact, it escalated the Cold War with the Soviet Union at a swift pace and attempted to contain Communism to prevent its spread across Europe. There was no significant legislation pertaining to aid to farmers and tariffs on imports. In fact, since World War II, trade has become more liberal than ever. Free trade, no matter how risky or harmful to the people of the United States or other countries, has become the economic policy of the United States called neo-liberalism. Due to this, the United States after World War II entered the greatest period of economic growth in its history and remains a world superpower.

107. **Which of the following is not a name associated with the Civil Rights movement?**
(Rigorous) (Skill 13.4)

   A. Rosa Parks

   B. Emmett Till

   C. Tom Dewey

   D. Martin Luther King, Jr.

C. Tom Dewey
(A) Rosa Parks was the black lady who wouldn't move to the back of the bus. (B) Emmett Till was the civil rights worked who was killed. (C) Martin Luther King, Jr. was a Civil Rights leader. (C) Tom Dewey was never involved in the Civil Rights movement.

108. **During the 1920s, the United States almost completely stopped all immigration. One of the reasons was:**
(Rigorous) (Skill 14.5)

   A. Plentiful cheap unskilled labor was no longer needed by industrialists

   B. War debts from World War I made it difficult to render financial assistance

   C. European nations were reluctant to allow people to leave since there was a need to rebuild populations and economic stability

   D. The United States did not become a member of the League of Nations

A. Plentiful cheap, unskilled labor was no longer needed by industrialists
The primary reason that the United States almost completely stopped all immigration during the 1920s was because their once, much needed, cheap, unskilled labor jobs, made available by the once booming industrial economy, were no longer needed. This has much to do with the increased use of machines to do the work once done by cheap, unskilled laborers

109. **A significant change in immigration policy occurred after World War II when the United States:**
     (Average) (Skill 14.5)

     A. Eliminated restrictions

     B. Prevented Japanese immigration

     C. Imposed policies based on ethnicity and country of origin

     D. Banned immigration

C. Imposed policies based on ethnicity and country of origin
(A) The policies that changed after the war did not include the elimination of restrictions. (B) Japanese immigration was not prevented and (D) immigration itself was not banned. (C) Policies were aimed at allowable limits based on ethnicity and country of origin.

110. **From about 1870 to 1900 the settlement of America's "last frontier", the West, was completed. One attraction for settlers was free land but it would have been to no avail without:**
     (Rigorous) (Skill 14.7)

     A. Better farming methods and technology

     B. Surveying to set boundaries

     C. Immigrants and others to seek new land

     D. The railroad to get them there

D. The railroad to get them there
From about 1870 to 1900, the settlement for America's "last frontier" in the West was made possible by the building of the railroad. Without the railroad, the settlers never could have traveled such distances in an efficient manner.

111. **The Electoral College:**
    (Average) (Skill 14.7)

    A. Elects the Senate but not the House

    B. Elects the House but not the Senate

    C. Elects both the House and Senate

    D. Elects the President

D. Elects the President
The Electoral College only exists to casts its votes for the President of the United States. Both Senators or Representatives are elected by majority vote.

112. **The Native American tribes of the Georgia area are:**
    (Rigorous)(Skill 15.1)

    A. Cherokee and Creek

    B. Cherokee and Hopi

    C. Creek and Seminole

    D. Seminole and Hopi

A. Cherokee and Creek
The Cherokee lived in the southern Appalachian Mountains in what is now northern Georgia. The Creek lived mainly along the Ocmulgee River which runs through Georgia.

113. **Which Native American tribe in Georgia was friendly to the British? (Rigorous) (Skill 15.2)**

    A. Creek

    B. Yamasee

    C. Navajo

    D. Cherokee

B. Yamasee
The Yamasee was the tribe that was friendly to the British until they had problems over the fur trade. When the Yamasee began to attack the colonists, they were driven into Florida.

114. **The first settlement in Georgia was: (Average)(Skill 15.2)**

    A. Macon

    B. Atlanta

    C. Valdosta

    D. Savannah

D. Savannah
When Oglethorpe received the charter to establish Georgia, he built a settlement on the Savannah River and named it Savannah. This was the first settlement in Georgia.

115. The first Constitution for Georgia was adopted in:
(Average) (Skill 15.3)

   A. 1776

   B. 1777

   C. 1778

   D. 1779

B. 1777
Georgia created a constitution three months after the Declaration of Independence was signed. The new constitution created a single elected assembly that in turn chose a governor and gave voting rights to a wide variety of citizens.

116. When did Georgia ratify the U.S. Constitution:
(Rigorous)(Skill 15.3)

   A. 1779

   B. 1785

   C. 1788

   D. 1790

C. 1788
Georgia opposed a strong federal government and insisted on the Bill of Rights being included before ratifying the Constitution in 1788.

117. The University of Georgia was:
     (Average) (Skill 15.4)

      A. founded as a private school

      B. founded as a military school

      C. the first state chartered university in the U.S.

      D. established in 1779

C. the first state chartered university in the U.S.
In 1785, the Georgia General Assembly set aside a tract of land to be used for the establishment of a college or seminary. In 1798, a portion of the land was sold to raise funds to establish a university and in 1799 the University of Georgia was officially founded. Classes began in 1801. The University of Georgia was the first state-chartered university in the United States.

118. The First and Second Great Awakenings refer to:
     (Rigorous)(Skill 15.4)

      A. religious movements

      B. political movements

      C. military movements

      D. industrialization

A. religious movements
Baptists have been present in Georgia since the first colonists arrived in 1733. At about that time, the Methodist denomination was developing in England and the American colonies during what is called the **First Great Awakening**. This protestant religious movement in the colonies emphasized a personal involvement in one's church and personal responsibility for sin and salvation. In Georgia, as elsewhere, protestant denominations gained in membership throughout the eighteenth century. The Second Great Awakening was a similar wave of religious zeal that moved through Georgia and the rest of the country in the early nineteenth century. Methodist and Baptist churches in particular saw huge growth. The Civil War cooled this revival in the North, but in the South, religious involvement was strengthened.

119. **The major crop of Georgia was:**
     (Average) (Skill 15.4)

   A. Cotton

   B. Corn

   C. Soybeans

   D. Wheat

A. Cotton
Georgia is well known for its cotton which it grew along the seacoast.

120. **During the Civil War, Georgia:**
     (Rigorous) (Skill 15.5)

   A. opposed slavery

   B. Opposed secession

   C. Abstained from the war

   D. Seceded from the Union

D. Seceded from the Union
Georgia like the rest of the South was an agricultural economy and dependent on slavery. They seceded from the Union and fought with the Confederacy.

121. **Jim Crow laws did all but the following:**
     (Rigorous)(Skill 16.1)

   A. Promoted segregation of blacks and whites

   B. Promoted integration of blacks and whites

   C. Provided for a poll tax

   D. Forced blacks to use inferior facilities

B. Promoted integration of blacks and whites
The Jim Crow laws promoted segregation and forced the blacks to use separate and inferior facilities. They also prevented blacks from voting due to the poll tax.

122. **Why did white Georgians try to prevent blacks from serving in World War I?**
(Rigorous)(Skill 16.2)

   A. Blacks were needed as sharecroppers for the agricultural crops

   B. They did not want to serve with blacks

   C. They felt that blacks were not qualified for military service

   D. They felt that the blacks would not return to Georgia after the war

A. Blacks were needed as sharecroppers for the agricultural crops
Georgia farmers used black sharecroppers for their land. If they went to fight in the war, they wouldn't have labor to work their land. Because of this, they opposed blacks in the military.

123. **Why did Georgia's Gov. Talmadge oppose the New Deal?**
(Rigorous)(Skill 16.2)

   A. He felt it wasn't needed

   B. He felt the New Deal programs were federal interference in local affairs

   C. He did not agree with the purpose of the spending policies

   D. He didn't like President Roosevelt personally

B. He felt the New Deal programs were federal interference in local affairs
Tamadge was strong and popular public figure. He opposed the New Deal programs even though they were popular with the people. Talmadge felt the New Deal programs were a form of federal interference in local affairs.

124. The Atlanta born man who became prominent in the Civil Rights movement was:
(Rigorous) (Skill 16.4)

A. Eugene Talmadge

B. Ellis Arnall

C. Herman Talmadge

D. Dr. Martin Luther King, Jr.

D. Dr. Martin Luther King, Jr.
(A) Eugene Talmadge, (B) Ellis Arnall and (C) Herman Talmadge were all governors of Georgia. (D) Dr. Martin Luther King Jr. was a Civil Rights leader.

125. All of the following are prominent Georgians except?
(Rigorous)(Skill 16.4)

A. Jimmy Carter

B. Rosa Parks

C. Maynard Jackson

D. Andrew Young

B. Rosa Parks
(A) Jimmy Carter was the President who came from Georgia; (C) Maynard Jackson was the first African American mayor of Atlanta; (D) Andrew Young was a key aid to Dr. King during the growth of the civil rights movement. (B) Rose Parks was the woman who refused to move to the back of a Montgomery bus that marked the beginning of the Civil Rights movement.

XAMonline, INC. 21 Orient Ave. Melrose, MA 02176
Toll Free number 800-509-4128
TO ORDER Fax 781-662-9268 OR www.XAMonline.com
GEORGIA ASSESSMENTS FOR THE CERTIFICATION OF EDUCATORS   -GACE - 2008

PO#   Store/School:

Address 1:

Address 2 (Ship to other):

City, State Zip

Credit card number_____-_____-_____-_____   expiration_____

EMAIL _____

PHONE   **FAX**

13# ISBN 2007	TITLE	Qty	Retail	Total
978-1-58197-257-3	Basic Skills 200, 201, 202		$59.95	
978-1-58197-528-4	Biology 026, 027		$59.95	
978-1-58197-529-1	Science 024, 025		$59.95	
978-1-58197-341-9	English 020, 021		$59.95	
978-1-58197-569-7	Physics 030, 031		$59.95	
978-1-58197-531-4	Art Education Sample Test 109, 110		$15.00	
978-1-58197-545-1	History 034, 035		$59.95	
978-1-58197-527-7	Health and Physical Education 115, 116		$59.95	
978-1-58197-540-6	Chemistry 028, 029		$59.95	
978-1-58197-534-5	Reading 117, 118		$59.95	
978-1-58197-547-5	Media Specialist 101, 102		$59.95	
978-1-58197-535-2	Middle Grades Reading 012		$59.95	
978-1-58197-545-1	Middle Grades Science 014		$59.95	
978-1-58197-345-7	Middle Grades Mathematics 013		$59.95	
978-1-58197-546-8	Middle Grades Social Science 015		$59.95	
978-158-197-573-4	Middle Grades Language Arts 011		$59.95	
978-1-58197-346-4	Mathematics 022, 023		$59.95	
978-1-58197-549-9	Political Science 032, 033		$59.95	
978-1-58197-544-4	Paraprofessional Assessment 177		$59.95	
978-1-58197-542-0	Professional Pedagogy Assessment 171, 172		$59.95	
978-1-58197-259-7	Early Childhood Education 001, 002		$59.95	
978-1-58197-548-2	School Counseling 103, 104		$59.95	
978-1-58197-541-3	Spanish 141, 142		$59.95	
978-1-58197-610-6	Special Education General Curriculum 081, 082		$73.50	
978-1-58197-530-7	French Sample Test 143, 144		$15.00	
			SUBTOTAL	
FOR PRODUCT PRICES GO TO WWW.XAMONLINE.COM			Ship	$8.25
			TOTAL	

Lilly:

Feeling like in your processing it is actually placing a belief system on me

I don't want a counselor but a friend ... not sure how to put this?

CPSIA information can be obtained at www.ICGtesting.com
Printed in the USA
LVOW010854250812

295842LV00004BB/81/P